AFRICAN HISTORICAL DICTIONARIES
Edited by Jon Woronoff

1. *Cameroon,* by Victor T. LeVine and Roger P. Nye. 1974. *Out of print. See No. 48.*
2. *The Congo,* 2nd ed., by Virginia Thompson and Richard Adloff. 1984. *Out of print. See No. 69.*
3. *Swaziland,* by John J. Grotpeter. 1975.
4. *The Gambia,* 2nd ed., by Harry A. Gailey. 1987.
5. *Botswana,* by Richard P. Stevens. 1975. *Out of print. See No. 70.*
6. *Somalia,* by Margaret F. Castagno. 1975.
7. *Benin (Dahomey),* 2nd ed., by Samuel Decalo. 1987. *Out of print. See No. 61.*
8. *Burundi,* by Warren Weinstein. 1976. *Out of print. See No. 73.*
9. *Togo,* 3rd ed., by Samuel Decalo. 1996.
10. *Lesotho,* by Gordon Haliburton. 1977.
11. *Mali,* 3rd ed., by Pascal James Imperato. 1996.
12. *Sierra Leone,* by Cyril Patrick Foray. 1977.
13. *Chad,* 3rd ed., by Samuel Decalo. 1997.
14. *Upper Volta,* by Daniel Miles McFarland. 1978.
15. *Tanzania,* by Laura S. Kurtz. 1978.
16. *Guinea,* 3rd ed., by Thomas O'Toole with Ibrahima Bah-Lalya. 1995.
17. *Sudan,* by John Voll. 1978. *Out of print. See No. 53.*
18. *Rhodesia/Zimbabwe,* by R. Kent Rasmussen. 1979. *Out of print. See No. 46.*
19. *Zambia,* by John J. Grotpeter. 1979.
20. *Niger,* 3rd ed., by Samuel Decalo. 1996.
21. *Equatorial Guinea,* 2nd ed., by Max Liniger-Goumaz. 1988.
22. *Guinea-Bissau,* 3rd ed., by Richard Lobban and Peter Mendy. 1996.
23. *Senegal,* by Lucie G. Colvin. 1981. *Out of print. See No. 65.*
24. *Morocco,* by William Spencer. 1980. *Out of print. See No. 71.*
25. *Malawi,* by Cynthia A. Crosby. 1980. *Out of print. See No. 54.*
26. *Angola,* by Phyllis Martin. 1980. *Out of print. See No. 52.*
27. *The Central African Republic,* by Pierre Kalck. 1980. *Out of print. See No. 51.*
28. *Algeria,* by Alf Andrew Heggoy. 1981. *Out of print. See No. 66.*
29. *Kenya,* by Bethwell A. Ogot. 1981.
30. *Gabon,* by David E. Gardinier. 1981. *Out of print. See No. 58.*
31. *Mauritania,* by Alfred G. Gerteiny. 1981. *Out of print. See No. 68.*

32. *Ethiopia,* by Chris Prouty and Eugene Rosenfeld. 1981. *Out of print. See No. 56.*

33. *Libya,* 2nd ed., by Ronald Bruce St. John. 1991.

34. *Mauritius,* by Lindsay Rivire. 1982. *Out of print. See No. 49.*

35. *Western Sahara,* by Tony Hodges. 1982. *Out of print. See No. 55.*

36. *Egypt,* by Joan Wucher King. 1984. *Out of print. See No. 67.*

37. *South Africa,* by Christopher Saunders. 1983.

38. *Liberia,* by D. Elwood Dunn and Svend E. Holsoe. 1985.

39. *Ghana,* by Daniel Miles McFarland. 1985. *Out of print. See No. 63.*

40. *Nigeria,* by Anthony Oyewole. 1997.

41. *Cote d'Ivoire (The Ivory Coast),* 2nd ed., by Robert J. Mundt. 1995.

42. *Cape Verde,* 2nd ed., by Richard Lobban and Marilyn Halter. 1988. *Out of print. See No. 62.*

43. *Zaire,* by F. Scott Bobb. 1988.

44. *Botswana,* 2nd ed., by Fred Morton, Andrew Murray, and Jeff Ramsay. 1989. *Out of print. See No. 70.*

45. *Tunisia,* 2nd ed., by Kenneth J. Perkins. 1997.

46. *Zimbabwe,* 2nd ed., by R. Kent Rasmussen and Steven L. Rubert. 1990.

47. *Mozambique,* by Mario Azevedo. 1991.

48. *Cameroon,* 2nd ed., by Mark W. DeLancey and H. Mbella Mokeba. 1990.

49. *Mauritius,* 2nd ed., by Sydney Selvon. 1991.

50. *Madagascar,* by Maureen Covell. 1995.

51. *The Central African Republic,* 2nd ed., by Pierre Kalck; translated by Thomas O'Toole. 1992.

52. *Angola,* 2nd ed., by Susan H. Broadhead. 1992.

53. *Sudan,* 2nd ed., by Carolyn Fluehr-Lobban, Richard A. Lobban, Jr., and John Obert Voll. 1992.

54. *Malawi,* 2nd ed., by Cynthia A. Crosby. 1993.

55. *Western Sahara,* 2nd ed., by Anthony Pazzanita and Tony Hodges. 1994.

56. *Ethiopia and Eritrea,* 2nd ed., by Chris Prouty and Eugene Rosenfeld. 1994.

57. *Namibia,* by John J. Grotpeter. 1994.

58. *Gabon,* 2nd ed., by David Gardinier. 1994.

59. *Comoro Islands,* by Martin Ottenheimer and Harriet Ottenheimer. 1994.

60. *Rwanda,* by Learthen Dorsey. 1994.

61. *Benin,* 3rd ed., by Samuel Decalo. 1995.

62. *Republic of Cape Verde,* 3rd ed., by Richard Lobban and Marlene Lopes. 1995.
63. *Ghana,* 2nd ed., by David Owusu-Ansah and Daniel Miles McFarland. 1995.
64. *Uganda,* by M. Louise Pirouet. 1995.
65. *Senegal,* 2nd ed., by Andrew F. Clark and Lucie Colvin Phillips. 1994.
66. *Algeria,* 2nd ed., by Phillip Chiviges Naylor and Alf Andrew Heggoy. 1994.
67. *Egypt,* 2nd ed., by Arthur Goldschmidt, Jr. 1994.
68. *Mauritania,* 2nd ed., by Anthony G. Pazzanita. 1996.
69. *Congo,* 3rd ed., by Samuel Decalo, Virginia Thompson, and Richard Adloff. 1996.
70. *Botswana,* 3rd ed., by Jeff Ramsay, Barry Morton, and Fred Morton. 1996.
71. *Morocco,* 2nd ed., by Thomas K. Park. 1996.
72. *Tanzania,* 2nd ed., by Thomas P. Ofcansky and Rodger Yeager. 1997.
73. *Burundi,* 2nd ed., by Ellen K. Eggers. 1997.

Historical Dictionary of Burundi

Ellen K. Eggers

African Historical Dictionaries, No. 73

The Scarecrow Press, Inc.
Lanham, Md., & London
1997

SCARECROW PRESS, INC.

Published in the United States of America
by Scarecrow Press, Inc.
4720 Boston Way
Lanham, Maryland 20706

4 Pleydell Gardens, Folkestone
Kent CT20 2DN, England

British Cataloguing-in-Publication Information Available

Library of Congress Cataloging-in-Publication Data

Eggers, Ellen K., 1955–
    Historical dictionary of Burundi / Ellen K. Eggers.
      p.   cm. — (African historical dictionaries ; no. 73)
    Includes bibliographical references.
    ISBN 0-8108-3261-5 (cloth : alk. paper)
    1. Burundi—History—Dictionaries. I. Title. II. Series.
DT450.68.E37   1997
967.572—dc21   96-44991

ISBN 0–8108–3261–5 (cloth : alk.paper)

♾™ The paper used in this publication meets the minimum requirements of
American National Standard for Information Sciences—Permanence of
Paper for Printed Library Materials, ANSI Z39.48–1984.
Manufactured in the United States of America.

For Paul

Contents

Editor's Foreword

Burundi, like its neighbor Rwanda, is a small, poor, remote country that, along with the usual political, economic, and social problems, must cope with the most serious of all: ethnic divisions and friction. So far, relations between the majority Hutu and minority Tutsi have been somewhat better, or rather less disastrous, than in Rwanda. But that is little solace in a society where ethnic conflicts could break out at any time. Given this situation, it is not surprising that the political scene has been broadly unstable, and little has been achieved in the economy, education, health, or other crucial sectors. Although Burundi is small, poor, and remote, it is important to the countries surrounding it, and Africa in general, that the situation be improved because otherwise the trouble could spill over.

As with Rwanda, nobody knows what will happen next. Fortunately, this new *Historical Dictionary of Burundi* offers some basis for evaluating the present situation and speculating more intelligently about the future. This is done by providing entries on many of the important national figures, the political parties, and the army, which dominate the foreground. It also includes entries on the other aspects of the country. Those reaching further into the past show the historical roots of many of today's problems and explain, if not how they can be resolved, at least why they have become so intractable. With so many twists and turns, the chronology is particularly useful. And the bibliography, while hardly vast (especially in English), helps the reader to round out the picture.

Due to the prevailing instability, it is extremely difficult to follow people and events in Burundi. This has been especially true of late. Thus, the author of this volume deserves special credit for having shed so much light on the present situation while also providing a good look at the past. Ellen K. Eggers, who teaches in the English Department at the University of Nebraska-Lincoln, is also a specialist on Bantu languages, including Kirundi. She lectured at the University of Burundi in 1985-86, and she has maintained close contact with the country ever since. This makes her one of the better guides to a place we should know more about before judging it.

Jon Woronoff
Series Editor

Acknowledgments

I would like to thank the following colleagues whose generosity has been of great help during the writing of this dictionary. From the University of Nebraska: Learthen Dorsey, Dieudonné Kwizera, Paul Olson, Oyekan Owomoyela, and George Wolf; from the University of Burundi: Jacques Bacamurwanko, former Burundi Ambassador to the United States.

This project was partially supported by a Maude Hammond Fling summer fellowship from the University of Nebraska-Lincoln.

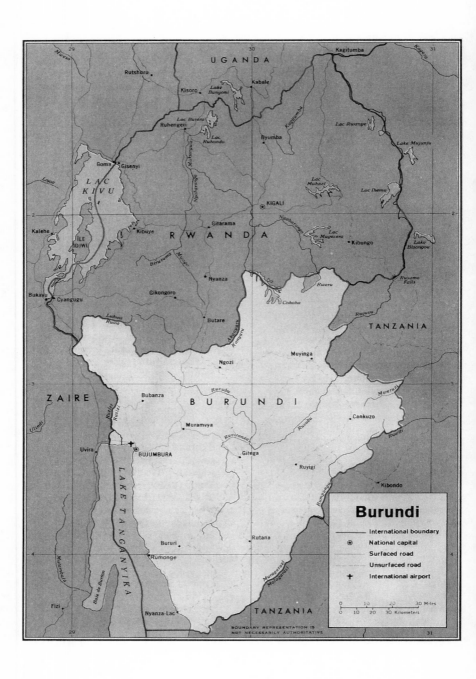

UGANDA

Rutshuru

Kisoro Lake
Bunyoni Kabale Kagitumba

Lac Bulera Byumba Lac Rwanye
Ruhengeri Lake Mujunju
Lac
Ruhondo

LAC Goma Gisenyi Lac
KIVU Muhazi Lac Ihema

KIGALI

ÎLE Kibuye Gitarama Lac
IDJWI R W A N D A Mugesera Kibungo
Lake
Kalehe Bisongou

Nyanza Rusumo
Falls

Bukavu Gikongoro
Cyangugu Cohoha Ruvuru
Butare
TANZANIA

Muyinga

Ngozi

Z A I R E Bubanza B U R U N D I Mweru

Cankuzo
Muramvya

Uvira Ruvironza
BUJUMBURA Gitega
Ruyigi

Kibondo

L A K E Bururi Rutana
T A N G A N Y I K A
Rumonge

Burundi

———— International boundary
⊛ National capital
———— Surfaced road
- - - - Unsurfaced road
+ International airport

0   10   20   30 Miles
0   10   20   30 Kilometers

Fizi Nyanza-Lac TANZANIA

Acronyms and Abbreviations

APRODEBA   Association des Progressistes et Démocrates Barundi/Associoation of Progressive and Democratic Barundi

CCB   Coopérative des Commerçants du Burundi/ Cooper-ative of Traders in Burundi

CEC   Centres Extra-Coutumiers/Extra-Customary Centers

CNR   Conseil National de la Révolutionnaire/ National Revolutionary Council

CPJB   Coalition for Peace and Justice in Burundi

CSP   Conseil Supérieur du Pays/Superior Council

CSR   Conseil Suprème Révolutionnaire/Supreme Revolutionary Council

EAC   East African Community

FDD   Front for the Defense of Democracy

FOREAMI   Fonds Reine Elisabeth pour l'Assistance Médicale aux Indigènes/Queen Elizabeth's Fund for the Medical Assistance of Indigenous People

Frodebu   Front Démocratique Burundi/Burundi Demo-cratic Front

FTB   Féderation des Travailleurs du Burundi/ Federation of Burundi Workers

FULREAC   Fondation de l'Université de Liège pour les Recherches Scientifiques au Congo Belge et au Ruanda-Urundi/Foundation of the

	University of Liège for Scientific Research in the Belgian Congo and in Ruanda-Urundi
ILO	International Labour Organisation
ISABU	Institut des Sciences Agronomiques du Burundi/Burundi Institute of Agronomic Science
JNR	Jeunesse Nationaliste Rwagasore/Nationalist Rwagasore Youth
JRR	Jeunesse Rwagasore Révolutionnaire/Rwagasore Revolutionary Youth
MIPROBU	Mission for the Protection of Democratic Institutions in Burundi
OAU	Organization of African Unity
OCA	Office des Cités Africaines/Office of African Cities
Palipehutu	Parti pour la Libération du Peuple Hutu/Party for the Liberation of the Hutu People
PARENA	Parti pour la Réconciliation Nationale/Party for National Reconciliation
PARMEHUTU	Parti du Mouvement de l'Émancipation d'Hutu/Party of the Movement of Emancipation of Hutu
PDC	Parti Démocrate Chrétien/Democratic Christian Party
PDJTB	Parti des Jeune Travailleurs du Burundi/Burundi Young Workers' Party
PDR	Parti Démocratique et Rural/Democratic and Rural Party
PP	Parti du Peuple/Party of the People
PRP	People's Reconciliation Party
UBU	Umugambwe wa'Bakozi Uburundi/Burundi Laborers' Party
UCJAB	Union Culturelle de la Jeunesse Africaine du Burundi/Cultural Union of the African Youth of Burundi
UDB	Union des Démocrates Barundi/Union of Barundi Democrats

UFB	Union des Femmes Burundaises/Union of Burundi Women
UNB	Union Nationale du Burundi/National Union of Burundi
UNDP	United Nations Development Programme
UNEBA	Union Nationale de Étudiants Burundi/National Union of Burundi Students
UNHCR	United Nations High Commissioner for Refugees
UNICEF	United Nations Children's Fund
UPRONA	Parti de l'Union et du Progrès National/Party of National Union and Progress
USAID	United States Agency for International Development

User's notes

Language

The adjective form can be found alternatively as *Rundi*, *Burundi*, and *Burundian*; here it has been standardized to *Burundi*, unless the material is quoted. Also for the sake of standardization, the simplified terms *Hutu* and *Tutsi* are used throughout to indicate the collective form of the ethnic groups as well as the adjective form. This usage is not meant to ignore or diminish the complexities found within each of the groups, but rather for ease of reference.

The verbal element in Kirundi is complex, as is characteristic of Bantu languages. It consists of a verbal root to which bound morphological elements are affixed. The basic prefixes of the verb are the subject prefix (obligatory, except in infinitives and imperatives), a tense marker, and optional focus and object markers in this order. Basic suffixes include all reflexive, applicative (allowing an already transitive verb to take two objects), locative, and causative markers (optionally), and an obligatory aspect marker as the final syllable. Primarily relevant to these entries, however, is the infinitive marker. The basic infinitive in Kirundi is the prefix *ku-*. In some words, the *ku-* changes to *gu-* following the rules of Dahl's Law; this law says that a morpheme beginning with a voiced consonant ([b], [g], [d], [z], [v], etc.) must precede one beginning with a voiceless one ([p], [k], [t], [s], [f], etc.). The verbs in these entries are listed by the initial letter of the word stem.

The noun is as complex in Kirundi as in other Bantu languages. The classification system (sometimes called a gender system) comprises 17 classes, most having semantic as well as historical value. For example, Classes 1 and 2 are the singular and plural respectively of words representing humans. The prefixes in Classes 1 and 2 are *mu-* and *ba-*; therefore, *Murundi* means Burundi person and *Barundi* means Burundi people. An entry such as this will be listed under *-rundi* with the relevant prefixes listed. If a word is used in one form only (such as *Kirundi* with *ki-* the prefix for languages), the full form will be listed. A single-vowel prefix is often added before the class prefix in discourse situations. For further information concerning the structure, sound system, and sound changes of Kirundi, which is beyond the intended scope of this historical dictionary, the reader will find numerous linguistic analyses listed in the bibliography.

Names
Kings of Burundi are listed under their dynastic names, with a cross-reference to their birth names. Also, please note that western texts have, over the last century, called Mwezi IV Kissabo, Kisabo, Gissabo, and Gisabo. In keeping with the modern rendering of Kirundi, the spelling here has been standardized to Gisabo.

Cross-referencing
When a word is in bold print in an entry, it can be found under its own heading.

Chronology of Important Events

Note: Place names are listed as they were known in the United States at the time. For example, the capital of Burundi is listed as Usumbura before its 1962 independence and Bujumbura since that date.

800-1000	Bahutu farmers, who belong to the Bantu group come to the area that is to become Ruanda-Urundi and establish their language and customs.
1300-1600	The Batutsi, who are said to be descendants of Nilo-Hamitic shepherd people, arrive from the north and achieve political domination through their feudal system. They found Burundi's first kingdom early in the sixteenth century.
1675	The Tutsi king, Ntare I, builds a kingdom in what is now Burundi. During his reign, the areas of Nkoma, Bututsi, Kilimiro, and Buyenzi are conquered.
1858	Richard Burton and John Hanning Speke arrive together at Lake Tanganyika, the first of the European explorers. They call it "ill-famed Urundi," as they explore, hoping to find the source of the Nile at the northern end of the lake. On April 14, they reach Wafanya in the far south of Urundi; Burton describes it as "the only port in that inhospitable land still open to travellers."
1860	Mwezi IV (Gisabo) begins his reign as *mwami* (king).
1871	During their exploration of Lake Tanganyi-

ka, Henry Morton Stanley and David Livingstone reach a point approximately ten miles from where Bujumbura lies today.

1879   An expedition of Cardinal Lavigerie's White Fathers arrives in Urundi, venturing along the eastern shore of Lake Tanganyika.

1881   A group of White Fathers is accused of befriending Arab slave traders and murdered in Rumonge.

1884
November 8   Germany recognizes the International Association of the Congo.

1885
August 25   Germany ratifies the boundaries described in the Declaration of Neutrality (of August 1). This ratification has two parts: recognition of the neutrality of the Congo State and recognition of its boundaries.

1890   This is the year of the Anglo-German partition of Africa, after which explorations become inseparable from colonial administration. Therefore, this is often considered the end of the era of great explorations of Africa.

1892   Oskar Baumann, an Austrian leading a Masai expedition of the German antislavery committee, is the first European to traverse the country from side to side.

1894   During this year, negotiations between Germany and Britain concerning a "Cape to Cairo" corridor of communications culminate, leading to a delineation of borders for German East Africa, including Ruanda-Urundi.

1896   Father van der Burgt and Father van der Biesen first arrive in Urundi to found a Catholic mission and are forced to flee from the attacks of a chief named Musabiko.
The first permanent Catholic mission is built at Muyaga.

1896-1897   Germans found the Usumbura military
               station.
1898   Richard Kandt leads an important
               expedition and makes the first detailed maps
               of the region of Ruanda-Urundi.
1899   German columns begin crossing the country
               in 1895, but following an attack against the
               Bethe column, the government of Germany
               decides to occupy Ruanda-Urundi.
               A second group of White Fathers settles at
               Mugera, the residence of Mwami Mwezi IV
               (Gisabo). The ruler attempts to remove the
               priests, but a religious leader (animist)
               persuades him to cease his attempts.
1900
December   A German contingent led by Captain
               Herrmann reaches Usumbura, where they
               join a Congolese group. Herrmann surveys
               the islands in the lake and the volcanic
               region. The result is the first reliable large-
               scale map of western Urundi and Ruanda,
               which confirms reports that Lake Kivu lies
               farther to the west than has been indicated
               on the maps.
1903   The Germans demand the passing of the
               Treaty of Kiganda to guard against further
               trouble for the missionaries. The treaty
               stipulates that missionaries are allowed to
               work with total freedom. Mwezi IV
               surrenders to the Germans.
               Father J. M. Van der Burgt publishes the
               first French-Kirundi dictionary.
1905
March 10   A Governor's Ordinance states, ". . . until
               further notice entrance to the sultanates of
               Ruanda and Urundi is permitted only from
               the military station of Usumbura, and only
               with written permission from the district
               office. . . ." This is in answer to what had

	become known as the *Inder Frage* or Indian Question, which had been construed as a trade problem of non-African and non-European merchants in Ruanda-Urundi.
1906	Military occupation of Ruanda-Urundi ends, and colonial administration begins.
May 26	A contract is signed between the Congo Free State and the Holy See, adding education to the evangelical activities of the Catholic Church.
1908	Mwezi IV (Gisabo) dies at the age of 63, and Mutaga IV begins his reign. Gisabo's death destroys German control over Urundi not by revolution, as had been feared, but by initiating what the Germans regarded as a period of chaos.
1909	A government school is established in Usumbura. The first year the school has 25 students, about three-fourths of whom are Rundi children; the rest are children of *askaris* (foreign businessmen) and traders.
1910	Ruanda-Urundi becomes completely German-administered.
1912	The Kivu-Ruanda-Urundi Vicariate is founded, and Monsignor Hirth, first apostolic vicar of the two countries, settles in Kabwayi, which becomes the spiritual center of the territory.
	The seat of the Urundi Residence moves from Usumbura to Gitega.
1914	
September 18	A German motorboat on Lake Kivu captures a Belgian boat, thus establishing German control of the lake.
1915	Mutaga IV ends his reign, and Mwami Mwambutsa, at the age of two, becomes the king of Burundi.
1916	Belgian troops enter Ruanda in two converging columns and, after successful battles, occupy all of Ruanda-Urundi.

1917	The arbitrary power of the *bami* and of the native authorities is abolished.
1919 May 30	The British and Belgian governments, under the Milner-Orts agreement, officially propose that Ruanda-Urundi be administered by Belgium. The Supreme Council of Allied Powers assigns the Ruanda-Urundi mandate to Belgium.
1923	Terms of the 1919 agreement are confirmed by the League of Nations. Domestic slavery is abolished.
1924	Terms of the 1919 agreement are finally approved by the Belgian Parliament, which formally accepts responsibility for Ruanda-Urundi under the conditions established by the League of Nations.
1925	A law is passed by the Belgian Parliament in August joining Ruanda-Urundi in an administrative union with the Belgian Congo. A separate budget is maintained for the Mandate Territory, but the administration, customs, and monetary systems are combined with those of the Congo. Prince Leopold of Belgium visits Ruanda-Urundi; the visit is repeated in 1933.
1926	The triple hierarchy of native authorities—the chief of crops, the chief of pastures, and the chief of armed units—is abolished and replaced by a single authority. Evidence of arrowheads and knives from the late Stone Age is discovered.
1932	Coffee, which is to become one of Burundi's largest exports, is first introduced by the Belgians as a cash crop under a compulsory cultivation system.
1936	Native justice is completely reformed ten years after some basic organization. The ad-

	ministrative funds of the chieftaincies are set up.
1938	Dr. Kurkhart Waldecker erects a pyramid at the southernmost source of the Nile in what is today Burundi.
1945	For four years Ruanda-Urundi contributes to the war effort of the allied nations. At the end of World War II, the United Nations make it a Trust Territory, ending the mandate.
1946 December 3	The United Nations General Assembly approves the Trusteeship Agreement for the territory of Ruanda-Urundi. The United Nations is more explicit than the League of Nations had been in stating the responsibilities of the administering authority. The agreement requires Belgium to work for the development of free political institutions and to assure the inhabitants of increased participation in administrative responsibilities. The agreement also requires progress toward appropriate forms of representative government and states that "the Administrating Authority shall take all measures conducive to the political advancement of the people of Ruanda-Urundi. . . ."
1947	The Prince-Regent Charles visits Ruanda-Urundi.
1948	The territory receives the first visit of a Trusteeship Council mission as relations between the United Nations and Ruanda-Urundi become effective. Missions follow at three-year intervals. The first two missions report that social and political advancements are proceeding too slowly, further stating that the administrative union with the Belgian Congo should not be al-

lowed to impede the political development of Ruanda-Urundi.

The first Homemaking Center to promote the education of women opens in Bujumbura.

1949
April 25   Belgium assumes the responsibility for the political, social, and economic development of the territory of Ruanda-Urundi "in order to guide it to autonomy in good time," based on a law approving the trusteeship agreement.

August 14   The vice governor general of the trusteeship publishes an ordinance that formally recognizes the boundary between the Residencies of Ruanda and Urundi. This political boundary remains the accepted one at independence and up to the present.

1951   In response to the reports of the first two missions of the Trusteeship Council, Belgium institutes a series of economic and administrative reforms. The economic reforms are embodied in the Ten-Year Plan, initiated the following year; administrative reforms involve reorganizing of indigenous political structures and instituting a limited degree of representative government.

1952   The Belgian administration sets up the Ten-Year Development Plan for Ruanda-Urundi (1952-1961), the first significant step taken toward the economic improvement of the country.

May 1   Polygamous marriages are legally abolished by the resident governor.

July 14   A decree establishing the hierarchy of sub-chieftaincy, chieftaincy, territorial, and country councils inaugurates a new political organization.

1954-1955   The almost exclusively Tutsi kingdom councils in Rwanda and Burundi (apparently with some prodding by the colonial administration) abolish cattle clientage. Skeptics later claim that, although this seemed to be a critical reform in the process of social change and development, the practice of cattle clientage had simply become outmoded.

1955   King Baudouin I makes what has become known as a "triumphant tour" through Belgium's African territories.

1957   A General Council replaces the Council of the General Vice-Government, highest consultative assembly of the territory. The new council, based on more democratic criteria, extends representation.

1959
November   A serious outbreak of violence between Hutu and Tutsi occurs in Rwanda and augments tensions in Burundi. The Belgian government issues a statement of its plans for the political future of the territory based on recommendations and proposals by the Groupe de Travail (Working Group) formed to aid in the transition to independence.

1960
October   Two university departments are opened in Usumbura, one in philosophy and letters, social, economic, and administrative sciences, the other in various scientific and agricultural disciplines.
            There is a political awakening in Urundi, with more than 20 political parties being formed and a temporary commission replacing the High Council of the country; a colloquy on Urundi is held in Brussels from August 23-31, and local (communal) elections take place from November 15-December 8.

1961
September   Legislative elections result in the wide-
                   spread allegiance among both Hutu and
                   Tutsi electorates to the Party of National
                   Union and Progress (Parti de l'Union et du
                   Progrès National) (UPRONA) under the
                   leadership of Prince Louis Rwagasore.
October 13   Crown Prince Louis Rwagasore, prime
                   minister-designate and leader of UPRONA,
                   is assassinated. The accused assassin is a
                   Greek national, allegedly part of a
                   conspiracy organized by a rival political
                   faction within the nobility. Andre Muhirwa
                   succeeds him.
1962
June 6   A special UN commission reports to the
                   General Assembly that it has "failed to
                   overcome the psychosis of mutual distrust
                   which has prevented the two sides [Rwanda
                   and Burundi] from taking a clearer view of
                   their long-term interests," and, therefore,
                   recommends that the two territories that had
                   been administered by Belgium as a single
                   unit should be given independence as
                   separate countries.
June 27   The UN General Assembly decides by
                   unanimous vote to give Rwanda and
                   Burundi full and separate independence.
                   They are admitted to the UN as the Republic
                   of Rwanda and the Kingdom of Burundi.
July 1   Burundi becomes independent and separates
                   from Rwanda.
September 18   Burundi joins the United Nations.
October   The Legislative Assembly of Burundi
                   approves a law outlawing all strikes in the
                   country until January 1963.
December 21   Mwami Mwambutsa IV of Burundi
                   becomes the first African sovereign to visit
                   Jerusalem in 2,900 years (when the Queen

of Sheba visited King Solomon). The Mwami and President Itshac Ben Zvi of Israel sign a treaty of friendship and a cultural accord.

1963
January 15   In spite of protests and appeals for a new trial from Amnesty International, five men, convicted of complicity in the murder of Louis Rwagasore, are hanged in Gitega as a crowd of 20,000 watches. One was a graduate of St. Antony's College, Oxford; one was a former minister; and one was a Greek businessman, the man originally accused of carrying out the assassination.

March 22   The government of Burundi announces the arrest of three prominent citizens accused of participating in a conspiracy to undermine the security of the state. They are Thaddee Sirynamunsi, president of the National Assembly; Dr. Pie Masumbuko, the only African physician in Burundi; and Ignace Ndimanya, former minister of public works.

June   Pierre Ngendandumwe, 31, becomes the first member of the Hutu majority to hold the post of prime minister. Andre Muhirwa, the outgoing prime minister, who has served as Burundi's chief of government since independence, is accused of "destroying national unity, installing a regime of terror and favoritism, managing the country's finances without a voted budget, showing public disrespect to the Mwami and his family, and of pursuing too 'independent' a role."

June 8   A deliberate attempt is made to shift power away from the government and to the court. The army and the gendarmerie are converted into secretariats of state and brought under the exclusive jurisdiction of the court.

July 29   The governments of Burundi and Belgium agree on terms of cooperation in areas of assistance, scholarships, and financial aid. In total, Belgium will provide 19 million francs in aid.

December 23   A bilateral economic conference between Rwanda and Burundi breaks down in total failure as the two delegations are unable to reach a mutually acceptable agreement for sharing of reserve currencies. Rwanda decides unilaterally to sever its economic ties with Burundi.
When the economic union with Rwanda breaks down, the Banque du Royaume du Burundi (Bank of the Kingdom of Burundi) is established. It is later changed to the Banque de la Republique du Burundi.

December 30   As a result of some threatening events of the last week of December on the borders of the two countries, Max H. Dorsinville, the officer in charge of UN operations in the Congo, visits Rwanda and Burundi for six days to assess the situation.

December 31   The government of Rwanda breaks the monetary union between the two countries, following the failure of talks on the questions of imports and customs. This takes effect from January 1, 1964.

1964
January 10   By Royal Decree of Mwami Mwambutsa IV, the Université Officielle du Bujumbura (the Official University of Bujumbura) is established. This decree transforms the former Collège du Saint-Esprit, established by the Roman Catholic Society of Jesus in Bujumbura in 1960, into a joint program of the church and the government.

March   Tracts of mysterious origin are circulated in Ngozi. These tracts announce the Mwami's resolution to dismiss four members of the Cabinet, all Hutu.

March 31   The Mwami dismisses the four ministers (finance, interior, public works, and justice) and asks Prime Minister Pierre Ngendandumwe to form a new government, but when agreement still cannot be reached on a new cabinet, Ngendandumwe resigns.

April 6   Mwami Mwambutsa calls on Albin Nyamoya to form a new government. Nyamoya has previously served as minister of agriculture and minister of the interior.

April 11   The Mwami presents the new government of Burundi, led by Prime Minister Albin Nyamoya, to the National Assembly.

April 28   A delegation, led by the National Assembly president, Thadee Siryuyumunsi, arrives in Peking for an official visit.

May 18   On a private visit to the United States to see the New York World's Fair, Mwami Mwambutsa IV meets with President Lyndon Johnson at the White House.

May 19   The National Banks of Rwanda and Burundi, successors to the *Banque d'Emission du Rwanda et Burundi*, open in Kigali and Bujumbura.

May 26   Tung Chi-ping, a Chinese diplomat, defects and asks for political asylum in the United States embassy in Bujumbura.

June 11   Peking Radio (quoting *The People's Daily*) reports the "kidnapping of Tung Chi-ping," staff member of the Chinese embassy in Burundi, by the U.S. embassy on May 26.

July 24   The secretary general and the permanent secretary of the federation of Burundi arrive in Peking as guests of the All-China Federation of Trade Unions and the Chinese Committee for Afro-Asian Solidarity.

July 31   The Burundi government blocks American efforts to arrange for Tung Chi-ping's departure from Bujumbura, and the U.S. embassy in Bujumbura discloses that Tung Chi-ping has disappeared. Burundi Radio denounces Tung's disappearance as "an unfriendly act which could damage relations between Burundi and the United States; the next day, a U.S. embassy spokesperson states that Tung had left "by his own choice."

August 17   The Burundi foreign minister wires the Secretaries General of the Organization of African Unity (OAU) and the UN, informing them that the situation between Rwanda and Burundi is "very tense," as well as protesting an alleged incursion by Rwandan troops on August 10. All servicemen on leave are ordered to return to their garrisons immediately.

September 1   Gregoire Kayibanda, president of Rwanda, and Mwami Mwambutsa IV, king of Burundi, begin an exchange of protests of alleged border violations.

September 8   Mwami Mwambutsa signs two royal decrees proclaiming martial law and a state of emergency in some regions of the provinces of Bubanza and Ngozi, "following the troubles which have broken out there."

The Burundi foreign minister wires the Rwandan foreign minister protesting an alleged incursion by Rwandan troops two days previously.

Senior officials of the governing UPRONA party meet under the chairmanship of the party president, Joseph Bamina. They call for the formation of a national committee and a political bureau.

September 17	Prime Minister Albin Nyamoya affirms that the new Bujumbura University will continue to admit Zairian students despite the expulsion of Burundi students from Zaire.
October 8	Prime Minister Albin Nyamoya cables the chairman of the OAU ad hoc commission on the Congo as well as the secretaries general of the OAU and the UN, charging that Zairian military aircraft have bombed Burundi communities twice.
November 13	Prime Minister Albin Nyamoya protests by cable to the prime minister of Zaire "aggressive acts" against the national sovereignty of Burundi, citing four specific occasions earlier in November on which armed Zairian troops allegedly crossed the border at Katumba.
December	A large quantity of arms and ammunition is discovered in the vicinity of Gitega, and rumors quickly spread of an impending Chinese-sponsored *coup d'état*. Just a few days later, the mwami withdraws.
1965	
January 7	Mwami Mwambutsa first dismisses the government of Prime Minister Albin Nyamoya and, five days later, asks former Prime Minister Pierre Ngendandumwe (June 1963-March 1964) to form a new government.
January 15	Prime Minister Pierre Ngendandumwe, 32, is assassinated by Tutsi extremists from Rwanda.
January 17	Former Prime Minister Albin Nyamoya and Communications Minister Pierre Ngunzu are charged in connection with the assassination.
January 21	Gonzalve Muyenzi, a Rwanda-born Tutsi employed as an accounting clerk at the U.S. embassy, confesses to the assassination of

the prime minister. Pie Masumbuko, the acting prime minister, announces that the assassination is the work of "Tutsi extremists," and that there is no evidence that either the U.S. or China is involved, as had been previously alleged.

January 24
Joseph Bamina, president of the UPRONA party, is appointed prime minister.

January 29
The Burundi government temporarily suspends diplomatic relations with China, and Ambassador Liu Yu-feng and his staff are ordered by the mwami to leave the country within two days.

February 5
Burundi's ambassador to Tanzania contradicts reports of Chinese complicity in the assassination of Ngendandumwe and states that Burundi has not broken off relations with China but only suspended them.

February 12
The International Monetary Fund approves a stand-by arrangement with Burundi, which authorizes drawing up to $4 million during 1965.

March 3
Mwami Mwambutsa dissolves the National Assembly "in view of the Assembly's bankruptcy." He appoints a 13-member Royal Commission to plan new elections.

March 4
Marc Manirarira, minister of foreign affairs, repeats that neither China nor the US was implicated in the assassination and that diplomatic relations would be resumed with China "as soon as the confusion is lifted."

April 13
Andre Nyankie, Burundi's chief delegate to the UN, states in New York that his country will resume full diplomatic relations with China "shortly."

May 10
The first postindependence elections to the National Assembly result in a Hutu majority.

July 27
The mwami states that all foreign investment projects since Burundi's

	independence in 1962 have been sabotaged and announces that he will call in foreign judges chosen by the International Commission of Jurists to insure impartiality in assigning blame.
September 13	Léopold Biha is appointed prime minister.
October	The Ecole Normale Supérieure, a second institution of higher education, is opened in Bujumbura to train secondary schoolteachers.
October 19	A putsch by Hutu military personnel, led by Gervais Nyangoma, is thwarted by army loyalists under the command of Captain Michel Micombero. Prime Minister Biha is wounded, and reprisals against the Hutu in the form of the slaughter of Hutu leaders follow.
November 2	Mwami Mwambutsa leaves for Europe.
1966	
January 5	A joint communique issued in Leopoldville announces the reestablishment of diplomatic relations between Burundi and Zaire that had been broken in August 1964.
January 8	The International Commission of Jurists reports in Geneva that 86 people, including all of the elected officers of both houses of Burundi's Parliament, have been executed following the abortive *coup d'ètat* of October 1965. Another report lists the number executed at 23, all Hutu.
January 10	The Burundi government expels the U.S. ambassador, Donald A. Dumont, and two other U.S. embassy officers, claiming that they were "rightly or wrongly" suspected of involvement with opposition conspirators. The government order states that relations are not being broken.
January 11	The U.S. Department of State protests the expulsion of Ambassador Dumont and asks

Burundi to recall Ambassador Léon Ndenzako from Washington.

January 12 Foreign Minister Marc Manirakiza of Burundi files a counterprotest, stating again that Burundi's action was aimed only at the three diplomats suspected of abetting the abortive coup of October 1965 and did not signify a break in relations with the United States.

January 17 The Burundi government charges to the OAU and the UN that armed bands (including Tutsi refugees from Burundi) have crossed the border from Rwanda, killed 14 people, and burned 30 houses.

January 20 Rwanda asks the UN to help repatriate 2,000 Hutu refugees who have recently fled into Rwanda from Burundi. A Rwandan spokesman also says that "bandits armed with automatic weapons" have crossed from Burundi into Rwanda.

March 7 The International Labor Organization (ILO) files a formal complaint with the UN Commission on Human Rights, charging the Burundi government with mass executions of political and labor leaders following the abortive coup of October 1965. This is the first complaint ever lodged against a government as a UN agenda item.

March 17 The Burundi government offers to send a mission to ILO headquarters in Geneva to discuss charges that Burundi has violated human rights.

March 24 The Mwami, while still in Europe, gives his son, Crown Prince Charles Ndizeye, substantial powers.

March 28 The Burundi mission to the UN announces that the ILO has agreed not to press its formal complaint before the UN Commission on Human Rights pending Burundi's explanation of "the true facts."

April 20	Talks between Rwanda and Burundi end in agreement on a stage-by-stage normalization of relations. Some of the subjects discussed include refugees, economic cooperation, and the establishment of diplomatic relations.
April 25	Burundi's ambassador to the UN states in Geneva that his country has been "judged and condemned unjustly." He claims that executions following the coup attempt had totalled "about 50" and not 86 as alleged in January by the International Commission of Jurists and that all had been given a trial.
July 8	The crown prince deposes his father (who is still in Europe), dismisses the government of Prime Minister Biha, and suspends the country's constitution, while leaving the constitutional framework virtually unchanged.
July 11	Prince Charles asks Defense Minister Michel Micombero, a Belgian-trained army captain and the senior officer in the army, to form a new government.
August 30	Foreign Minister Dr. Pie Masumbuko announces in Kinshasa that Burundi has signed a mutual security agreement with Rwanda and a trade and cultural agreement with Zaire. He also states that Burundi will resume diplomatic relations with China.
September 1	Crown Prince Charles Ndizeye, is installed as Mwami Ntare V. In Geneva, the deposed Mwami condemns the "open rebellion against my authority" and claims that his son is being manipulated by extremist elements. The new Mwami calls on the people to heal their tribal divisions.
November 20	Radio Burundi broadcasts a decree (dated November 18) that restores the Biha government and abrogates the July 8 decree which had suspended it.

November 24   A royal decree establishes UPRONA as the sole political party in Burundi.

November 28   Micombero deposes Mwami Ntare V and proclaims Burundi a republic of which he is the first president. The military coup is peaceful.

November 30   The military regime confirms UPRONA's status as the sole political party, with Micombero as its leader.

December 3   Ntare V, from Kinshasa, says that he expects to live in Brussels or join his father in exile in Geneva. Micombero says that "the King can return in a few months if he wishes, but only as an ordinary citizen. He must realize now that the monarchy is ended."

December 6   Former Mwami Mwambutsa IV issues a statement in Geneva, describing the new regime as having only superficial authority and being "doomed to disappear." He says that his son had been naive enough to believe in the sincerity of his advisors, despite warnings from his father.

               The National Revolutionary Council of military personnel announces that Micombero's term as president will be seven years and promotes him to the rank of colonel.

December 20   Micombero announces that all governmental directives will be issued as presidential decrees, on the advice of ministers, and after consultation with the attorney general.

1967
February 1   Representatives of the Burundi Ministry of Information and the Soviet news agency Tass sign an agreement under which Tass agrees to supply information equipment to Burundi at no cost and to provide news service at nominal cost.

February 10   Radio Bujumbura reports that all of the country's youth organizations have merged into one group: the Jeunesse Rwagasore Révolutionnaire (JRR).

March   After a major reshuffling of his cabinet, President Micombero decrees that the police should be integrated into the national army.

March 20   The presidents of Rwanda and Burundi decide to try to limit the long, bloody conflict on their common frontier by disarming refugees on both sides of the border.

May 8   President Micombero dismisses Major Albert Shibura from command of the army and replaces him with Captain Thomas Ndabemeye. When he announces the change, Micombero says that there is reason to believe that "a small group of irresponsible men" has found accomplices in the army in efforts to "take advantage of the Republic."

November 5   Agence France-Presse reports that President Micombero has dismissed three ministers and two senior officials. No reasons have been given for the dismissals; no replacements have been announced.

December 1   The East African Community (EAC) is formally inaugurated in a ceremony at EAC headquarters in Arusha. Presidents Jomo Kenyatta of Kenya, Julius Nyerere of Tanzania, and Milton Obote of Uganda attend. A Burundi delegation attends as guests.

December 16   Burundi makes formal application to join the EAC.

December 21   The Supreme Court of Burundi acquits for lack of evidence four men accused of the January 15, 1965 assassination of Prime Minister Pierre Ngendandumwe.

1968

January — Micombero dissolves the National Council of the Revolution.

March — After meeting in January and February, an East African negotiating team states that no new members will be admitted to the EAC "for at least two years."

June 7 — President Lyndon Johnson appoints George W. Renchard as U.S. ambassador to Burundi. The post has been empty since the expulsion of Donald Dumont in January 1966.

July 11 — The Burundi government announces that it is expelling (on 48 hours' notice) seven officers and an enlisted man belonging to the 44-member Belgian military assistance group in Burundi.

August 1 — Gilles Bimazubute replaces both Cyprien Smbiyara as secretary-general of UPRONA and Pierre Apozensi as secretary of interior and civil service.

December 24 — A Bujumbura court pronounces sentences on 13 former political leaders of the monarchical regime who were arrested in in May 1968 on charges of writing and distributing "open letters" hostile to the government of Michel Micombero. This is described two days later by *La Libre Belgique* (Brussels) as Burundi's "most important political trial since the change of regime."

1969

September — An abortive Hutu plot against the government is discovered.

October 11 — Burundi Foreign Minister Labare Ntawurishira, discloses that at least 20 people have been arrested in Bujumbura for plotting against the regime of Colonel Micombero. The foreign minister also states that "the plot was financed by an embassy

	in Bujumbura as was clearly confirmed by the confessions of the plotters arrested."
December 17	The Burundi government announces that 26 people, including three former ministers, have been sentenced to death for taking part in the September coup attempt and for planning a massacre of Tutsis. Those sentenced form the new Hutu elite that has emerged since the mass slaughter of Hutu leaders in 1965.
1970 November	Several operations are undertaken against Tutsi guerrillas operating against Rwanda from northern Burundi in the Burundi government's attempt to improve relations with the Hutu government of Rwanda. Tutsi refugee leaders have been arrested and forced to return to special refugee camps or to leave Burundi.
	Africa Report prints an anonymous article (the journal's policy if the author chooses) titled "Burundi: Political and Ethnic Powderkeg." Terence Nsanze, the Burundi ambassador to the UN, protests strongly, accusing the article of lacking "the most elemental academic integrity."
1971	A 30-member Supreme Council of Revolution of is set up.
October 13	China and Burundi restore diplomatic relations. A communique signed by representatives of the two governments in Dar es Salaam says: "With a view to developing friendly relations and co-operation between the two countries, the Government of the People's Republic of China and the Government of the Republic of Burundi have decided to restore diplomatic relations at the ambassadorial level."

1972
March   Idi Amin helps arrange a written guarantee of amnesty for Ntare so that the deposed king can return to Burundi as a private citizen. One of Micombero's letters to Amin states that Burundi will meet "all conditions" set by Amin. It adds that, "Your Excellency can be assured that as soon as Mr. Charles Ndizeye (Ntare) returns to my country, he will be considered as an ordinary citizen and that as such his life and his security will be assured."

March 30   Ntare returns to Burundi and is flown to one of his father's former residences in Gitega to be detained. Hours later, the Voice of the Revolution Radio announces that Ntare has been arrested trying to lead West German white mercenaries in an invasion. The Burundi Embassy in Dar es Salaam denies the invasion report. Other radio reports say that the former king has plotted, but not led, the invasion.

April 29   Micombero dismisses his entire government and the executive secretary of the ruling party, UPRONA. Within hours of the dismissal of the government, the Voice of the Revolution announces that "imperialist stooges and traitors who support the monarchy tried to overthrow the Republican rule and its Constitution." The radio also reports riots in Bujumbura, saying that dissidents have set fire to cars, killed civilians in their homes, and killed soldiers returning to their barracks.

The radio also reports fighting in Gitega (where Ntare has been under house arrest since his return to Burundi), during which the former king was killed when an attempt was made to rescue him.

April 30   By the end of this day, fighting is reported to be very heavy in the South, with bands of Hutu attacking members of the ruling minority Tutsi. Burundi radio says that the dissidents had "organized massacres" in Bururi and appeals to the Burundi people to heighten their vigilance and "stamp out the last vestiges of monarchism" in the country. In a second broadcast, Micombero appoints military governors to each of Burundi's eight provinces. The report promises that those responsible for the coup attempt ("monarchists and mercenaries") will be hunted down and punished without mercy.

May 3   Madrandele Tanzi, director of Zaire's political bureau, says Zaire is sending a company of troops to Burundi at the invitation of Micombero to help "overcome agents of imperialism" and will provide the Burundi army with ammunition and put fighter aircraft and other "needed elements" at its disposal.

May 4   The Voice of the Revolution Radio reports that the whole country is calm and that those responsible for the coup attempt have been arrested.

May 5   In a rebroadcast of the announcement of May 4, the passage stating that calm prevails throughout the country is left out. Scattered fighting is reported.

May 7   The government radio announces that an unspecified number of people have been executed for their part in the coup attempt. Diplomatic sources in Kampala say that the death toll in Burundi has reached several thousand and that about 10,000 refugees have fled to Tanzania and Zaire. It is officially confirmed in Dar es Salaam that more than 3,000 refugees have entered Tanzania.

May 9   British missionaries in outlying parts of Burundi say that new and serious trouble has broken out in at least three areas of the country.

May 29   The Belgian prime minister states that Burundi is faced "not with a tribal fight but with a veritable genocide."

June 12 U.S. Senators Edward M. Kennedy and John V. Tunney call for international action to deal with the situation in Burundi. Kennedy, chair of the Senate Judiciary Subcommittee on Refugees, says he hopes the UN will expedite requests for aid by neighboring countries that have received refugees from Burundi. He adds, "Inevitably, it has been labelled an internal affair of Burundi. But when people are being slaughtered at a rate of nearly 3,000 per day, shouldn't there also be some international concern? Shouldn't governments condemn the killing? Shouldn't more concerted efforts be made by regional organizations or the UN to offer their good offices to end the strife and human suffering?" Tunney, referring to press reports estimating that more than 100,000 people have been killed, says that even if the conflict does fall within the UN definition of a domestic matter, "the international community cannot escape its moral responsibility to act."

June 13 Micombero denies that his government is engaged in a policy of genocide against the country's Hutu. He reiterates that all of the 50,000 or more people said to have been killed by the rebels were Tutsi and compares the attacks to previous unsuccessful coup attempts by the Hutu in 1965 and 1969.

June 21   A telegram from the U.S. embassy in Burundi (later published in the *New York Times*) reports "selective genocide" and describes live burial, the "summary" slaughter of returning refugees promised safe conduct, and executions not only of the Hutu elite, but also of "masses of villagers and refugees throughout the country." At about the same time, an intelligence memorandum circulating within the State Department concludes that, "There is no doubt the government [in Burundi] is engaged in selective genocide."

July 4   UN Secretary General Waldheim confirms that the first UN team to Burundi has found awful suffering and that the dead might number as high as 200,000. The reactions to this announcement are angry rebuttal in Burundi and silence in Washington and among the other African states.

August   An American Universities Field Staff report on Burundi, which U.S. officials judge accurate, summarizes the killings of the last several months as follows: ". . . the four Hutu members of the cabinet, all the Hutu officers and virtually all the Hutu soldiers in the armed forces; half of Burundi's primary schoolteachers; thousands of civil servants, bank clerks, small businessmen and domestic servants. At present, there is only one Hutu nurse left in the entire country, and only a thousand secondary school students survived."

December   The disaster relief office of United States Agency for International Development concludes that "In human terms, Burundi was the worst disaster to occur in 1972."

1973
March 21   Tanzania protests the bombing of three northwestern villages by Burundi. A report

filed from Bujumbura by *Christian Science Monitor* correspondent Frederic Hunter claims that Burundi has neither bombs nor bombers, but puts together the following explanation from fragmentary reports: "On March 16, a Burundi army patrol was ambushed near the Tanzanian border by a guerrilla band of approximately 30 Hutu armed primarily with spears; one of the military was killed and three injured. A detachment was sent to the area, using mortar fire and one helicopter for strafing. This anti-guerrilla action resulted in 30 dead and many chased across the Tanzanian border. As the border in this area is ill-defined, a Tanzanian village could have been hit."

April 3   Burundi (which has crucial transportation lines through Tanzania) extends a formal apology to the Tanzanian government, admitting the incursion of March 16 and offering to pay compensation for loss of life and property.

August   The UN Subcommission on the Prevention of Racial Discrimination and the Protection of Minorities complains about Burundi as a situation that possibly reveals a persistent pattern of human rights violations.

1974   Early this year, full diplomatic relations are resumed between the United States and Burundi in spite of persisting reports of the ruling Tutsi carrying out a policy of genocide against the Hutu. The United States plans to renew an aid fund for $100,000 that was suspended in 1972. A new constitution this year confirms Burundi as a one-party state.

1975
February   Former U.S. ambassador to Burundi, Thomas Melady, publishes a letter in the

New York Times criticizing the lack of UN action over the massacres: "I was present in Burundi in 1972 when most of the at least 90,000 Hutu were killed in what was a selective genocide. Why did the UN General Assembly not speak about this horror?"

1976

May   Micombero places the national university under Simbananiye's jurisdiction, a move interpreted as a major victory for Simbananiye and a serious setback for the more development-minded Tutsi and for those close to the Micombero "Family Corporation."

November 1   Micombero's government is overthrown in a bloodless coup by the military. The commander in chief of the Burundi Army, Lieutenant-Colonel Thomas Ndabemeye, is dismissed, and UPRONA, Burundi's only political party, is dissolved. An armed forces' broadcast says that the country is calm, but there is no word of Micombero's fate.

November 6   Voice of the Revolution radio announces that the country has returned to complete normality, and a Supreme Revolutionary Council headed by Lieutenant-Colonel Jean-Baptiste Bagaza is embarking on a national and international campaign to explain its aims. Micombero, who has been under house arrest, will be imprisoned.

1978

January   Prime Minister Ndugu Nzambimana says the country's military rulers plan to hand over power to civilians in 1981, five years after the overthrow of Micombero.
The office of prime minister is abolished, and the president becomes the head of the

government. The president chairs an 11-member Executive Committee, responsible to the newly formed Supreme Revolutionary Council of army officers.

1979
June

52 Protestant and Roman Catholic missionaries are expelled from Burundi, accused of encouraging rebellion against Bagaza's military government.

September

Bagaza heads the delegation from Burundi to the 34th General Assembly of the UN in New York, becoming the first Burundi head of state to officially visit the United States since Mwami Mwambutsa IV in 1964.

1980
March

The first national congress of the revived UPRONA party, Burundi's only legal political party, chooses the head of state, Bagaza, as the only candidate for party president and head of the Central Committee, which recently took over from the Supreme Revolutionary Council of army officers.

1981
November

A new constitution, approved by a national referendum, provides for a national assembly to be elected by universal adult suffrage.

1982
October

The first elections under the new constitution are held.

November

In a cabinet reshuffle, 11 new ministers are named, including, for the first time, two women.

1983
July 16

Michel Micombero dies of a heart attack in Mogadishu, Somalia, where he has lived since shortly after the overthrow of his

	government and his arrest in November 1976.
1984	
August 31	Bagaza is re-elected in the first presidential election since he gained control of Burundi eight years earlier. He had been re-elected to the presidency of UPRONA in July, and under the constitution, the party leader is the only candidate for the national presidency.
1985	
August	More than 150 local priests are detained. The government cites defiance of a recent ban on church services between 7 A.M. and 5 P.M. as the reason.
1986	A new political party named Burundi Democratic Front (Frodebu) is founded by Melchior Ndadaye.
1987	
September 3	Pierre Buyoya leads a bloodless coup, overthrowing Bagaza's government, suspending the constitution, announcing the formation of a ·31-member Military Committee for National Redemption, and dismissing all government ministers. Bagaza was attending a Francophone summit in Canada.
1988	
August 5	A Hutu uprising occurs in Marangara. Hutu villagers demand the removal of four Tutsi civil servants and then panic when three military vehicles arrive. One refugee in Rwanda later says, "We knew what they were going to do. Everyone was saying 1972! 1972!"
August 6	The Hutu arm themselves with arrows, spears, and machetes, fell trees across roads and dismantle a bridge in order to block the army.

August 7   When soldiers arrive with a chain saw to clear the road, several dozen Hutu, the first of the refugees, flee to Rwanda.

August 5   The provincial governor, Colonel Cyriac Kobako, begins to meet daily with the local population of Marangara. He says, "They just kept saying that they were frightened, but they would not say what of." Hutu refugees claim that they were very specific; they want the four civil servants removed and the governor to act against Tutsi plotters.

August 14   This is considered the flash point of the 1988 massacres. A wealthy Tutsi coffee merchant in Ntega refuses to pay a group of Hutu peasants money that he owes them, taunting and killing five of them. In an enraged response, the Hutu mobilize, surround and stone his house, and besiege him for many hours. When he defends himself with a shotgun, they break in and kill him and his family. After this, pandemonium erupts.

August 22   In an open letter to the president, 27 Hutu intellectuals ask for an inquiry into the massacres and point to gaps in the official account. Seven are promptly imprisoned, and 12 university students are suspended.

October 6   Buyoya presses on with reforms, creating a Consultative Commission on National Unity with 12 Hutu and 12 Tutsi members to investigate the recent massacres.

October 19 Buyoya reshuffles his cabinet, increasing the number of Hutu ministers from six to twelve, now a majority. He also re-creates the position of prime minister and fills it with former provincial governor, Adrien Sibomana, a Hutu.

1991
February 1

The Charter of National Unity is adopted by 89.2 percent of the electorate in a national referendum. The document was written under the auspices of the ruling UPRONA party and had been highly criticized by some opposition groups. Among those opposing the charter was the new and now principal Hutu party, Party for the Liberation of the Hutu People (Palipehutu).

1993
March

A new constitution, paving the way for multi-party democracy, is approved by over 90 percent of the electorate. The constitution disallows political organizations that advocate "tribalism, divisionalism, or violence," and states that parties must be representative of both the Hutu and Tutsi groups.

June 1

The first free presidential election takes place, resulting in the election of Melchior Ndadaye with 64.7 percent of the vote, against 32.5 percent for Buyoya.

June 29

The first free legislative elections take place.

July 10

Melchior Ndadaye takes power in Burundi. He is the first democratically elected president, as well as the first Hutu and the first civilian to hold that office.

July 18

Ndadaye announces an amnesty for about 500 political prisoners. This is seen as a conciliatory gesture to both Tutsi and militant Hutu. Under the amnesty, hundreds of Hutu prisoners accused of having taken part in ethnic clashes in November 1991 will be released, as will a group of Tutsi soldiers accused of having taken part in a March 1992 coup attempt aimed at thwarting Buyoya's reform process.

September-
October   In the September-October issue of *Africa
                 Report*, a reporter states that the new
                 government is safe because an army coup
                 would set the country on fire. She further
                 states that Frodebu enjoys "rapturous
                 support" and that "if Ndadaye or his team
                 were harmed, every Tutsi family in Burundi
                 would be in danger."

October 21   Melchior Ndadaye is assassinated in an
                 attempted coup.

October 22   The killings of Tutsi are under way with
                 intensity across many provinces of Burundi
                 and in Bujumbura; thousands of Hutu and
                 anywhere between 100,000 and 200,000
                 Tutsi are reported killed. This would be one
                 quarter to one third of the entire Tutsi
                 population.
                 Leaders of the attempted coup establish a
                 Committee of National Salvation to run the
                 country temporarily, sealing the borders,
                 closing the airport, shutting down the Lake
                 Tanganyika port, and cutting phone service.
                 The temporary government is being led by
                 François Ngeze, a former interior minister.
                 Ngeze tells the official Burundi radio station
                 (Burundi Radio) that he was forced into a
                 leadership role.

October 23   Lieutenant Colonel Jean Bikomagu,
                 Burundi's chief of the army, says the troops
                 who took part in the attempted coup are
                 willing to surrender power in return for
                 amnesty. Bikomagu tells Burundi Radio
                 that he was not involved in the coup.
                 From Rwanda, Jean Minani, health
                 minister, proclaims a government in exile.

October 24   Reports of mass violence begin to circulate.
                 A doctor with the Red Cross says, "It's a
                 mess—the war is going on with machetes."
                 The same doctor reports peasants attacking

and burning farms, large groups of refugees fleeing, and bodies lying in now-deserted villages. The violence appears to be primarily Hutu against Tutsi. Prime Minister Sylvie Kinigi has taken refuge along with seven other ministers in the French embassy. She says that the remaining ministers known to be alive are hiding in the city or have fled the country. She says to reporters, "It's very difficult to say who has power now. The army does not seem to want to lose it. I have no military, no police force, and no control of the media. I have nothing." She asserts, however, that 60 percent of the army is still loyal to her and that the coup was organized by officers mainly from the province of Bururi, long the home of the ruling Tutsi aristocracy.

October 26   The army leadership urges government ministers to come out of hiding and resume control. The government, led by Prime Minister Kinigi, refuses to give amnesty to soldiers involved in the coup and refuses to negotiate until the soldiers disarm and return to their barracks.

November 15   Dozens of Hutu villagers are killed by the military in Kiganda district. Despite evidence such as this, the military claims that the country is calming down and that the troops have remained neutral.

1994
January   Cyprien Ntaryamira is appointed head of state (now president) by the National Assembly. The appointment is challenged in the Constitutional Court by the opposition.

February   Amnesty International receives reports that more than 40 civilians have been killed and many homes destroyed since January 31. The latest violence is reported to have started when Tutsi opposition leaders called on their supporters to dissolve the Constitutional Court, which was done.

February 3 The government and opposition parties meet in the capital and agree that Ntaryamira will take the oath of office on February 5. The agreement also calls for the president to reinstate the Constitutional Court judges and appoint a new prime minister from among the ranks of the opposition.

February 4 The Coalition for Peace and Justice in Burundi (CPJB) is formed by a group of Burundians gathered in Ithaca, New York.

February 5 Ntaryamira is inaugurated and, during the ceremony, says the main goals of his government will be "to do everything possible so that peace, tranquillity, and mutual trust return among Burundians."

March 5 Missionary and Amnesty International reports claim that several hundred people have been killed in Bujumbura in the continuing tribal conflict set off by the October coup.

March 12 News in the Western press is very sketchy. Some relief agencies and diplomats say that more than 1,000 may have been killed in the current ethnic violence; others say the number is far fewer than that. Relief agencies, including the office of the United Nations Office of High Commissioner for Refugees (UNHCR), also say that the fighting since the October coup may have forced as many as a million people to flee to neighboring countries, where dozens are dying each day from disease and starvation in makeshift camps.

The United States suspends its $16 million aid program to Burundi after the coup and later rejects an appeal to send troops there as part of a UN peacekeeping mission.

April 6
President Cyprien Ntayamira and Rwandan President Juvenal Habyarimana are killed when their plane crashes near the airport in Kigali (Rwanda). Rwanda's UN ambassador, Jean Damascene Bizimana, tells the Security Council that the crash was not an accident but an assassination. He reports that the plane was hit by rocket fire. This incident sparks massive and widespread violence in Rwanda, while Burundi remains relatively calm. Pockets of fighting and killing have been reported continually since the attempted coup of last October.

April 24
Fighting intensifies in the Bujumbura suburb of Kamenge, where Hutu militants are said to be staying. More ethnic clashes are reported in the countryside, where Hutu have barricaded themselves behind roadblocks and trenches intended to stop army vehicles. Most of Bujumbura is now segregated into Tutsi and Hutu neighborhoods.

April 25
Sylvie Kinigi, a moderate Tutsi, who was prime minister under President Ndadaye and briefly head of state, says the only hope for peace is for Burundians to become exhausted by the fighting. She says, "We entered into democracy without having the means of dealing with it. The process was too rapid. There was no time to form political leaders, so parties formed on the simple criteria of ethnicity. With Rwanda, we have in common inexperience in democracy and ineptness in managing power."

August 7
Tutsi opposition leader, Mathias Hitimana, is arrested, bringing Bujumbura to a two-day standstill and sparking clashes by his followers that leave up to 15 people dead.

August 11   A grenade from an unknown source is thrown into Bujumbura's main market, injuring at least seven people.

September 10   A coalition government, comprising members of the country's 13 political parties is set up. Under an agreement achieved with UN help, it is decided that the prime minister of Burundi must be a member of UPRONA.

September 12   Gun battles begin to break out in the suburb of Kamenge. Military officials say gunmen attacked troops at Nyabiraba, 11 miles from Bujumbura, and five attackers were killed.

October-
November   Hundreds of people in Burundi are killed by Hutu extremists and army reprisals.

December 1   Jean Minani, a Hutu and former exile in Rwanda, is elected speaker of the National Assembly.

December 20   About 20 people are killed in two days of ethnic attacks that bring Bujumbura virtually to a standstill. No strong military presence is visible on the streets of the capital.

December 21   A 7 P.M. curfew in Bujumbura is initiated in an attempt to curtail the violence in the city.

December 22   The UN Security Council calls for a halt to violence in Burundi, fearing a repeat of the ethnic mass killings in Rwanda earlier this year.

December 23   UPRONA withdraws from the coalition government for as long as Minani remains speaker of the National Assembly. UPRONA accuses Minani of inciting Hutu against Tutsi following Ndadye's murder in October.

December 24   Looting breaks out in abandoned parts of Bujumbura; authorities say calm is being restored.

1995

January 29   U.S. envoy to Burundi Robert Kruger announces in an interview that scores of people have been killed in a new outbreak of violence between Hutu and Tutsi. After seeing 67 corpses during a tour of rural areas, Kruger says that the total number of dead is probably "much higher." He also says that the victims appear to be Hutu; the local villagers blame the killings on troops of the Tutsi-dominated army.

February 4   Opposition leader Charles Mukasi threatens to topple the fragile coalition government, but backs off, saying he never intended to use violence to achieve his aims. At the same time, former President Pierre Buyoya says, "Things are worse here in Burundi than they were in Rwanda in April last year just before the plane crash."

February 8   Bujumbura is virtually shut down for six days under a general strike called by UPRONA to press for the resignation of Prime Minister Anatole Kanyenkiko.
Burundi Radio quotes Kanyenkiko as saying he will not resign until the two parties agree on a successor, while Charles Mukasi, the opposition chairman, says the strike will continue until Kanyenkiko's government collapses.

February 11   In a radio address, American president Bill Clinton urges Burundi to "say no to violence and extremism" and seek peace.

February 16   Kanyenkiko resigns, and shooting and grenade blasts break out in Bujumbura. A resident says, "It was almost like every other night. We hear this all the time."

February 22   President Ntibantunganya appoints a new prime minister, Antoine Nduwayo. Nduwayo tells reporters that nothing can be achieved until peace is restored in Burundi:

"Peace and tranquility constitute the most important program. . . . Those who don't want peace are the very ones who keep saying Burundi is about to ignite, that Burundi is about to become like Rwanda."

March 1   Prime Minister Nduwayo names seven new government ministers.

March 6   Twenty-nine Hutu are slain by Tutsi near the provincial capital of Muyinga, about 80 miles northeast of Bujumbura.

March 8   Ten raiders from Zaire, who the Burundi authorities say are extremist Hutu who believe Ntibantunganya sold out to Tutsi by agreeing to a coalition government, are killed in an attack against a military post in Butara, about 30 miles north of Bujumbura.

March 9   A seven-person mission that had been dispatched to Burundi by the UN Security Council in February calls for increased UN presence to help the Burundi government strengthen its legal system and train civilian police.

March 11   Mines and Energy Minister Ernest Kabashemeye is shot by a lone gunman in downtown Bujumbura. Following the shooting, gunfire and grenade explosions can be heard in Bujumbura, and young Tutsi militiamen begin congregating at street corners.

March 13   A Tutsi government official, Lucien Sakubu, is kidnapped, allegedly by Hutu militants.

March 14   President Ntibantunganya asks the international community to help his country avert genocide: "The world must help Burundi, not with military intervention, but by stopping the same thing from happening in Burundi as in Rwanda."

March 15   The mutilated and crucified body of Lucien Sakubu is found. Tutsi riot to avenge the

	killing, attacking Hutu with grenades and knives, wounding many.
March 17	Four grenades explode in Bujumbura, killing one and injuring dozens, following the burial of Kubasheneye.
March 19	Two Burundi soldiers and three Belgians are killed outside Bujumbura by a Hutu gang.
March 20	The killing sets off fighting in Bujumbura's market in which five people are reported killed. Jean Minani, head of the Frodebu party, says he wants the attackers tracked down quickly and punished, to make them an example.
March 21	Burundi state news agency says that six people were killed in the attack outside Bujumbura, and 11 were wounded.
March 23	Burundi's army clashes with armed civilians believed to be infiltrators from Zaire. The civilian fighters are thought to be followers of former Interior Minister Leonard Nyangoma (in exile in Zaire), who opposes the inclusion of Tutsi in Burundi's coalition government.
March 26	Burundi Radio reports that the Frodebu party headquarters in Bujumbura was burned down. Thousands of residents flee Bujumbura following a night of fighting between security forces and supporters of Nyangoma. President Ntibantunganya says that at least 150 were killed and as many as 50,000 have fled. The Bujumbura suburbs of Bwiza and Buyenzi, where the clashes occurred, are virtually empty.
March 27	UN Secretary General Boutros Boutros-Ghali meets with ambassadors of the United States, Russia, France, Great Britain, and China. Ntibantunganya says he fears genocide has started in Burundi.

March 28   Amnesty International says that Burundi is "poised on the brink of another cycle of horrific slaughter."

March 29   More than 500 dependents of American and European diplomatic staff fly out of Burundi in what is described as a "low-key" evacuation.

A United Nations Children's Fund (UNICEF) study of 2,769 (of the more than 14,000) children orphaned by ethnic killings since October 1993 found that 58 percent had been personally attacked, 77 percent of those knew their attacker, and in 81 percent of those cases, the attacker was a neighbor.

March 31   President Ntibantunganya and Prime Minister Nduwayo sign an agreement to pursue stability, protect lives, and encourage the return of about two million refugees living in camps.

April 1   Tanzania closes its borders to Burundian and (mostly) Rwandan refugees.

April 3   One hundred fifty people, mostly Hutu women and children, are reported killed in a single village (Gasorwe) in northeastern Burundi. Survivors say their attackers wore army uniforms.

Robert Krueger, U.S. ambassador, visits the area and reports: "one child had been shot in the face and had lost an eye." He adds that he saw another child beaten so badly that his brain had been exposed. As many as 450 have been reported killed in this province of Muyinga in the past two weeks; the Burundi army says it knows of only 20 deaths.

April 4   More than 60 civilians are killed in ethnic fighting in northern Burundi, raising the number of deaths reported to more than 500 in the last two weeks.

April 5	The government says it will investigate reports of ethnic massacres in northeastern Burundi. Amnesty International says in a report that Burundi's justice system is dominated by Tutsi and has done little to establish who is responsible for political killings.
April 6	President Ntibantunganya leads hundreds of mourners, including government officials, diplomats, and military leaders in prayer in Bujumbura on the first anniversary of the deaths of his predecessor, Cyprien Ntaryamira, and Rwanda's President Juvenal Habyarimana.
April 10	The French Cooperation Minister Bernard Debré accuses the American ambassador, Robert Krueger, of warmongering; according to Debré, Krueger advocates military intervention in Burundi but refuses to send in American troops. Debré opposes foreign armed intervention.
April 18	Hutu gunmen (reported to be of Rwandan origin) kill two soldiers in an assault on an army post in Gasorwe in northeastern Burundi; five of the attackers also die.
April 22	The Associated Press prints some comments by Burundi leaders concerning the present state of unrest. President Ntibantunganya says, "These militias are not created out of thin air. They are essentially political, and there are politicians who fund and direct them." Pierre Buyoya, Burundi's former military ruler, says, "The real problem isn't the power of extremists. It's the weakness of moderates who are afraid to denounce violence." UN representative, Ahmedou Ould Abdallah, says, "This is a very unstable country, and the more we talk about genocide, the more we provoke it. People will think genocide is

coming so they had better attack their neighbor before he attacks them." Emmanuel Ndabarushimana, a Protestant minister in Bujumbura, says, "Even the children's hearts are full of hate." Jean-Baptiste Bagaza, a former president who now leads a hard-line Tutsi political party and finances an extremist newspaper, says elsewhere that "everyone here is sharpening their knives." Over a year ago, Bagaza proposed partitioning Burundi into a "Hutuland" and a "Tutsiland"; "At the time, people thought I was an idiot," he continues. "Today it's happening with machete blows."

April 25   Two soldiers and at least ten other people are reported killed during fighting between security forces and Hutu militia members in Bujumbura. The fighting begins when security forces search the Kamenge district of Bujumbura for five young members of a Tutsi militia known as Sans Echec [without fail] who had been kidnapped the day before allegedly by "Hutu elements."

April 26   Burundi Radio says that, in fact, 24 people were killed in the latest violence.

May 1   The international group, Reporters Without Borders, urges President Ntibantunganya to close six newspapers that have "stirred up for many months, in a blatant and deliberate way, ethnic hatred." For example, a Tutsi newspaper claims that Hutu kill Tutsi and then feast on their corpses; a Hutu newspaper calls Hutu to arms. Innocent Muhoze, president of the Association for the Promotion and Protection of Freedom of Speech, says, "These newspapers are dangerous. They are the lifeblood of extremists." The Tutsi extremist press recently has directed its anger at the U.S.

ambassador, Robert Krueger. *L'Etoile* accuses Krueger of being a Hutu supporter who was "fanning the flames." The paper said last month, "The day may come when patriotic Burundis will make him pay. This would be a legitimate act."

May 5   Unidentified gunmen attack a bus with guns and grenades in northern Burundi, killing 18 and wounding 13 others. 36 people are reported injured by a grenade thrown into Bujumbura's central market.

May 9   Burundi denies asylum to 317 Rwandan refugees and expels them back to their country. By doing so, Burundi has breached the 1951 UN refugee convention, according to the UNHCR.

The body of Dmitri Lascaris, an employee of Catholic Relief Services (CRS) (Greek-born, but raised in Burundi), is discovered near a camp for Rwandan refugees in Kirundo province in northern Burundi. He had been shot.

May 11   President Ntibantunganya appeals to the international community to support his government, which he says runs a country "sick in all parts." The Burundi News Agency announces that a grenade explosion at Busoni prison in Kirundo province has killed 14 people and wounded four. An attack on an official's car in Kamenge killed a soldier on guard.

May 15   Foreign relief groups suspend all but essential humanitarian assistance in Burundi for one week in reaction to the death of the CRS aid worker.

May 18   Leonce Ngendakumana, president of the National Assembly, reports that a gang armed with rifles and grenades has attacked a public bus outside Burundi's Parliament building, killing at least five people. He blames the attack on a Tutsi militia.

May 19   The main market and most shops in Bujumbura close for a peaceful protest against the arrival in Burundi of Rwandan Hutu blamed for the last year's genocide in Rwanda. About 10,000 people march through the capital in the protest, organized by members of Burundi's main opposition party (UPRONA).

May 22   Unidentified extremists successfully close down Bujumbura for three days with gunfire, grenade blasts, and barricades.

May 24   Sans Echec, a Tutsi youth militia, claims responsibility for the general strike in Bujumbura; they demand the release of their leaders, arrested over the weekend by security forces. Prime Minister Nduwayo says on Burundi Radio: "I am personally ready to meet youth delegations and other groups of people so that together we can find peaceful and reassuring solutions."

May 25   Virtually no shooting overnight and a reopening of Bujumbura's central market follow Prime Minister Nduwayo's speech.

May 26   Gunfire and grenade explosions resume in Bujumbura when members of Sans Echec are not released.

May 28   Businesses reopen, and normal activities resume in Bujumbura.

May 30   An OAU peace mission arrives in Burundi seeking to promote reconciliation between Tutsi and Hutu; it is the second visit since last month by the team. The OAU currently has approximately 50 military observers in Burundi. The team will meet with former President Bagaza, who currently leads the radical Tutsi Party for National Reconciliation (PARENA), the only political party not part of the agreement to share power that was signed last year.

May 31   Radio Burundi reports that one soldier is killed when fighting breaks out in Kamenge between government troops and Hutu militiamen. Mayor Pie Ntiyankundiye of Bujumbura says it is not coincidental that violence has flared up again after the arrival of the OAU delegation: "Every time we have a foreign delegation here shots are fired at soldiers and the clashes in Kamenge start again." Salim Ahmed Salim, the secretary-general of the OAU and the head of the visiting mission, says that after some hopeful signs, "things go back to square one." Salim also says that the people of Burundi "must capitalize on the present good will of the international community."

June 2   Gunfire continues in Hutu areas of Bujumbura; the casualty total remains unknown because soldiers have banned reporters and other outsiders from entering Kamenge. There is also shooting in the Tutsi districts of Cibitoke and Bwiza and another Hutu district, Kinama. The OAU mission leaves Bujumbura after failing to enter Kamenge to negotiate a cease fire.

June 4   Military sources report that in the last six days of fighting 11 people including four soldiers have been killed, but a postal worker says that 25 bodies have already been buried.

Aid agencies are still unable to enter Kamenge, but thousands of Hutu from Kamenge have sought shelter in nearby areas, where they are being helped by the Red Cross.

June 6   Prime Minister Nduwayo orders the army to prepare to move into Kamenge. He says on Burundi Radio, "Today we can no longer wait. The government cannot accept that a portion of Burundian territory, however sick it is, should be occupied by terrorists who kill and chase away the population." The Burundi Press Agency says that "rebels of the hardline Palipehutu have stepped up attacks on the Tutsi army in the Cibitoke region."

Nduwayo urges civilians to evacuate Kamenge and offers them refuge at a soccer stadium. As of late afternoon, no one has taken up the offer.

June 7   At dawn army troops begin pushing into Kamenge in armored vehicles. One report says that the sweep was delayed while troops and officials tried to evacuate civilians; a dispute is witnessed where Foreign Minister Jean Marie Ngendahayo demands to know why the military operation has started much earlier (13 hours), before the end of the interval that the civilians had been given to flee.

June 8   The bodies of at least 25 children, women, and elderly are reportedly found after the army offensive against militiamen. However, the militia apparently retreated into the hills before the operation; none of the dead are reported to be young men. A Tutsi soldier claims that Hutu militiamen killed their own people in order to implicate the army.

In an apparent revenge attack, armed Hutu kill eight or nine Tutsi in suburban Musaga.

June 9   The UN calls for an investigation by the Burundi government into the massacre of Hutu civilians; President Ntibantunganya agrees to it. The UN puts the death toll of innocent people at 30; foreign press representatives count at least 40 dead. Army spokesman Longin Minani denies that Tutsi troops are responsible, saying that Hutu gunmen are capable of murdering other Hutu in order to ruin the army's reputation.

June 12   At least 13 Hutu students are killed at the Matanga campus of Bujumbura University when Tutsi students throw grenades into dormitories. The Tutsi students suspected one of the Hutu of having taken part in an earlier attack on the Saint Esprit secondary school near Kamenge in which four Tutsi students were killed.

June 14   Gunmen ambush a convoy between the villages of Rusenda and Bukinanyana in the province of Cibitoke near the Zaire border in northwest Burundi, killing an OAU observer from Burkina Faso and wounding another observer and six Burundi soldiers. The foreign minister of Burundi, Jean-Marie Ngendahayo, and the U.S. ambassador, Robert Krueger, also in the convoy, are unharmed in the attack. A UN spokesman says it is not known who is responsible for the attack, but the group of dignitaries were in one of the most dangerous areas of Burundi, Cibitoke. Krueger, along with UN special envoy Ahmedou Ould Abdallah, had been threatened earlier this year by an extremist Tutsi newspaper, which accused them of siding with Hutu.

June 15   Amnesty International reports that immediate international action is necessary to stop Burundi's army and other armed groups from killing civilians. The report states that "the overriding human rights concern in Burundi is the mass murder of defenseless civilians. Extrajudicial executions by the army are continuing unabated. Most of the victims are Hutu."

June 18   In an attempt to lessen ethnic violence, President Ntibantunganya announces a nationwide 5 P.M. to 9 A.M. curfew (expanding the dusk-to-dawn curfew in effect in Bujumbura since December 1994), a requirement for travel documents and special permission to travel outside of one's home province, bans on political meetings, demonstrations, and broadcasts; government censorship of all television and radio programs. He also asks Parliament for power to rule by decree until October.

June 20   Aid agencies come under attack and halt operations in Burundi as fighting continues in Kamenge.

June 21   Tutsi militants murder a Hutu professor and director of research, Ruzemza Stanislav, at Bujumbura University. Prime Minister Nduwayo says that civilian casualties in the current fighting in Bujumbura are inevitable because Hutu guerrillas are using civilians as shields.

June 24   Hutu militias attack a Tutsi neighborhood in Bujumbura, killing at least nine people; new emergency laws give the army more power to crack down on violence throughout the country.

Foreign ministers of the OAU pass a resolution in Addis Ababa, urging countries bordering Burundi to stop the flow of illegal arms into the country.

June 25   Foreign Minister Jean-Marie Ngendahayo, who escaped injury in an attack on his convoy last week, resigns and seeks temporary refuge in South Africa. He tells Belgian radio that he quit because he has lost faith in the government of Burundi to protect its citizens.

At the OAU summit meeting in Addis Ababa, the Rwandan foreign minister expresses fear that there will be an explosion in Burundi like that in Rwanda. "Our fear is total. . . . Please, wasn't Rwanda's example enough for you? Do you want to commit the same madness?"

June 28   By a vote of 38-13 with 11 abstentions and 19 absentees, Burundi's parliament rejects President Ntibantuganya's proposal for extra emergency powers to curb the ethnic violence. In the vote, all 38 negative votes were from Frodebu (the president's party). Frodebu party members say it would give the military too much power; UPRONA members vote unanimously in favor of it. At the OAU summit conference, other African leaders threaten military intervention in Burundi to restore peace. Ntibantuganya says the other heads of state were "extremely severe toward Burundi's politicians."

June 29   Fifteen Frodebu members of parliament flee the country and go into hiding amid death threats following their defeat of the president's bill for emergency power.

June 30   Heavy gunfire in Bujumbura forces between 30,000 and 50,000 Hutu to move farther into the hills surrounding the capital.

July 1   Tutsi and Hutu celebrate independence day peacefully but separately. President Ntibantuganya leads celebrations in Gitega, which is mostly Hutu, and Prime Minister Nduwayo leads festivities in Bujumbura, now almost completely Tutsi.

July 11   Charles Mukasi says the UPRONA party will not attend talks in Addis Ababa aimed at ending bloodshed. He says mediation to end fighting should be held in Burundi: "It is a question of patriotism. We must forge a strong current of peace and national unity here in Burundi, not in a hotel environment hundreds of kilometers away."

July 12   About 50 people are killed in Muyinga province when masked gunmen shoot guns and throw grenades into a market; the victims are both Hutu and Tutsi. The president of Frodebu says that when all reports are added up, the daily death toll is approximately 100. An OAU team leaves Bujumbura after failing to persuade Tutsi opposition parties to participate in peace talks in Addis Ababa.

July 15   Tens of thousands of Hutu flee Bujumbura after overnight clashes.

July 16   Boutros-Ghali arrives in Burundi, where he plans to talk to the current president, prime minister, and commander of the military as well as to former Presidents Bagaza and Buyoya.

July 17   President Ntibantunganya tells Parliament that no nation in history has been able to commit collective suicide, so at some point the bloodshed in Burundi must stop. Defense Minister Firmin Sinzoyiheba says that since the democratic elections in June 1993, there have been three attempted coups—in July 1993, October 1993, and April 1994. He says that the attempts failed only because of army action.

July 21   The OAU postpones the Burundi peace conference indefinitely because the Tutsi opposition parties refuse to attend.

July 25   Ten Hutu are killed and three wounded on their way home from work in what are possibly revenge killings for the death of four Tutsi students two days before.

July 28   Thousands flee Kamenge as renewed fighting breaks out. A senior army officer says that the fighting was started by Hutu gunmen in order to coincide with the arrival in Bujumbura of South African Archbishop Desmond Tutu and German Foreign Minister Klaus Kinkel. "Each time a foreign delegation arrives in Bujumbura, Kamenge explodes," he says. Kamenge residents, however, say the fighting was started by the army.

July 29 — Another army officer says that there has not been fighting in Kamenge. Rather, the residents fled when they heard gunfire three miles to the north and feared being caught once again in the crossfire.

August 3 — Two South African peacemakers (Meshack Radebe of the African National Congress and Sipho Mlaba of the Inkatha Freedom Party) leave Burundi, saying that they found little commitment to peace during their six-day visit. They are "worn out by taking on so much ethnic hatred." They recommend grass-roots peace committees and say they will return to Burundi in October.

August 19 — Jean Minani, president of Frodebu, tells news services that government and provincial leaders from the Hutu majority are being systematically assassinated and threatened by extremist members of the Tutsi minority. He says that nine high-ranking Hutu officials have been killed or have survived assassination attempts in the last two weeks.

August 22 — Zairean troops continue herding Barundi refugees back across the border to Burundi. Most of the approximately 2,000 people expelled from Zaire are women, children, and the elderly; some claim they have been living in exile since the 1972 massacres. The UNHCR says it expects thousands more to be expelled.

August 28   The UN Security Council creates a commission of five jurists to probe the 1993 death of President Ndadaye.

August 29   Innocent Nimpagaritse, minister of transport, posts, and telecommunications, announces his resignation in a news conference from Kenya. He says there have been three attempts on his life, the last one approximately two weeks ago.

September 5   Hutu villagers accuse soldiers of the Tutsi-led army of massacring up to 50 people, as reported by the U.S. ambassador, Robert Krueger. Krueger meets with military officers to demand a full investigation into the incident.

September 9   Prime Minister Nduwayo censures the U.S. ambassador over allegations that the army was involved in the killing of civilians. The prime minister says that the ambassador only wants to discredit the government and army and that he presents his allegations in a biased manner with no evidence to back them up.

September 14 UN sources say that North Korean military experts are training the Burundi army in the use of heavy weaponry in the northwestern regions of Cibitoke and Bubanza. A Western security source tells Reuters, "The presence of the North Koreans may not be unrelated to the recent shipment of 152 metric tons of Chinese weaponry into Burundi."

September 19 Pope John Paul II appeals to refugees from Burundi and Rwanda for an end to the "terrible tragedy" in the two countries.

September 21 The OAU welcomes former U.S. President Jimmy Carter's plan (presented on September 20) to discuss with African leaders how to end conflicts in Burundi and Rwanda.

September 26   Angry Tutsi vow to avenge the slaughter of a family of five and the wounding of seven other Tutsi in a suburb of Bujumbura on September 25. The attack occurred just hours before the president, prime minister, and other cabinet ministers were to visit the suburb to try to encourage Hutu to return to their homes.

September 30   Five people are wounded in the heaviest night of gunfire to hit the suburbs of Bujumbura in weeks. The initial attack is on a camp for displaced Tutsi. President Ntibantunganya suggests the attack may have been intended to sabotage a government campaign to persuade tens of thousands of Hutu to return to Kamenge.

October 5   Cibitoke Governor Sylvestre Mvutse says that his province is trapped in a spiral of violence. "Extremists on both sides have personal and political interests in maintaining the bloody status quo" because they know that if peace ever returns, they could face arrest.

October 11   Ahmedou Ould Abdallah, UN special envoy to Burundi, leaves after a two-year assignment. He says he does not despair for the future of Burundi. He is given one of the great drums meant for the one who has power as a parting gift.

October 12   President Ntibantunganya reshuffles the Cabinet.

October 27   President Ntibantunganya says he wants former U.S. President Jimmy Carter to convene a conference to deal with the crisis in Burundi. Carter, former Tanzanian President Julius Nyerere and South African Archbishop Desmond Tutu will serve as mediators.

Burundi's Defense Minister Firmin Sinzoyiheba vows to wage a "merciless

war" against both Hutu and Tutsi
extremists.

November 1   More than 250 Hutu are killed in a raid near
the northern town of Ngozi; the raid appears
to have been the work of Burundi
government soldiers, according to a senior
government official.

November 4   Burundi's army says it killed 11 Hutu
rebels near the capital; an army commander
in the South, Fidele Baramburiye, was
killed.

November 7   The Red Cross suspends operations in
Burundi after unknown gunmen shoot at a
convoy and kill a Burundi employee.

November 8   The UN appoints Aziz Hasbi of Morocco as
its new special representative in Burundi.

November 21   Jimmy Carter says, "The visit to Burundi
has been completely successful. The
president, prime minister, and others have
approved a draft of the agenda for the
conference in Cairo." The conference,
attended by leaders of Uganda, Tanzania,
Rwanda, Burundi, and Zaire is to begin
later in the month.

November 27   The Burundi army steps up its military
campaign against suspected Hutu rebels;
diplomats say the strategy is likely to cripple
peace prospects.

December 2   One government soldier and 20 suspected
Hutu rebels are killed in a clash near
Bujumbura.

December 8   The U.S. State Department strongly
condemns the reported massacre of 430
civilians, 90 percent women and children,
by the Burundi military. The massacre is
supposed to have taken place on November
14, but the State Department waited for
corroboration before commenting.

December 15   The International Committee of the Red
Cross suspends all activities in Burundi, cit-

	ing too much danger to its workers. A spokesman says, "One accepts security risks. But beyond a certain level it would be crazy."
December 19	International Action Against Hunger also suspends activities in Burundi, following the wounding of two of its workers in a grenade attack on their residence in Gitega.
December 20	Juvenal Manyrambona and Innocent Ndikumana, two prominent Hutu Burundi politicians of Frodebu, are murdered in Bujumbura.
December 22	A UN human rights investigator says that gunmen killing at will in Burundi are dragging the country into a "genocidal trend."
1996 January 1	In a New Year's Day address, President Ntibantunganya says that Burundi is on the brink of collapse and appeals for an end to confrontation and destruction. He says, "Extremists in the ethnic Hutu majority attack the army, minority Tutsis, and Hutus who do not agree with them, while Tutsi extremists kill innocent people and loot their property." He also says, "Undisciplined elements in the Tutsi-dominated army also loot and kill."
	Doctors Without Borders, a relief agency, estimates that the death toll in 1995 was 15,000.

Introduction

> The political system [of Burundi] did not favor historical memory. . . . It was in everyone's interest to forget the past, whether it was the *ganwa* who had taken the land, the subchief who had been dismissed, or the king himself who relied now upon one faction, now upon another. The former senior regent of the country told me that history was of no interest at the court so there were practically no historical accounts. The political system shows why. (Vansina 1985, 115).

Vansina's view of the history of Burundi may very well be the correct one. Certainly, this is not the first historical work on Burundi that quotes him, nor, in all probability, will it be the last. However, Vansina speaks mostly of a country's oral tradition, a primary method by which a country becomes familiar to the rest of the world, but not necessarily the only method; and he seeks the truth. Perhaps the truth is something that is never known precisely; historical truth, at least, is dependent upon the givers and the receivers of it. Earlier, Vansina says of truth:

> Not all societies have the same idea as to what historical truth is. . . . In the Congo, "truth" is what has been transmitted by the ancestors as having really happened . . . .The Rundi have the same idea of historical truth, and as soon as something is accepted as a historical truth, they do not trouble to think whether it could have happened or not, or whether it really happened in the way the tradition describes. In their eyes, analysis of a testimony is meaningless. (1965, 102-3)

It is difficult to ever know if what we learn of a people and of a culture is "true." Do those inside the culture have a better perspective, or does the necessary objectivity come from outside? These questions may never be answered to everyone's satisfaction, but they will still be asked as history continues and unfolds to the world. This historical account of Burundi seeks to find facts rather than truth; unfortunately, the line between the two is not always as clear as we may like. Some of the facts, however, follow.

Burundi is located in the east central portion of the continent of Africa (between 2 and 4 1/2 degrees south and 29 to 31 degrees east, bordered to the north by Rwanda, to the east and south by Tanzania, and to the west by Lake Tanganyika. The country is one of the smallest on the continent, approximately 10,746 square miles 6,448 square kilometers) in area. It is in a mountainous area; in fact, part of it falls into the area named "The Mountains of the Moon" by Sir Richard Burton during his explorations of the region. As a result of the elevation, temperatures average about 73 degrees Fahrenheit in the Rift Valley region and between 65 and 67 degrees Fahrenheit in the central plateau. Rainfall averages between 40 and 60 inches per year with the heaviest rainfall in March and April and the least in June, July, and August. Coffee and cotton are the most important commercial agricultural products and the main sources of foreign exchange, but the economy of the country has been based almost entirely on subsistence-level agriculture throughout most of its history and up to the present.

Burundi became an independent monarchy separate from Rwanda on July 1, 1962, and it was proclaimed a republic on November 28, 1966. Prior to independence, it had had a long history of European colonization. It was a part of German East Africa from 1894 to 1919 and then administered by Belgium as part of the League of Nations Mandate Territory and the United Nations Trust Territory of Ruanda-Urundi. These years followed a much longer history of a feudal system of patronage between indigenous Hutu and more recently arrived Tutsi.

The national language of the country is Kirundi, and this member of the Bantu language family is spoken by all members of the population. French is the European language that was the official language of the government and post primary education. Swahili, the *lingua franca* of much of East Africa, was used as a trade language in the urban centers. At least 60 percent of the population practices Christianity (mostly Roman Catholicism), and there is a small following of Islam as well, but traditional religions remain a part of everyday life in Burundi.

Until 1966 when the monarchy ended, Burundi's kings (*bami*; singular, *mwami*) came from four dynastic lines, giving the country's history a cyclical nature. Some traditions say that as one king succeeded another, history ran its course and began again. A member of the Batare (Ntare I) was the first known king of Burundi, but the cycle is said to have begun with the Bambutsa family. A Ntare followed a Mwambutsa, then came a Mwezi (from the Bezi clan), and finally a Mutaga (of the Bataga). Each of the kings was supposed to have an ideal character: Ntare was the conqueror, Mwezi was the maintainer of the power in the face of rebels, Mutaga was good but often unlucky, and Mwambutsa was the king who prepared the country for the cycle to begin again. Perhaps ironically, a Ntare also ended the cycle in 1966.

Three ethnic groups that are not tribes in the traditional sense comprise the population. The groups, for the most part, share a language, kinship system, and spiritual belief system, but have been considered as separate groups from the earliest known time of the country. The breakdown of the population is a source of controversy even today, but the census numbers generally given are the Bahutu (Hutu) at 84 to 85 percent, the Batutsi (Tutsi) at 14 to 15 percent, and the Batwa (Twa) at only about 1 percent. Membership in the groups was apparently clear in the country's earliest days; the Tutsi came to the region later than the Hutu, but became the landowners and, eventually, the royalty. It remains an interesting mystery that this apparently invading group (thought to be originally from the Nile region) adopted the language of the indigenous group. The Hutu generally were closer to the land as workers and did not gain as great a degree of monetary wealth or political power, leading to a patronage system that, in turn, led to a system of minority rule in the twentieth century. In the present, in spite of continued violence between the ethnic groups, physical membership is less clear due to generations of intermarriage. And indeed, the divisions between the ethnic groups have been perhaps the primary driving force in the modern history of Burundi and the cause of at least four enormous civil wars resulting in the deaths of thousands. The vast majority (probably about 95 percent) of the national army is Tutsi, and this continues to be a controversy within the country as well as among outside observers.

The first sign of ethnic violence on a massive scale occurred in 1965. Many international observers thought it was the obvious sign of unrest and unequal political dominance that it was, but also thought that it was an isolated event. However, large ethnic massacres occurred again in 1972, 1988, 1991, and 1993. The last one has perhaps tapered off somewhat but continues up to the present in acts of violence, sometimes killing hundreds of people at a time.

Since its independence, Burundi has had very few peaceful times of development, leaving it one of the poorest nations in the world. In the last 35 years, there have been 13 heads of state (first prime ministers and, since 1966, presidents); the first prime minister, Prince Louis Rwagasore, was assassinated before independence and so before he was able to take office. Only one (Melchior Ndadaye) was elected in a free democratic vote in 1993; therefore, only one (his predecessor, Pierre Buyoya) left office as the result of losing the votes of his constituents. Ndadaye was assassinated only months after taking office. All of the others were overthrown in *coups d'etat*, some peaceful, some violent, or assassinated while in office. The years following independence also saw a crown prince usurping his father for the monarchy, although the last king remained in power for only a few months.

Burundi's neighbor to the north, Rwanda, has a similar ethnic makeup, but the two countries evolved quite differently after becoming independent from each other. Nevertheless, the situation in Rwanda is still ethnically volatile as well. The government of Burundi remains in flux as some parties of a weak coalition, installed in December 1994, struggle to achieve and maintain peace. The country remains an object of the world's speculation.

The Dictionary

-A-

Abadasigana. This was the original Kirundi name for the **UPRONA** party, meant to evoke elements of tradition. Traditionally, *abadasigana* refers to a group of people who were the personal entourage of the *mwami*. More specifically, it refers to the followers of Mwami **Mwezi Gisabo** and is usually translated by Barundi as "the followers of Mwezi." The **PDC**, during the period just preceding independence, called itself Amasuka u'Mwami, which refers traditionally to the same category of royal officials. This name, however, is more closely associated with Mwami **Ntare Rugaamba**, giving it a pro-**Batare** meaning, rather than the pro-**Bezi** connotation of the Abadasigana.

Abasapfu. See **Musapfu.**

Action Sociale. This program for women was inaugurated in 1949 and was taught by **White Sisters** and European wives. The purpose was to teach women of Burundi skills that would raise them "to the level of their husbands" (according to the charter of the program). These skills included sewing, knitting, home management, and gardening; the classes were open only to women with families. The enrollment was 244 women at the onset of the program and rose to 2,332 by 1957.

Agriculture. Except for a very few small industries, Burundi's economy has, for the most part, been based primarily upon agriculture at a subsistence level. The ratio of arable land to population was documented around the time of independence at 1.18 acres per capita; since then, it has become even smaller due to population growth and spread as well as the erosion of the soil. Generally, however, except for occasional periods of severe drought, Burundi has been self-sufficient in terms of food. The main subsistence crops have been sorghum, corn, millet, beans, peas, potatoes, cassava, tobacco, peanuts, and various fruits such as bananas and papayas. Honey is also popular and is gathered throughout the country. Additionally, coffee and cotton have become the most important commercial agricultural products and the main sources of foreign exchange.

Albert, Ethel. A linguistic anthropologist, Albert did extensive research in Burundi in the late 1950s and early 1960s. Her research provided some new insight into many social practices of the Barundi; it also provided linguistic insight into the class structure of the country. She writes: "Speech is explicitly recognized as an important instrument of social life; eloquence is one of the central values of the cultural world view; and the way of life affords frequent opportunity for its exercise. . . . Argument, debate, and negotiations, as well as elaborate literary forms are built into the organization of society as means of gaining one's ends, as social status symbols, and as skills enjoyable in themselves" (1964). Albert also writes that the formal speech of the Tutsi and the Hutu differ; Tutsi men receive formal training in the practice of eloquence, and Hutu men are made aware that the production of eloquent, "aristocratic-type" speech before a "superior" is tactless. She says that caste stereotypes prevent members of the upper caste from raising their voices or allowing anger or other emotions to show. She also says that "the Batutsi herders prefer to bear a grudge silently and to take revenge when opportunity permits, even if it comes 20 years after the affront has been suffered."

Amasuka u'Mwami. See **Abadasigana.**

Anglo-Congolese Agreement. This agreement was important in eventually deciding the borders of Ruanda-Urundi in 1894 and after. Between 1890 and 1894, Cecil Rhodes popularized the notion of a "Cape to Cairo" line of British communication. The difficulty was that the telegraph would have to pass through German East Africa, which included Ruanda-Urundi. The **Germans** protested against the British corridor although, at that time, European trade in the Ruanda-Urundi area was nonexistent. To the Germans, the Cape-to-Cairo route was a symbol of British domination of the African continent—something the Germans wanted to prevent at all costs. Ironically, this corridor was originally subordinate to other parts of the 1894 agreement and was included—some say almost accidentally—as Article III. The original objectives of the 1894 agreement were quite similar to those of an 1889 agreement concluded by the Imperial British East Africa Company and the Congo State: both allowed for a British corridor to Lake Tanganyika through Ruanda-Urundi, but the later agreement focused on the prevention of French advancement to the Nile. By June 1894, the British were convinced that the Germans were targeting Article III and that they wanted it completely withdrawn. All of this, including the withdrawal of Article III, led to further exploration and delineation of the European and Congolese claims in the region of Ruanda-Urundi.

Army. The army of Burundi has long been a source of controversy. At first, around the time of independence, it was closely controlled by the government. In the months immediately following independence, for example, all non-**UPRONA** officers were weeded out of the corps. The army started out as ethnically neutral, but by around 1965 this was no longer as true.

Starting from 1965, members of the army have carried out or attempted at least six coups. Gradually, the number of **Hutu** army officers has lessened until today, when there are fewer than 5 percent Hutu in the army at any level. This has renewed the atmosphere of controversy and distrust; many say that a Hutu president is unable to control a **Tutsi** army. In fact, the first elected Hutu president, Melchior **Ndadaye**, was assassinated by the army. He was also the first civilian head of state in three decades. However, his predecessor, President **Buyoya**, was also plagued by a disgruntled army, including a group that plotted in 1989 against the regime. The assumption remains that the purpose of that coup was to return President **Bagaza** to power, although that has never been proven.

Art. As with many traditional cultures, the art forms of Burundi revolve primarily around oral histories of the country. **Vansina**, however, argues that there is very little of historical value in the stories of Burundi, unlike in those of neighboring countries. Nevertheless, there is a body of oral literature, songs, and proverbs that has now been collected and written down.

Additionally, Burundi has a history in the musical arts, including such traditional instruments as the musical bow, the flute, types of horns, and an instrument similar to a small violin. Of course, drums have been important in the cultural history of Burundi and remain so; one can still see performances by the royal drummers in Gitega, and these drummers have gained worldwide acclaim.

In the visual arts, Burundi is less developed by Western standards. As with much of East and Central Africa, decorative art tends more toward geometric motifs, consisting of lines and circles, than toward other types of nonrepresentational designs. Sculpture and figure painting are not popular forms of expression, but the geometric designs painted on otherwise utilitarian basketry and pottery are unique and quite beautiful.

Association des Progressistes et Démocrates Barundi (APRODEBA). In the very early days of independence, a number of **Hutu** politicians were supported in their quest for democratic rule by some **Belgian** functionaries. Two of the most enthusiastic were Resident de Fays and the court inspector named F. L. Asselman. These two actively participated in the launching of the pro-Hutu APRODEBA; when the organization's vice-president later joined **UPRONA**, the two Belgians gave their full support to the **Parti du Peuple**.

-B-

Bacamurwanko, Jacques. As ambassador to the **United States** in 1994, Bacamurwanko wrote extensively of his views of the crisis that plagued Burundi since the assassination of President **Ndadaye**. In his document, "Burundi: Which Way Out? (Perspective of the Crisis)" he wrote about the need for security throughout the country as well as for the elected officials; he discussed reforming the military to correct the near lack of **Hutu** soldiers; in fact, he stated that the "biggest threat to Burundi's emerging democracy has been, still is, and will ever be the configuration of the **army**." He proposed long-term plans for peace and democracy, which included improved security forces, an independent judiciary, an independent legislature, a more solid civilian society, viable political parties, a free press, civilian control of the military, self-support of the military, an increase of small enterprise, and a more competitive educational system.

Bagaza, Jean-Baptiste. Lieutenant-Colonel Bagaza, a **Tutsi-Hima** and deputy **army** chief of staff and a member of the **"Family Corporation"** under Michel **Micombero**, overthrew Micombero's government in a bloodless coup in November 1976. Bagaza charged the "clans of self-interested politicians" had used their office to gain personal wealth. In the aftermath of the coup, the new government's first appointments included Bagaza as president and Lieutenant-Colonel Edouard **Nzambimana** as prime minister. As well, a special executive council led by Bagaza would conduct the administration, with a 30-member Supreme Revolutionary Council, consisting exclusively of army officers. Micombero, who had been under house arrest was imprisoned. Just five days after the coup, Burundi's **Voice of the Revolution** stated that the country had returned to complete normality and the supreme council had embarked on a nationwide and international campaign to explain its aims.

Although the period of Bagaza's presidency was outwardly relatively peaceful, it was nevertheless full of ethnic and religious strife. For example, in June 1979, a group of 52 Protestant and Roman **Catholic** missionaries was expelled from Burundi after being accused of encouraging rebellion against the military government. A report from Bagaza's office stated that the missionaries had been urging young people to flee the country by telling them that a civil war was about to break out. The incident was one of many in a series of tensions between Bagaza's government and the church in Burundi. The month before this incident, Bagaza had issued a decree limiting Roman Catholic Masses to Sundays only; the church bishops protested the move in a letter questioning the restrictions of their religious freedom, to which Bagaza responded with a statement accusing the bishops of spreading antigovernment propaganda and contributing to the division of the population. From 1985 to 1987, Bagaza continued his attempts to diminish the influence of the church in Burundi. The government charged that the missionaries inject politics into their health and education work by supporting the Hutu. Religious colleges were taken over by the government, and new measures were imposed to close catechism classes in primary schools, ban instruction based on religious texts, and outlaw Catholic youth movements. From 1980 until the end of Bagaza's presidency, more than 450 foreign missionaries were forced to leave Burundi, and several other members of the clergy were detained for varying periods of time. The government also shut down the Catholic radio station and newspaper, prohibited religious gatherings without prior approval, and closed a network of church literacy groups that taught an estimated 300,000 children and adults in rural regions.

In a move to boost the national economy in the 1970s, Bagaza arrested 70 former officials on charges of misappropriating public funds. In an effort to keep the country's meager wealth from going abroad, Bagaza then forbade any Burundi national from holding foreign investments and any company owned by Barundi from using overseas bank accounts or acquiring foreign property. In 1980, the First National Congress of the **Union for National Progress (UPRONA)**, Burundi's only legal political party at that time, chose Bagaza as the only candidate for party president and head of the **Central Committee**. In July 1984, Bagaza was overwhelmingly re-elected as the president of UPRONA. Under the constitution, the party leader was the only candidate for the national presidency. The following month, as the only candidate, Bagaza won 99 percent of the 1.7 million votes in the first presidential election since he had seized control of the country. This election was a step in Bagaza's efforts to reestablish a measure of democratic rule in Burundi; he had promised upon taking over the government to restore civilian rule and to ease the deep animosities and long-standing ethnic rivalries partly caused by the violence in 1972.

Among indications of ethnic strife in Burundi during this period was, ironically, the total denial of ethnic strife. Bagaza is said to have believed that by not mentioning the long-standing division between Hutu and Tutsi citizens, the problems would cease to exist; foreign nationals working in Burundi during this period were forbidden by their embassy officials to even use the words "Hutu" and "Tutsi" in public for fear of expulsion from the country.

Bagaza promised to heal the ethnic strife and to promote policies of national reconciliation when he seized power. According to some past critics of Burundi's treatment of the Hutu, who had become newly hopeful, he toured the country to promote reconciliation and urge officials to facilitate the return of as many as 150,000 Hutu refugees who had fled during the years of repression; he issued land reforms to help Hutu acquire more property and desegregated the national university to encourage more interchange between Hutu and Tutsi. In fact, however, these few reforms to counter the existing institutionalized discrimination against the Hutu were not enough. In September 1987, Bagaza's government was overthrown in another bloodless coup led by Pierre **Buyoya**. Bagaza found refuge in Uganda, where he was granted temporary asylum. He said that the coup had been carried out by "young boys without a great deal of political experience," and he vowed to return home. In November, however, he attempted to fly to Burundi, and the government refused the plane permission to land in Bujumbura. After being denied permanent asylum in Uganda, he took up exile in **Belgium**. In 1993, he was accused of masterminding the coup in which **Ndadaye** was killed, but denied involvement.

Bambutsa and Bataga. While the **Bezi** and **Batare** were the central figures in the conflicts around and after independence, the two other dynastic families, the Bataga and the Bambutsa, were not sufficiently important in terms of influence or numbers to make a significant contribution to the conflicts. The Bataga were represented by Mwami **Mwambutsa** and his late brother **Kamatari** almost exclusively; the Bambutsa, who were descendents of Mwami Mwambutsa II, were still quite young at the time of independence, while their distant cousins, descendants of Mwambutsa I (*mwami* from 1765-1795), had long been absent from the political scene.

Bami. See *Mwami.*

Bamina, Joseph. After **Ngendandumwe**'s death in 1965, the mwami appointed Bamina as prime minister. Bamina was a university-educated Hutu, considered to be from a high-status lineage, and married to a Tutsi. Bamina had briefly served as a compromise **UPRONA** president in late 1962; he was acceptable at that time to both Tutsi and Hutu. At the time of his appointment as prime minister, it was thought that Bamina's strength lay in his unique position as a Hutu who had been a prominent member of the Casablanca group; his racial origins should enable him to rally the support of many in the Monrovia group as well. Finally, his political ties should make it possible for him to extract concessions from the Tutsi minority. Bamina was one of 23 people (all Hutu) found guilty of leading the abortive coup of October 1965; all 23 were executed in January 1966.

Bandwa (mu-, ba-). These are initiates or participants in ceremonies honoring **Kiranga**. The verb that corresponds to this noun, *kubandwa*, means to invoke Kiranga. Kiranga then communicates with the living through intermediaries known as *bishegu*. Bourgeois traced the roots of this religious practice to the arrival of Bantu-speaking people in **Rwanda** and Burundi, because it seemed to be more popular among the **Hutu** than among the **Tutsi**. Others have agreed that the practice of worshipping Kiranga probably predates the arrival of the Tutsi.

Bangemu, François. Just before—and while—an almost entirely new cabinet was being formed in November 1967, a series of firings and arrests took place, ridding the country of many left-wing elements to whom the military had become averse. Among these were Bangemu, known to be a **JNR** zealot and, at the time of his arrest, the director-general in the ministry in charge of party affairs. He was arrested for the assassination of Prime Minister **Ngendandumwe** (in 1965), but was later acquitted for lack of evidence along with the other accused conspirators.

Bangiricenge. See **Mwambutsa IV**.

Barahinduka, Jean. A brother-in-law of **Micombero** and a member of the "**Family Corporation**," Barahinduku became the governor of Muyinga Province in 1972.

Baranyanka. Once the personal secretary of Richard Kandt, the first **German** diplomatic resident in Ruanda-Urundi, Baranyanka became a chief during the early years of **Belgian** colonial rule. Known for his very Western outlook, Baranyanka was one of the most eminent representatives of the **Batare** family. The Belgians thought him to be brilliant and so chose him to rule over one of the largest chiefdoms; at the height of his career, he almost surpassed the Mwami's (Mutaga) prestige in the eyes of the

Belgian administration and was regarded by the **Bezi** as a threat to the monarchy. Baranyanka became the protégé of several later residents of Burundi, most notably Resident Schmidt (1944-54), who demonstrated a systematic policy of favoritism toward the Batare. For example, Schmidt gave an important chiefdom to Joseph **Ntitendereza**, Baranyanka's eldest son. Jules Sasserath wrote the following about him, a passage revealing of what the European Residents looked for in their favored chiefs:

> Paramount Chief Baranyanka is one of the coffee-kings of Ruanda-Urundi and a great connoisseur of Burgundy wines . . . owns his own chateau, drives an American car of the latest model, and is known to have a famous cellar. He makes a charming impression and has a refined intelligence. But if Baranyanka leaves an excellent impression, some of the other chiefs are full of deceit and deviousness, impregnated as they are with a typically oriental sense of duplicity.

Baranyanka, Pierre. Great-grandson of Mwami **Ntare** (II), he was the founder of the **PDC** and helped to carry on the family politics of his clan.

Baribwegure, Joachim. In late 1962, young Tutsi militants affiliated with the **JNR** made threats against Hutu trade unionists and politicians. Baribwegure, then president of the **Parti du Peuple** (PP) was an object of these often violent threats.

Barusasyeko. Although Mwami **Mwambutsa** was the son of **Mutaga**, he chose to identify with the **Bezi** instead of allying himself with his own people. A powerful chief during the early reign of Mwambutsa, Barusasyeko claimed that the Bezi managed to persuade the mwami that he was of Bezi origins, rather than the **Bataga** lineage that was truly his. Several historians (including Lemarchand) believe that Mwambutsa was fully aware of his origins, but chose to align himself with the more powerful Bezi as a means of solidifying his rule.

Bataga. See **Bambutsa and Bataga**.

Batare and Bezi. Before independence, the primary political problems still reflected conflicting interests and goals of several princely families associated with a class of traditional Tutsi rulers known as *baganwa*. The most important of these were the Batare and Bezi families, the descendants of whom were associated around the time of independence with, respectively, the *Parti Démocrate Chrétien* (Democratic Christian Party) **(PDC)**, with whom the **Belgian** administration identified, and the *Union du Progrès National*, (Union for National Progress) better known as **UPRONA**. At that time, both of these Tutsi-led parties vied for support of the Hutu majority. The roots of the Batare-Bezi conflict lie in the distribution of power that characterized the traditional politics of Burundi, where political competition often took the form of periodic struggles among the different dynastic segments of the royal line. During the time of independence, the authority of the Bezi grew at the expense of the Batare, their immediate rivals, but complete elimination of the Batare from the political arena was a process that was slow and, in fact, according to many historians, incomplete. They continued to be vital and resourceful, at least limiting the Bezi sphere of influence somewhat. It was these traditional princely feuds that caused cyclical tensions within the political system of the early 1960s which led to a dispersal of power between the factions as well as within each of them. At the time that Mwezi **Gisabo** was mwami, his primary preoccupation was to evict his predecessor (Ntare) descendants (the Batare) from their positions to the profit of his sons (the Bezi). This struggle, which was so much an established policy as to become institutionalized, continued quietly during the colonial period and intensified in the months preceding independence. By then, the Bezi had established themselves as dominant with the Batare holding a position clearly inferior in power. Eventually, the links between the Mwami and the Bezi family created a network of mutual obligations that continued to influence royal policies long after independence; in fact, according to Chief **Barusasyeko**, who was interviewed by Lemarchand, the Bezi managed to "persuade Mwambutsa that he was of Bezi origins." Lemarchand himself believed that the mwami was "fully aware of his Bataga origins but deliberately chose to align himself with the Bezi because they were the only ones whom he could trust to solidify his rule."

Baumann, Oskar. In 1892, this Austrian became the first European to traverse Burundi from side to side. Leading a Masai expedition of the **German** antislavery committee, he claimed to have received a friendly welcome from the Hutu, who thought of him as a liberator from Tutsi domination.

Belgium, Relations with. Belgian plans for the territories conquered in 1916 involved using them as pawns in postwar negotiations. The Belgians hoped to cede Ruanda-Urundi to Great Britain; they then hoped the British would cede a portion of German East Africa to Portugal and that the Portuguese would cede the southern bank of the lower Congo River to be joined to Belgium's Congo colony. First, however, Belgium's claims to the possission of the conquered territories needed to be recognized by the Allied Council, consisting of the **United States**, Great Britain, France, and Italy.

In August 1919, the council recognized Belgium's claims to Ruanda-Urundi. With approval by the League of Nations following shortly, Ruanda-Urundi became a mandated territory of the League of Nations under the supervision of Belgium. A law joining Ruanda-Urundi in an administrative union with the Belgian Congo (**Zaire**) was passed by the Belgian Parliament in 1925. The seat of the colonial administration was in Brussels; the chain of command passed to the governor-general in Léopoldville (Kinshasa), and from there to the Usumbura-based Governor of Ruanda-Urundi who held the title of vice governor-general of the Belgian Congo. Many officials in Brussels began to consider the territory another province of the Belgian Congo.

The Residency of Burundi was then divided into nine territories, each under a Belgian territorial administrator. The country's traditional political organization of approximately

36 chiefdoms under the *mwami* was subordinated to the Belgian administration. All chiefs and subchiefs were subject to the approval of the administering authority.

The government **education** policy during the early years of the Belgian administration was geared toward the training of the sons of the *ganwa* and other lesser **Tutsi** chiefs. As with the **German** administration, the intent was to equip these boys and young men to fill positions in the administration and civil service. For the rest of the population, emphasis was placed on primary education and mostly carried out through subsidizing the **Catholic** missions. This goal of the predominance of upper-caste elements in the higher councils was achieved and raised anxieties among the **Hutu**.

After the **United Nations** was formed, Ruanda-Urundi was made a Trust Territory. This new arrangement encouraged the political development of the people and the development of a democratic system, things not present in the League of Nations mandate.

Since Burundi's independence in 1962, Belgium's intervention and involvement has been sporadic. They have given financial aid and technical assistance to a degree. In 1987, President **Bagaza** did not renew residency visas for missionaries, Brussels "reviewed" its technical assistance program in Burundi, and there was a strong anti-Belgian campaign in Burundi's news media. Also since independence and primarily beginning with the massacres of 1972 (and continuing until the present), Belgian imperialism is often cited as the cause for the ethnic divisions in both Burundi and **Rwanda**.

Bezi. See **Batare and Bezi**.

Bigayimpunzi, Pierre. A *ganwa* of **Bezi** origin, Bigayimpunzi founded the **Parti Démocratique et Rural** (PDR) in 1961 during the time when many of the old **UPRONA** chiefs were severing their ties with the party. He, along with **Biha**, was a member of the Mwami's inner circle, but his favored position was not sufficient to gain votes, and he and his party finally had to concede defeat.

Later, however, possibly because of this favored status, he was appointed to the post of director of the Institut des Sciences Agronomiques du Burundi (ISABU). In 1972, as a member of President Micombero's **Family Corporation** (the uncle of Micombero's sister-in-law), he became minister of agriculture and often chaired cabinet meetings in Micombero's absence.

Biha, Léopold. Chief Léopold Bihumugani, who became popularly known as Biha, was the founder of the **UPRONA** party in 1957. A favored member of the Mwami's inner circle, he eventually conceded defeat to the prime minister designate, Prince Louis **Rwagasore**, for the party's leadership. Rwagasore's return to Burundi from Europe coincided with these beginnings of UPRONA. After several years of political turmoil, often influenced by the ethnic strife between **Hutu** and **Tutsi**, Biha, still a leading **Bezi** courtier (and the Mwami's personal secretary) was named as interim prime minister on September 13, 1965. As the Hutu had won an electoral majority in the National Assembly in May of that year, the Hutu parliamentarians concluded that the Mwami intended to deny them the fruits of their victory. On October 18, a group of Hutu **army** and gendarmerie officers tried to take over the royal palace, but encountered too much resistance from the Mwami's personal guard. As this attempted takeover was occurring, another group attacked Biha at his home, injuring him severely. On November 20, although Biha was still recovering and physically incapable of performing his duties, the Mwami restored the Biha government, which had been suspended during the emergency. In August of the following year, after Mwami Ntare had taken over from his absent father, Biha was arrested and, along with others who had been ministers of state under the previous regime, lost his title and all of the political power he had enjoyed for nearly a decade.

Bikomagu, Jean. As **army** chief, Lieutenant Colonel Bikomagu, who had been called the leader of the 1993 coup attempt that resulted in the death of President **Ndadaye**, both denied that he had a hand in the activities and, shortly after the violence began, designated himself as a mediator. Since the 1992 **Palipehutu** attack, he had acquired a distinguished human rights record. He also claimed that he managed to bargain for the lives of the president's wife and children during the uprising. In the role of mediator, he announced on a Burundi radio station that the soldiers who had seized power were ready to give up in return for amnesty. At this time, he also said, "The government must have confidence in its army. I control the entire army. Everything is now in order. But as for civil war, everything now depends on the government." A government spokesman, Jean-Marie Ngendahayo (a Tutsi and the minister of communications) replied, "How can I trust the army?" In 1994, several weeks after President **Ntayamira** was killed along with the **Rwandan** president, Bikomagu claimed to have foiled an attempt by Tutsi paratroopers to oust the interim government of President **Ntibantunganya**.

Bimazubute, Gilles. In 1959, while a student in Lubumbashi (then Elizabethville), Bimazubute along with another student, Prime Nyongabo, founded the **UCJAB**, later known as the **JNR**. While still a student abroad, he was the principal spokesman for the student organization, Union Nationale des Etudiants Barundi (**UNEBA**). His criticisms were at first directed against specific characteristics of the monarchy's policies, later against people closely involved with the Mwami, and finally against the Mwami himself. In one of his tracts, he stated that he was speaking on behalf of the "millions of citizens, abandoned to their fate, the intellectuals bullied by their elders who claim to be more deserving, and the young . . . who are no longer naive enough to balance their interests against those of a crown that has become ever more tarnished." He said, "Let there be no mistake—*we* are the rebels." Later he became the chief of the cabinet of the minister of external affairs and commerce; in this capacity, he publicly commented on the ethnic nepotism that had been occurring in government organizations. In January 1967, he was made secretary-general to the presidency, yet his sympathies for left-wing causes were not diminished; March of that year brought a major reshuffling of the cabinet, after which Bimazubute was appointed to the post of director-general in the Ministry of Information. He held that post until he was put in prison in May 1967 on President **Micombero**'s orders, under suspicion of being involved in a coup attempt. Bimazubute was a member of the **Abasapfu** clan. However, in 1968, he became secretary-general of **UPRONA**, as well as the secretary of the interior and the secretary of civil service. He was killed in the coup attempt of October 1993 that also killed President Melchior **Ndadaye**.

Bimpenda, Germain. Like **Biha**, Bimpenda was a descendant of the princely **Bezi** clan. After independence, they were among the most important personalities at the court and used their kinship affinities with the royal family to strengthen their leverage on royal decisions.

Biroli, Joseph. Some historians, for example, Lemarchand, note that the historical conflicts and antagonisms between the **Bezi** and **Batare** families flared up with renewed strength as independence and self-government approached. In addition to this, however, were other factors that reinforced these traditional rivalries. The president and one of the founders of the **PDC**, Biroli (Batare), and **Prince Louis Rwagasore**, the leader of **UPRONA**, disliked each other personally and intensely, a fact that was not concealed from the public eye during this time. Biroli was known to be a brighter student than Rwagasore at the Institut Universitaire des Territoires d'Outre-Mer in **Belgium**, and he attended Oxford and Harvard before going to work for the European Common Market organization. He was highly regarded in European circles, and his social graces tended to make Rwagasore appear awkward and backward by comparison. Political convictions notwithstanding, Biroli received greater sympathy and support from the European administration.

Apparently well-established are the facts surrounding the death of Rwagasore just prior to independence. The gunman, Jean **Kageorgis**, was a tool in the hands of the PDC leaders, and the assassination was the result of a political conspiracy organized by Biroli and **Ntitendereza**. The aim was to create disturbances throughout the country that would be exploited by the **PDC**; their actions were actively encouraged by some Belgian functionaries. Although the case was tried by judicial authorities of the Belgian administration, a retrial was ordered after independence. In the new trial, Biroli, who had previously been sentenced to penal servitude, was sentenced to death. On January 14, 1963, the sentence was carried out in front of an estimated 10,000 witnesses.

According to Lemarchand (and others), although the crime was due to a combination of motives both political and personal, it was also a settling of "old scores" between two rival dynasties. Lemarchand said it well: "Only if one remembers the historical dimensions of the conflict can one understand the feelings of rage of the Batare in the face of a situation which denied them once and for all the opportunity to make good their traditional claims to power."

Biru (mu-, ba-). Historically, these were the guardians of tradition and the royal counsellors. The *ubwiru* was the ritual code of the monarchy and the *abiru*, the interpreters of the code.

Biteyamanga. This was the name of the court jester, who was always with the ***mwami*** even in his travels. Some sources say that the jester was traditionally a dwarf; others maintain that the occupation was filled by members of the **Twa** ethnic group. The jester was responsible for the expected activities such as reciting silly speeches and poems, gesturing wildly, and generally playing the fool.

Bomunzu. Clans are subdivided into lineages, the descendants of a grandfather or great-grandfather. These are called *bomunzu* or *abo bunzu imwe*, "those in one household," or people living in one ***rugo*** presided over by an elder (*umujuru*). The council that makes a group decision is generally composed of lineage heads who speak with authority for all members of their group.

Bududira. This is the spirit of the traditional family and represents an orientation of all members to the lifelong welfare of the whole. Plural marriage was traditionally preferred because it made possible an estate system in which property could be kept in the family more easily. Therefore, the nuclear family comprising the spouses and their children could be quite large.

Bungere (mu-, mi-). Amulets and charms (*iviheko*) used to bring good fortune and ward off evil were a very important part of Burundi tradition. These particular amulets carried by women to ensure good fortune during their pregnancy were made of a hollow tube (often a reed) with a piece of quartz set into it. The quartz represented the unborn infant.

Bururi. Just before the aborted **Hutu** revolt in 1972, the southern **Tutsi**, known as the Bururi group, were on the verge of a violent clash with Tutsi from central and northern Burundi (known as the **Muramvya** and **Ijenda** groups, respectively). This conflict had historical roots; the southern Tutsi had been kept out of the political system in traditional Burundi, and under more than 60 years of European colonial rule, these same southern Tutsi were kept from the more important posts. In 1966, when the **army** seized control of the state, its commander (**Micombero**) and many officers and regular troops were from various southern districts, which put Bururi in a position of advantage.

Buryenda. This special house was traditionally built in the *mwami*'s compound for the purpose of guarding the *Karyenda*.

Butanyerera. After finishing his studies at the Institut Universitaire des Territoires d'Outre-Mer in Antwerp, **Rwagasore** returned to Burundi and was given this chiefdom to administer. Not satisfied with this power alone, Rwagasore virtually took control of the newly founded **UPRONA** party in 1958.

Buyoya, Pierre. In 1967, Buyoya went to **Belgium** for secondary and university education in social science. He then did military training before returning home to become commander of a local armored squadron; this was followed by further military training at Cavalrie, France from 1976 to 1977. Upon this second return home, he was again made a commander of an armored battalion and became the chief training officer for the chief of staff in the **army**. He also pursued political interests, being an important member of **UPRONA**, and was elected to the central committee of the party in 1979 and reelected in 1984. In the meantime, he continued his military training at the West German War School from 1980 to 1982.

In September 1987, while President **Bagaza** was attending a Canadian summit of Francophone countries, Major Buyoya led a bloodless coup, overthrowing Bagaza's government. Since Buyoya was formerly chief of operations and training in the defense ministry and was a central committee member of the ruling UPRONA party he was a natural leader for the country. The change in government was welcomed by many Barundi as well as by the country's Roman **Catholic** Church. Buyoya immediately suspended the constitution, announced the formation of a 31-member Military Committee for National Redemption, and dismissed all government ministers. Several of Buyoya's colleagues who had previously helped Bagaza overthrow **Micombero** in 1976 were named to the new ruling committee, including the government's second in command and new army chief, Colonel Edmond Ndakazi. Although Bagaza had pledged to heal the ethnic strife, there were few reforms to counter the existing institutionalized discrimination against the Hutu. When Buyoya took over, three-quarters of the cabinet and National Assembly, about two-thirds of all university students, 13 out of 15 provincial governors, all army officers, and 96 percent of all enlisted soldiers and police were Tutsi.

In his takeover speech, Buyoya emphasized that his reasons for the coup were almost identical to those of his predecessor: "We could, almost word for word, trace them in the declaration which 11 years ago justified the fall of the

First Republic. These statements denounced the acquisition by one person of all party and state powers, blocking of all institutions, constant violation of the constitution . . . and an incoherent economic policy." He concluded, "We are unfortunately forced to note that just a few years later, the regime of the Second Republic had fallen into the same errors." Also according to Buyoya, a major factor that encouraged the coup was Bagaza's clampdown on political dissent in the country and more specifically, repression of the Roman Catholic Church. As a result, one of his first moves as president was to release several hundred political prisoners whom, he alleged, Bagaza had jailed "without justification and without trial," and to promise a more conciliatory policy toward the Church.

In August 1988, there were, again, ethnic massacres in the countryside of Burundi that apparently escalated from a local event that got badly out of hand. Western diplomats did not think that the atrocities were ordered by the president, nor did they think that they were centrally planned by Buyoya, considered a sincere moderate. Nevertheless, his regime, seemingly committed to reform, was somewhat tarnished.

In October 1988, Buyoya re-created the position of prime minister and named a Hutu, Adrien **Sibomana**, to the post. At the same time, pressing on with reform, he created a consultative Commission on National Unity with 12 Hutu and 12 Tutsi members to investigate the massacres. Perhaps even more importantly, he reshuffled his cabinet, increasing the number of Hutu ministers from six to 12, now forming a majority.

The Buyoya government worked very hard to lay the groundwork for multiparty, nonethnic politics to take hold in Burundi. In February 1991, the Charter of National Unity, a document that transcended all laws including the Constitution, was adopted. The reforms were unprecedented and widely welcomed by Barundi as well as Western aid donors. In June 1993, Buyoya was defeated in a democratic election by Melchior **Ndadaye**. He was reported to be gracious in his defeat and remained fully supportive of the change in government. He continued to be an important spokesperson for Burundi.

-C-

Casablanca and Monrovia. Upon the death of **Prince Louis Rwagasore**, his dream of a truly nationalist party unifying all people of Burundi was also lost. **UPRONA** broke into factions competing for control of the party, one led by Andre **Muhirwa**, a Tutsi *ganwa* who succeeded Rwagasore as prime minister, the other by Paul **Mirerekano**, a Hutu, sometimes described as a merchant and mystic. The two factions took on very different ideological orientations. The Tutsi-led faction, which came to be known as the "Casablanca" group, was strongly anti-Western, partly because of the active role played by **Belgium** in support of the Hutu revolution against the Tutsi rule in **Rwanda** in 1959. The Casablanca group was divided between traditionalists and modernists, monarchists and republicans, civil servants and politicians. The Hutu group became known as the "Monrovia" group and was generally neutral or pro-Western in its orientation. The two names derived from two conferences of African states, one held in Casablanca, Morocco and the other in Monrovia, Liberia, and the two major African blocs that resulted from them. Other than the generally anti- and pro-Western sentiments, there was no direct connection between the factions in Burundi and these two blocs. The original "Casablanca" group reflected the views of participants at a conference in Casablanca in 1961 that resulted in the "African Charter of Casablanca," affirming that its signatories were determined to liberate and unify all of Africa; the "Monrovia" group participated in a conference later the same year, and participants agreed on five principles. Among them was noninterference in the affairs of other African states.

By March 1963, the Monrovia group was under the leadership of National Assembly President Thaddée **Siryuyumunsi**; the group delivered a series of attacks against the policy of the government and applied enough pressure on the court to have the minister of interior removed from office. The effect of this was short-lived. Prime Minister Muhirwa arrested three Monrovia leaders, including Siryuyumunsi, on the grounds that they were conspiring against the security of the state. The Mwami, however, intervened and ordered the three released, a short time later dissolving the Muhirwa government and appointing as the new prime minister Pierre Ngendandumwe, a Hutu of the Monrovia group.

Nearly a year later, under pressure from the Casablanca group, the Mwami issued a decree that restricted the powers of the government and centered greater control in himself and a few of his close associates. Instead of stabilizing the situation, this entrenchment of the traditional elements of the royal court made opposition to the monarchy more pronounced than it had been, and both factions of UPRONA considered the Mwami an obstacle to their political control. In March 1964, the Mwami dismissed four Hutu members of the Cabinet; when Ngendandumwe was unable to replace them, the Mwami gave the job to Albin **Nyamoya**, a member of the Casablanca group, former minister of agriculture, and a veterinarian. The anti-Western orientation of the Casablanca group and the Nyamoya government resulted in the establishment of close ties with the Communist Chinese government as well as with other Communist bloc nations. These moves were meant to provide additional leverage against the monarchy, which continued to be supported by some Western nations.

In late 1964, political tension in the country was rising; at this time a cache of arms was discovered, and fears spread of an impending coup allegedly supported by pro**China** elements. In reaction, the Mwami dismissed the Nyamoya government and reappointed Ngendandumwe as prime minister; three days later, Ngendandumwe was assassinated. The assassination confirmed the Mwami's fears of an impending coup; the Chinese ambassador, Liu Yu-feng and other members of the Chinese embassy were expelled from the country, diplomatic relations were broken, a number of politicians from the Casablanca group were arrested, and the leftist labor union, **Fédération des Travailleurs du Burundi**, and the youth wing of UPRONA, **JNR**, were ordered to suspend their activities. Joseph **Bamina**, chairman of the UPRONA central committee and a Hutu who had maintained political ties with the Casablanca group, was named prime minister, but the Mwami continued to restrict the powers of the government.

Catholic Church. An estimated 60 to 70 percent of the Barundi have been converted to Christianity, most of these Catholic. The Catholic clergy (**White Fathers**) came to Burundi in the mid- to late- nineteenth century and were accompanied by the **White Sisters**. The two groups set up missionary centers and in 1900 began to set up schools.

The church has had a great deal to do with the conflict between **Hutu** and **Tutsi**. Although there are now many Tutsi priests and bishops in the church, it is said that the majority of Tutsi have ambivalent feelings toward Christianity. This is partly due to the belief that the church in **Rwanda** was closely connected to Hutu leaders of that country. In the postcolonial years, in fact, the church attracted more rural Hutu than Tutsi for literacy training.

President **Bagaza** had shaky relations with the church; his successor, President **Buyoya**, attempted to normalize relations somewhat by repealing most of the restrictions on church-sponsored activities.

Central Committee. In 1980, the first national congress of the only political party then legal in Burundi, **UPRONA**, chose **Bagaza**, the head of state, as both the only candidate for party president and also as head of the Central Committee, which had taken over power from the **Supreme Revolutionary Council** of **army** officers earlier this year.

***Centres Extra-Coutumiers* (CEC).** In 1941, the **Belgian** Residency set up two *centres extra-coutumiers* (extra-customary centers or CECs) in the vicinity of Bujumbura, known as "Belge" and "Village des Swahili." This represented an extension of a royal decree of 1934, which made possible the creation of CECs in the urban centers of the Congo; as in the Congo, these later CECs were administered by a "chef," assisted by an "adjoint" and an advisory council, all picked by the administration. According to Léopold **Biha**, **UPRONA** was founded in 1957 in protest against the decision of the administration to reintroduce a system of CECs in Bujumbura, Kitega, Nyanza Lac, and Rumonge. Such a system would have removed these areas from the jurisdiction of the crown and would have deprived the mwami of opportunities for patronage. While earlier administrators once thought the system of CECs was an imaginative initiative of the Belgian administration, the chiefs who sat on the **Conseil Supérieur du Pays** (**CSP**) now saw it as an attempt to interfere with the Mwami's traditional role and prerogative.

Chanyo (i-). The French equivalent, *colline*, meaning "hill" is the more commonly used word even in the writing of modern Barundi; however, it is a complex notion and crucial to an understanding of the traditional as well as the modern social system of Burundi. Because of the geography of the country, there are few villages of the type familiar to other African countries and to Westerners. Instead, socioeconomic communities are built around the series of hills scattered throughout the countryside, often isolated or hidden by banana trees. On each of the hills is a group of *urugo*, the inhabitants of which collectively use the surrounding pastures (*ubunyovu*).

Charter of National Unity. On February 5, 1991, the Charter of National Unity was adopted by 89.2 percent of the electorate in a national referendum, although the document, written under the auspices of the ruling **UPRONA** party, had been highly criticized by opposition groups, including the externally based and then principal **Hutu** party, the **Party for the Liberation of the Hutu People (Palipehutu)**. Jacques Bacamurwanko, Burundi ambassador to the **United States** in 1994, wrote in his tract, "Burundi: Which Way Out?" that the time spent on the "ritualization" of the concept and the symbols of national unity could have been utilized more usefully and economically. He saw the Charter of National Unity as an opiate concocted by President **Buyoya** to keep a firm grip on Burundi's fluid politics for a long time to come.

China, Relations with. See **China Syndrome**.

China Syndrome. This title was coined by Lemarchand in 1970 as a description of China's involvement in Burundi politics. Burundi was attractive to China as a base for Communist penetration in Africa because of its location close to Zaire, the 1963-1964 revolutionary activities of which were an important reason behind the Chinese involvement. At independence in 1962 unofficial contacts had already been established between certain Barundi politicians and Chinese diplomats, but it was not until December 1963, after the Mwami yielded to the pressures of the **Casablanca** faction, that mainland China received official recognition. The deterioration of the Zaire situation at this time caused the mutual courtesies to crystallize into an alliance of sorts. Peking was determined to take full advantage of what Chou En-lai described as "an excellent revolutionary situation" in reference to the Congo. The motives that inspired Peking's policies in Burundi were clearly formulated by **Tung Chi-ping**: "Because it is the gateway to the Congo, this small, underdeveloped, overpopulated nation is important to Mao's long-range plans to dominate as much of Africa as he can. Before I was sent to Burundi, I had been thoroughly briefed on the progress being made there and the plans for the future. Again and again my superiors repeated Mao Tse-tung's statement: 'When we capture the Congo, we can proceed to capture the whole of Africa.' Burundi is the stepping stone for reaching the Congo."

Diplomatic relations between Burundi and China were shaky at first. Relations were first established in December 1963, but were "temporarily" suspended in early 1965 by Mwami **Mwambutsa**, who was aware of China's use of Burundi to contact revolutionaries in Zaire. At this time, China also lost its contacts with **Rwandan** exiles, who had been training in Burundi under Chinese experts in the hope of returning to Rwanda and seizing power. The suspension occurred two weeks after the assassination of **Hutu** moderate Prime Minister **Ngendandumwe**, an act that escalated a crisis between **Tutsi** and Hutu. Although no specific charges were made against China at that time, there had been speculation that the Chinese were involved. Burundi's new prime minister said that China had interfered with internal affairs, but had had nothing to do with the assassination; he stressed that relations would resume when the political situation was clarified. In fact, diplomatic relations remained suspended until 1971.

Coalition for Peace and Justice in Burundi (CPJB). Organized in February 1994 by a group of Burundians gathered in Ithaca, New York, the CPJB is a nonprofit organization. In March 1994, they produced a response to the tract written by then ambassador (to the **United States**) **Bacamurwanko**. They accused the ambassador of using statistics taken from a 1934 survey of ethnic populations in Burundi in a modern context. They criticized some of the ambassador's other ideas, for example, recognizing that the **army** needed to undergo changes, but disagreeing with the ambassador's suggested methods. Finally, they accused the ambassador of relaying false information. In their first newsletter of April 1994, the following organizational goals are listed: to strengthen the relationship between its members in order to partake in the restoration and maintenance of peace and justice in Burundi; to facilitate discussions between its members on any questions related to peace and justice in Burundi; to reflect upon and express the opinion of its members on any issue capable of compromising peace and justice in Burundi; to make a lasting contribution to the maintenance of peace and justice in Burundi by submitting to whom it may concern its opinions and information about matters of peace and justice; to call upon appropriate institutions anytime that peace and justice will be compromised in Burundi; to organize and participate in debates having to do with peace and justice in Burundi. In this same newsletter, the organization's president also called upon "all extremists in the country and outside to come back to their senses so as to avoid another bloodbath that would consummate the split among the Burundian population. This way, we can guarantee peace and justice not only for ourselves, but also for younger generations whose future is being gambled by a power struggle between the **Hutu** and **Tutsi** political elites."

Committee of National Salvation. After the coup attempt of 1993 and the assassination of President **Ndadaye**, François **Ngeze**, the minister of interior in **Buyoya**'s government and one of the rare **Hutu** who held a position of power from 1965 to 1993, was made head of this new ruling committee and claimed that he had been forced to support the coup.

Conseil National de la Révolution (CNR) (National Revolutionary Council). When Prime Minister Michel **Micombero** deposed the absent Mwami **Ntare V** in a peaceful coup in November 1966, he proclaimed a republic with himself as president. He dissolved the government, replaced the eight provincial governors with **army** officers, and established a provisional 12-man National Revolutionary Council of military officers. Micombero said the CNR would rule until a new government had been formed, "probably within two months." The council's first task would be drafting a new constitution; the mwami had suspended the former constitution earlier that year when he dismissed Prime Minister **Biha**. In December 1966, the council announced that Micombero's term as president would be seven years, and they promoted him to colonel. Although set up as a provisional unit, until its dissolution in 1968 the CNR functioned as a supreme advisory body, influencing all nominations to the upper levels of the administration including the appointment of army officers. The CNR was opposed by leftist members of the **UNEBA** (later **JNR**). In 1967, Micombero dismissed Major Albert **Shibura**, a member of the council, from command of the army; when he announced the change, he said that "a small group of irresponsible men" had found accomplices in the judiciary and army in efforts to "take advantage of the Republic."

Conseil Supérieur du Pays (CSP) (Superior Council). In 1952, a Belgian decree provided for the establishment of representative bodies at every level of the administrative hierarchy; it was the first hint of democracy in native administration. Advisory councils were set up at the subchiefdom, chiefdom, district, and territorial levels and were called, respectively, "conseils de sous-chefferie," "conseils de chefferie," "conseils de territoire," and "conseils supérieurs du pays." In Burundi in 1953, Tutsi controlled 80.7 percent of the seats in the conseil supérieur du pays. The situation did not change markedly in 1956 with the advent of universal male suffrage. In 1957, the CSP strongly protested the administration's decision to institute a system of **centres extra-coutumiers** (CECs), almost unanimously urging the resident to reverse the decision, citing the historical claims of the crown and the sacred character of kingship. The CSP members addressed a petition to a **UN** visiting mission; the text of the petition was nationalistic and promonarchy.

Coopérative des Commerçants du Burundi (CCB) (Cooperative of Traders in Burundi). During the pre-independence period, **Rwagasore** established cooperatives in order to build up support for his party. The Cooperative of Burundi Traders was set up in the hope of using it to enlist support of the so-called "Swahili" population of Bujumbura. The CCB hardly got off the ground due partly to mismanagement and partly to the administration's refusal to extend its financial backing to the cooperative, which they considered a "front organization." The CCB initially received about six million francs from various European firms in Bujumbura, but by 1958 most of the money had vanished. According to a report by the **Conseil Supérieur du Pays**, almost two million francs had been lent to another cooperative, 450,000 francs had been lent to "an influential TANU personality," and the rest "to a number of businessmen who failed to observe the terms of reimbursement."

Coreke (in-, in-). This generally means a servant or follower, but the word (with the nonhuman prefixes) was traditionally used to refer to the *mwami*'s concubines. They were considered grand ladies who remained with the *mwami* even during his travels. They helped in teaching the ancient religious beliefs and practices to the royal children.

Cuma (i-, i-). Literally translated as "iron," but this word was used in the sense of gifts surrounding a marriage. It could be anything from beer to cattle. Even after the marriage, the *icuma* might continue as a sign of good relations between the principal families. After the marriage, the gift was almost always beer, but money for the new couple's house was also often offered.

Cuti (bu-, in-). This is a very close relationship, usually beginning with two people or families needing each other economically and coming to appreciate the partnership. It is variously described as kinship, an in-law relationship, friendship, neighborliness, and trade partnership.

-D-

Dasigana (mu-, ba-). In traditional usage, *abadasigana* refers to a group of individuals who formed the personal entourage of a mwami, but, more specifically, it refers to the entourage of Mwezi **Gisabo**. It is usually translated by the Barundi as "the followers of Mwezi"; because of its attachment to the **Bezi** family, it implies a strong attachment to the crown as well. Another Kirundi name, *amasuka u'Mwami*, refers to the same category of individuals, but is associated with followers of Mwami Ntare **Rugaamba**; these followers became the **PDC** and because of its pro-**Batare** connections, carried a somewhat antimonarchic bias.

Deuxième Manifeste du Parti Politique. In the days shortly before independence, **UPRONA** made an effort to identify with the crown, but also tried to live up to the "Unity and Progress" of its name. **Rwagasore**, therefore, made it clear that his support of the monarchy was conditional. In the party's second manifesto, he said that his party was prepared to "endorse a monarchic regime only insofar as this regime and its dynasty favoured the genuine emancipation of the Murundi people." The manifesto further stated that "UPRONA notes that the Burundi monarchy is *constitutional*, and wishes to see the constitution of the realm adapted to a *modern state*. UPRONA favours the democratisation of institutions . . . and will firmly and tenaciously combat all forces of social injustice regardless of the system from which they may come: *feudalism*, *colonialism*, or *communism* . . . . UPRONA favours the election of the chiefs and subchiefs by the population, and will combat with all its forces those who seek to destroy the *unity* of the country.

Dirimbo (in-, in-). This popular type of song was traditionally performed by one person or a very small group and was considered appropriate for the expression of personal feelings.

Dongoranywa (in-, in-). In addition to the bride price (**inkwano**) paid by the groom to the bride's family, the bride's family also gave this dowry. The parents of the bride traditionally provided in some way for the new couple's home and furnishings. In fact, the dowry could be small livestock, farming implements, or money. The primary purposes of the dowry were to ensure an alliance between the two families by consolidating the bonds between them. If the husband died, the *indongoranywa* went to his legitimate heirs, rather than back to the wife's family.

Dorsinville, Max H. At its 15th session in 1960, the UN General Assembly endorsed the UN Trusteeship Council's statement that the "best future for Ruanda-Urundi lies in the evolution of a single, united, and composite state with such arrangements for the internal autonomy of Ruanda and Urundi as may be agreed upon by their representatives." The General Assembly established a three-member commission headed by Haitian Ambassador to the UN Max

Dorsinville to supervise the elections in the two countries. In December of that year, the permanent representative of **Belgium** to the UN told the secretary general that a conference of political parties of Ruanda-Urundi—based on the results of communal elections, which gave eight delegates to the **Front Commun** and two to **UPRONA**— would be held in Ostend, Belgium on January 6, 1991 and that the UN was invited to send observers. At the conference, the Belgian government announced that elections would be held in Burundi on January 18 and in **Rwanda** on January 23. On behalf of the UN, Dorsinville protested this as an attempt to circumvent the UN resolution. On January 21, the Belgian government announced that it had agreed to follow the recommendations of the UN and that the elections would be postponed until the Dorsinville Commission had the opportunity to carry out its work of supervising the arrangements. The commission registered strong objections to the Belgian actions in general. It stated that democracy had not been strengthened in Burundi in spite of Belgium's indication of its desire to cooperate with the UN. Instead, according to the commission, the Belgian administration had simply favored "one feudal group over another."

Dumont, Donald. On January 10, 1966, the Burundi government ordered the expulsion of this **United States** ambassador and two other American embassy officers on grounds that they were "rightly or wrongly" suspected of involvement with opposition "conspirators." The order emphasized that relations with the United States were not being broken; in fact, the statement from the Foreign Ministry stated that the relations between the two countries were going to improve after the recall of the three diplomats. However, the United States retaliated the following day by ordering the expulsion of Leon Ndenzako, the Burundi ambassador to the United States. The ambassador was called to the State Department, and a note was handed to him that contained a strong protest against the expulsion of the diplomats from Bujumbura. On January 12, Burundi filed a counterprotest. In a news conference, Foreign Minister Marc Manirakiza explained that his government suspected that

Dumont and the others had abetted the abortive coup of October 1965. He emphasized again that Burundi's action was aimed only at the three individuals and did not signify a break with the United States.

- E -

East African Community (EAC). The EAC was formally inaugurated in December 1967 in a ceremony Arusha. It was attended by Presidents Jomo Kenyatta of Kenya, Julius Nyerere of **Tanzania**, and Milton Obote of Uganda. Guests included a delegation from Burundi, which also made formal application to join the EAC. However, in March 1968, an EAC spokesman said that no new members could be admitted for at least two years from that time.

Economic Community of the Great Lakes. In 1975, Burundi joined **Rwanda**, **Tanzania**, Zambia, and **Zaire** in this organization, which was formed in order to work closely with the **UN** Economic Commission for Africa to develop the economic potential of the basins of Lakes Kivu and Tanganyika. This turn toward neighbor states for help in achieving economic progress was also a temporary turning away from the internal ethnic rivalries that plagued the country.

Economy. The national economy has been based almost entirely on subsistence-level **agriculture**. Coffee and cotton are the most important commercial agricultural products and the primary sources of foreign exchange. The **United States** has been the primary buyer of Burundi's coffee beans; **Belgium** and Luxembourg have been the primary buyers of cotton. Mineral resources include gold, bastnaesite, cassiterite, wolfram, and columbium, but ore reserves are very small. Burundi has been heavily dependent upon foreign financial aid and technical assistance, with Belgium as the main donor in the period following independence. The United States, France, **Germany**, and the **UN** have also granted financial and technical assistance.

The monetary unit is the Burundi franc, created in 1964 after the economic union between **Rwanda** and Burundi ended. The Bank of the Republic (Banque de la République du Burundi) is the central bank.

Currently, there are no records or statistical data available on the distribution of income of **Hutu** and **Tutsi**. However, many claim that the so-called ethnic division is, in fact, an economic one with "Tutsi" naming the upper caste and "Hutu" naming the lower ones. It should be noted that there are poor Tutsi as well as wealthy Hutu, but the above description remains dominant.

Education. Most of the precolonial education of Barundi was provided in the home. Later, the bulk of the formal education was in mission schools administered by the **Catholic** and Protestant churches and subsidized by the government. In the early postcolonial years, primary education was provided almost exclusively by these mission schools. Secondary education remained based on the **Belgian** system. The national university (Université Officielle de Bujumbura) was founded in January 1964, and the postsecondary teacher training school (Ecole Normale Supérieure de Bujumbura) was founded in October 1965. Many students also studied in other countries on various grants and scholarships. Today, the national university has 11 faculties, including medicine. There is also the Institut Supérieur d'Agriculture and the Institut Supérieur des Techniciens.

There was a great deal of ethnic discrimination in secondary and higher education; as a result, the majority of bureaucratic posts went to **Tutsi**. Under the **Bagaza** administration, there was a movement of "Kirundization," which insisted on the use of **Kirundi** as the sole medium of instruction in primary and secondary schools. This is not an unusual nationalistic move, but in Burundi, it perpetuated the ethnic discrimination. Access to French, the international language (considered the elite language) was restricted to privileged families whose members already spoke it, and Tutsi continued to dominate the bureaucratic posts.

By 1986, fewer than one third of the students at the national university were **Hutu**. By 1988, only a fraction of the Hutu population was qualified for employment in the modern sectors of the economy. Of these, from a population already decimated by the 1972 massacre, many were killed or forced into exile during the 1988 and 1991 massacres.

-F-

Family Corporation. Captain Michel **Micombero**, who was named prime minister in 1966 and later named himself president, appointed a great many friends and relatives to his cabinet, thus securing his grip on power. Micombero's wife was an aristocrat and became his link to many in this group. Among these people, some of whom later overthrew Micombero's government, were Pascal **Kashirahamwe**, Pierre **Bigayimpunzi**, Athanase **Gakiza**, Colonel Sylvère **Nzohabonayo**, Colonel Jean-Baptiste **Bagaza**, second in command of the armed forces and a close neighbor of Micombero, and Jean **Barahinduka**. This group, often called the "family corporation," controlled the economy, the **army**, and the judicial system.

Fasoni (mu-, ba-). See *Ganwa.*

Féderation des Travailleurs du Burundi (FTB). Around and just after the time of independence, Burundi like much of Africa had an emerging, activist counterelite. In the case of Burundi, this counterelitism often manifested itself as antimonarchy. The FTB was made up a handful of trade union leaders, but, despite the efforts of the organization's secretary general Augustin **Ntamagara** to build up a mass following, it never became a central force in the politics of the country. In spite of the small number of members, however, the FTB developed into a very vocal group that was clearly Marxist in outlook. According to their own organizational statements circulated in 1964, they were committed to the liquidation of "colonialism, neo-colonialism, imperialism, reaction, and feudalism." It was thought that two potential major allies of the **Casablanca** group would be the **army** and the trade unions; however, the FTB did not build up enough grass-roots support among the people to be a strong tie with the Casablanca group. When Prime Minister **Ngendadumwe** was assassinated, Mwami **Mwambutsa's** fears of an impending coup were escalated, and the FTB was ordered to suspend its activities.

Fondation de l'Université de Liège pour les Recherches Scientifiques au Congo Belge et au Ruanda-Urundi (FULREAC). The Foundation of the University of Liège for Scientific Research in the Belgian Congo and Ruanda-Urundi sent a team of educational specialists to the territory in 1957 to study and report on the impact of European education on the population, the future of children who are successful in elementary school but fail to complete secondary school, and the possible modification of educational measures in order to make educated students better farmers. The final report discusses concerns about the education of women and moral education as well. The report also points out, among its suggestions, that education is "but a single element—of capital importance, it is true—of the civilizing action of Europe in Africa."

Fonds Reine Elisabeth pour l'Assistance Médicale aux Indigènes (FOREAMI). The Queen Elisabeth Native Medical Assistance Fund grew out of a study trip made to the Belgian Congo by King Albert I and Queen Elisabeth in 1928. The purpose of the fund was to promote social and medical services for the benefit of the indigenous populations in the Belgian Congo and Ruanda-Urundi. The project was funded by investments, government subsidies, and charitable contributions.

Foyers Sociaux. In 1948, the first of these Homemaking Centers opened in Bujumbura. Because the women of Burundi and **Rwanda** were traditionally closely tied to farming, the colonial government sought ways to educate them in their new roles as urban women. Social workers taught women "household arts" because it was assumed that the woman arriving in the city did not know how to organize her household or even how to spend her leisure time. Among the skills taught in the centers were sewing, knitting, darning, fabric cutting, washing, and ironing; when these basic skills were achieved, the women learned principles of hygiene, thrift, and child care. After completing the courses, women were encouraged to return to the centers often for advice as domestic problems arose. These centers grew rapidly and spread to other towns and the rural areas; eventually, the need for more teachers led to a school for homemaking monitors. The Union des Femmes du Congo Belge et du Ruanda-Urundi also opened a home in Bujumbura where women could complete their homemaking and social training.

Front Commun. At the time of independence, this was the only opposition group to **UPRONA** in the National Assembly. Founded in September 1960, it was a loose electoral coalition (sometimes described as a cartel), which included the **Parti Démocratique Chrétien**, the **Parti du Peuple**, the **Parti Démocratique et Rural**, the Parti de l'Emancipation Populaire, the Voix du Peuple Murundi, and several other minor political parties.

Front for the Defense of Democracy (FDD). This is one of several emerging **Hutu** militia groups (and one of the more visible and active ones) formed to fight the national **army** of Burundi. The army is estimated to be approximately 90 to 95 percent **Tutsi**. Leonard Nyangoma is the leader of the FDD.

Front Démocratique Burundi (Burundi Democratic Front) (Frodebu). For much of the history of post-independent Burundi, **UPRONA**, dominated by **Tutsi**, was the only legal political party; power within the party was synonymous with power in the country at large. However, in 1986, Melchior **Ndadaye** formed Frodebu, a party dominated by moderate **Hutu**. The party included many Hutu intellectuals, many of whom had been in exile in **Rwanda** since the massacres of 1972. For a brief time, it was reported that Frodebu enjoyed what Catherine Watson called "rapturous support" in the country, and in 1993, the party, with Ndadaye at its head, won by a two-to-one margin over UPRONA in Burundi's first multiparty election. Ndadaye became several firsts in Burundi's history: the first elected president, the first civilian president, and the first Hutu president. After Ndadaye's assassination, *Le Citoyen*, previously considered one of Burundi's most balanced newspapers, reported without adequate support that Frodebu members had been the killers in many ensuing massacres throughout the country.

Fumu (mu-, ba-). In the traditional religious beliefs, these medical practitioners have the power to ward off misfortunes caused by malevolent spirits. The symbols of the position are a leopard skin, a headdress made from a cow's tail, and a gourd rattle. These, as well as various curing techniques, are either passed from father to son or earned by apprenticeship to a practicing *umufumu*. In addition to these powers and duties, *abafumu* predict the future, call together spirits during seances, and interpret dreams. Some perform rainmaking ceremonies. The *abafumu* were highly respected members of society and often became wealthy and politically powerful.

-G-

Gabekazi (in-, in-). Traditionally, this royal bull and his cows always accompanied the *mwami* wherever he went.

Gabire (bu-, mu-, ba-). When the nomadic, pastoral **Tutsi** migrated into the lake region, they gradually achieved economic, social, and political dominance over the **Hutu**. The Hutu, in a sense, mortgaged themselves to the Tutsi minority in exchange for cattle and protection through a contract called *ubugabire*. This patron-client system was similar to a feudal relationship in that the Tutsi *shebuja* (lord) entrusted his Hutu *mugabire* (serf) with cattle (see *inka*). This was not ownership, but symbolized a contract between the parties. The relationship allowed the *shebuju* to expect services and produce; it allowed the *mugabire* to expect protection and favors. If the *mugabire* neglected his duties, the *shebuju* had the option of demanding the return of the cattle; in fact, the *shebuju* could break the contract at the slightest provocation. The stipulations imposed on the *mugabire* were extensive: for example, although the milk and the calves born of the cattle entrusted to them generally were considered the property of the *mugabire*, he could not kill or dispose of cattle, nor could he leave the territory of the *shebuju*. The *shebuju* also had the right to set aside a specific cow and all of her calves as his own. But if the *mugabire* was a good manager of his own property, he could eventually become a manager of a larger area by contracting cattle to others. The contract usually passed from father to son for both patron and client.

The land tenure system, considered feudal by many, was theoretically abolished in 1955. In 1956, the **Conseil Supérieur du Pays** presented a program that suggested that grazing land be owned communally and that independent agriculturalists be allowed to consider their cultivated land as private property. This proposal was never actually made into law, and some analysts believed at least as late as 1969 that unless it was made into law and the *ubugabire* system officially eliminated, the people of Burundi could not achieve a significant improvement in their standard of living.

Gabiro (ki-, bi-). These historical sites in Burundi are unusual in that they are neither stone nor metal, but vegetation. Trees planted on tombs are testimony to the ancient presence of people—kings, grand chiefs, ceremonial leaders—invested with grand powers.

Gabo (bu-, ku-). While the same root with a different set of prefixes is used to mean "husband" (*umugabo*), this word represents many things traditionally masculine in the literal sense. It could mean courage, virility, strength, and ability. It could also mean male genitals. With yet another prefix, *intwarangabo*, it means the chief of the **army**, and *urugabo* is a strong, growing youth.

Gacoreke. In the traditional courts of the *mwami* or the *ganwa*, these young girls were charged with the maintenance of the royal palace or residence and the care of and attending to the princes. Variations of the name were *gicoreke*, *mucoreke*, and *nyancoreke*.

Gahigi. He is the one, in the traditional royal court, responsible for hunting. This was an important post because, according to some legends, **Kiranga** was killed during the course of a hunt. This position was usually held by a **Twa**; variations on the name were Inagahigi and Semuhigi.

Gakiza, Athanase. A member of **Micombero**'s "**Family Corporation**," and Micombero's wife's uncle, Gakiza was the director of the president's personal spy network.

Ganuro (mu-, no plural). During traditional harvest ceremonies, women were honored in the fertility ceremony called the *umuganuro*. Traditionally, women were believed to be symbolically one with the earth; as such, traditional beliefs had women act accordingly. For example, a woman could not jump, climb ladders, or step over brooks. It was thought that every woman held inside all the potential of life. She fulfilled her role in society by bearing children, and it was also thought that if she performed her duties well, fertility would be transmitted to the seeds she planted, thus bringing prosperity to her entire kin group. It is this belief that was demonstrated in the *umuganuro* ceremony. The ideal woman was fertile and modest, having been trained in silence and reticence. Many women were trained to be such careful listeners that they could repeat whole conversations verbatim. However, husbands also appreciated it when their wives were good at bargaining, negotiating, or managing their property if they had to be away. In this way, intelligent women often became powerful matriarchs. In spite of this, as well as the great respect mothers receive, women traditionally had very little authority in decision-making. Traditionally, a women's position in the society was mainly determined by the marriage that she contracted. Women of all social classes were expected to act subservient and obedient and to follow the dictates of their husbands and fathers. A few upper-class women were known historically to have achieved considerable independent wealth and authority, but this was very rare in a society in which men virtually monopolized the right to inherit cattle and land. Although voting rights were accorded to women in the 1962 constitution, few women took advantage of them. There is record of the *umuganuro* being held as recently as 1964, with a format somewhat modified from the traditional. The program included members of the National Assembly, military leaders, international diplomatic personnel, and religious representatives. The royal drummers performed, and various youth groups marched in a parade.

Ganuza (mu-, ba-). Generally, this is a master of ceremonies during traditional religious rituals and festivals; originally, however, this was specifically the guardian of the sacred **Karyenda**.

Ganwa (mu-, ba-). When a *mwami* ("king") came to power in traditional Urundi (but not Ruanda), he received one of four dynastic names: Ntare, Mwezi, Mutaga, or Mwambutsa. Their descendants were named **Batare**, **Bezi**, **Bataga**, and **Bambutsa**, respectively, and these were the princes of the royal blood, or *ganwa*, until the accession of a king who received the same name as their ancestor; then they became *bafasoni*, a less important honorary title. Rank and privilege played an important role in allocating power and authority, but these were primarily the prerogatives of the *ganwa*; since the *ganwa* were regarded as a group separate from the **Hutu** and the **Tutsi**, political competition was traditionally rare between these two groups. This changed along with the traditional opportunity structure as democratic ideas and practices began to spread. In the early years of independence, Burundi politics reflects conflicts involving struggles between *ganwa* clans, the monarchy and its opponents, *ganwa* and antiroyalist Tutsi, regional Tutsi and **Hima**, and Tutsi and Hutu. By the 1970s, the monarchy had disappeared, and the *ganwa* as a hegemonic elite had lost their role.

Garama (ki-, no plural). This is the winter solstice during which the sorghum festival occurs. During this time, the *mwami* presents the dynastic drum, the **Karyenda**, and cattle are said to be made more fertile.

Gendanyi (bu-, ba-). Under the system of ubu**gabire**, the court contained many levels of patronage. These were young attendants who would eventually gain positions of authority and prestige. They were trusted members of the court and followers of the king whose activities and responsibilities varied considerably but included being escorts, warriors, dancers, messengers, and police. The English word "courtier" is probably the closest translation.

Geni (bu-). As with any society, there are many traditional regulations and tabus around the institution of marriage, *ubugeni*. Burundi had the expected incest tabus between people and their parents or grandparents, between people and their uncles or aunts, between siblings, and between first cousins; they also had regulations against marriage with one's father- or mother-in-law, but not against other in-law relationships. Marriages could also be forbidden if the two people were from very different social or economic classes, if the two families were feuding, if one of the families had developed a bad reputation, or if the bride was pregnant before the wedding. Many tabus against marriage were also based on physical reasons. Marriage was forbidden if either member of the couple had syphilis (*mburugu*), tuberculosis (*igituntu*), mental disorders (*ubusazi*), or leprosy (*imibembe*), among others. Marriages were also forbidden or dissolved if the young man had chronic impotence (*umwange*). Traditionally, Barundi married around the age of puberty, usually between the ages of 13 and 15. In fact, marriage was forbidden before the young woman developed breasts suitable for child-bearing, had a regular menstrual cycle, and had pubic hair. The majority of Barundi remained monogamous, but polygamy was accepted as part of the culture as well, usually among the upper classes.

Genge (bu-, ma-). **Ethel Albert** translates this as "successful cleverness," which seems to trivialize both its range of meaning and range of importance in Burundi society. Actually, a better translation might be "verbal sophistication." It is a key concept to the norms and values associated with the uses of language. *Ubugenge* primarily applies to the verbal intellectual management of important situations. The specific manifestations of *ubugenge* are diverse. According to Albert, "the cleverness of a rogue; the industriousness of a virtuous man whose overlord gives him a cow as a reward for virtue; the skill of a good psychologist-rhetorician in persuading a generous, impulsive, or inebriated superior to give him a cow although he has done nothing to earn it; the skill of a medical healer; the success of a practical joker who has victimized a simple-minded peasant or feeble-minded boy; the wise and just judgments of the *umubashingantahe*; and the technological accomplishments of Europeans are equally good examples of *ubugenge*—for they all succeed in bringing something good to their designers."

Germany, Relations with. The Conference of Berlin designated Ruanda-Urundi as a sphere of German interest in 1885, but it was not until the 1890s that the government of German East Africa extended its authority to the territory. In 1896, a military post was established in Usumbura, which remained the administrative center for both kingdoms until two separate German Residencies were established in 1906 and 1907.

After the death of Mwami Mwezi **Gisabo** in 1908, as well as due to the lack of a replacement for the successful Resident Von Grawert, the German administration was only able to firmly control Usumbura and the immediate area; German authority diminished in proportion to the distance from the military post. This led to the moving of the Residency to the more central Gitega in 1912.

German colonial policy provided for missionary **education** of the sons of chiefs in order to equip these boys to later be part of the administration. There were, in fact, only about 190 Germans in both **Rwanda** and Burundi by 1914, about 130 of whom were missionaries. There were, at that time, only 40 soldiers and six civilian officers.

Although some senior German officers saw World War I as an opportunity to create a great German empire in Central Africa, this was not to be because of the vastly inferior numbers of German forces and weapons. By January 1916, Germany offered only token resistance to the **Belgian** occupation of the region, and by June of that year, Burundi was under Belgian control.

Gihanga. Some myths that are part of Burundi's oral tradition trace the origins of **Rwanda** and Burundi to a common ancestor, Gihanga. In these myths, Gihanga's two sons, Kanyaburundi and Kanyaruanda, founded the two kingdoms. There are other myths as well that deal with the origins of the country; some say that Kanyaburundi, who ruled as **Ntare I Rushatsi**, was the great-grandson of Kanyaruanda. Yet another myth traces the origin of Ntare I to the small **Tutsi** kingdom of Buha, located at what is now the southeastern border of Burundi. All of these myths and popular traditions are important in understanding of the history of Burundi. Burundi did not have official court historians as did Rwanda, so many details about several of the earlier monarchs are missing. In fact, because of the frequent wars between the two countries, some information about Burundi has been gathered from the oral traditions of Rwanda.

Gisabo (Kisabo/Kissabo/Gissabo). See **Mwezi IV.**

Gitega Scheme. This was an integrated rural development project in the late 1970s and early 1980s. In the project, sponsored by the UNDP, a special component financed by UNICEF was entirely devoted to the training of women as farmers. Excellent results were achieved in better yields when the women used improved farming techniques and selected seeds and fertilizers in the co-operative. The World

Bank was so impressed that a major loan was approved for a much larger program based on the Gitega Scheme.

Goma (in-, in-). These are the royal drummers of the Burundi dynasties.

Gorore (in-, in-). When generally used, this is simply a tribute or fee (perhaps for rent or a license of some sort). In terms of Burundi royalty, however, it is the word for the tribute that was given to the ***mwami.*** All who visited the court were under an obligation (considered part of a person's moral duty) to bring a gift of cattle to the *mwami* as well as to his mother.

Groupe de Travail. In the late 1950s, the **Belgian** government appointed this parliamentary study group to investigate the conditions under which a transfer of authority to Ruanda-Urundi could be accomplished peacefully. It was probably in anticipation of a visit from this group that **Rwagasore** virtually took control of **UPRONA**.

Guru (in-, in-). These smooth, round stones and their purpose are apparently unique among traditional charms and amulets that have been studied in the region. They are symbolically regarded as **Imana**, although there is a distinction between them and the actual creator, and they have the power to hurt as well as to bless. It seems that only **Hutu** keep them just outside the entrance to the **rugo** (compound). It is usually a hereditary symbol, but anyone might be told to keep them (by the *mupfumu*) if his wife or crops are not fruitful. A small, circular patch is smoothed out on the ground outside of the entrance, and it is spread with cut grass; occasionally, a tiny hut is built over the *inguru*. At first only two or three were put in this area, but later more can be added; when this happens, the *inguru* are said to have given birth. Over the course of many years, the number of *inguru* may increase to 20 or 30. Before sowing or planting, a few grains of seed were traditionally scattered over the *inguru* or else the fields would not bear crops. After harvesting millet, a basket of the early fruits was placed on top of the *inguru* and left for several days; the millet was then dried, and beer was made from it. The family's closest friends were called to sit in a circle around the *inguru* with their feet pointed toward them; the head of the house then sprinkled the *inguru* and the feet of the participants with the beer.

Guthrie, Malcolm. See **Kirundi**.

-H-

Hanza (ba-, **rarely used in singular).** The Abahanza were a noble **Hutu** clan, who were often charged with guarding the property within the *Mwami*'s enclosure. Court singers and soldiers were also chosen from among this lineage.

Heko (ki-(gi-), bi-(vi-)). According to the traditional religious beliefs, *iviheko* (charms, amulets) made of sticks and the hair of animals are used both to ward off evil and to generate power for the one who wears them. Special practitioners transfer supernatural energy to the material object through magical formulas; of course, the more powerful the diviner, the more potent the charms. Even after the majority of Barundi were converted to Christianity, most still used charms for a variety of purposes, such as luck in hunting, finding a wife, and curing sick cows. Special amulets are still often made for infants to protect them against such things as intestinal worms, diarrhea, skin irritations, and snakebites. A positive talisman, one bringing good luck and long life, is *ikimazi* (plural: *ibimazi*).

High Council of Burundi. A decree of 1952 that included administrative reforms was looked upon as a cautious first step in representative government. A 1943 decree had established a system of councils, whose members were appointed, to advise the Mwami and the chiefs, particularly on matters of budget and taxation. The later decree broadened the functions of these councils and established a limited degree of elected representation. Councils existed for each administrative level: subchiefdoms, chiefdoms, districts, and the High Council of Burundi. This last was presided over by the Mwami. Part of the membership of each council was chosen by the members of the council immediately below it. In 1956, the governor of Ruanda-Urundi decided to interpret the 1952 decree so as to allow the subchiefdom electoral colleges to be chosen by universal male suffrage. There were 3,904 seats to be filled, and the balloting resulted in the election of 1,664 Tutsi electors. Observers believed that these results indicated that there was rapport between the **Hutu** and the ordinary (non-**ganwa) Tutsi**.

Hima. Another pastoral people and ethnically related to the **Tutsi**, the group is often considered to be Tutsi. But its original home is not agreed upon. Names given to groups do not always define the limits of a tribe in the accepted sense. They can link a number of peoples that are located far apart and sometimes considered to be separate tribes, or else link only special categories of population among several different peoples; the Hima of Uganda are the more widely written-about Hima. Some Western historians and anthropologists say that both the Tutsi and the Hima have ethnic affinities with the Galla tribes of southern Ethiopia; in Burundi, both groups were believed to have migrated from a different direction. Perhaps as a result of this second opinion, the Hima were traditionally set apart from the Tutsi socially. They, for example, did not have the privileges associated with forming alliances with the *mwami* such as marriage to a family member of the *mwami* or the receiving of cattle. They also did not participate in the traditional structures of Tutsi hegemony over **Hutu**. Some political analysts say that it was the Hima who planned the arrest of **Ntare** in 1972, one of the events that set into motion a series of massacres within the country. Hima officers have controlled the **army** since 1972.

Hindure (gi-, bi-). These are evil spirits that have changed themselves into some kind of wolf or hyena.

Hinza (mu-, ba-). Knowledge of the **Hutu** before the arrival of the **Tutsi** is limited, but oral traditions indicate that the early Hutu social system was based on the clan and kings ruling over very limited domains; all of this was centered around small-scale agriculture. The kings were known as *bahinza*, "those who cause things to grow," and, according to the stories, their strength was based on the popular belief that they were endowed with supernatural powers that allowed them to control the fertility of the earth, domestic animals, and people, as well as cause rain, protect crops from insects, and protect cattle from disease.

Hoza umwana (gu-). Burundi lullabies are very important parts of the country's oral tradition. Sometimes they are filled with historical allusions, and very often they are filled with allusions to the baby's parents or grandparents. They then serve as a source of information within a family about that family's history. Lullabies are used to comfort babies, but never to put them to sleep; in fact, it is traditionally tabu to sing to a baby at night for fear that it could cause nightmares.

Hume (gi-, bi-). In traditional Burundi culture, these souls of people who died violent deaths played a major role; they were said to be malevolent and to wander around seeking humans to disturb. Many people still wear charms for protection against their curses.

Hutu and Tutsi. Historically, at least in the view of many Western scholars and readers, the relationship between these two major ethnic groups is a primary factor in the culture of Burundi. Because of this, they will comprise this joint entry, the purpose of which is to describe the individual historical development as well as the relationship. It is important to note that the groups are not so simply defined as any description might imply; there are many factions and belief systems within each group, as well as those that span both or parts of both groups. Formally, each group name would carry the prefixes attached to Classes 1 and 2 for humans (see the user's notes earlier in this volume). Therefore, they would be, in the plural, Bahutu and Batutsi, but the simple forms will be used here. The relative populations of Hutu and Tutsi have been a source of controversy; the usual figures given are that the Hutu number about 85 percent of the population and the Tutsi about 14 percent. Formal census figures are hard to find; some modern politicians say that those figures were never true, but were the mistaken figures of Europeans who assumed that anyone who owned cattle was a Tutsi. It should also be noted that Hutu and Tutsi have intermarried for many generations, thus blurring ethnic distinctions. In any case, whatever census figures do exist are certainly quite old and probably outdated.

The two groups came to the region of Burundi at different times probably very far apart, but these times are disputed. The Hutu came first (but after the **Twa**), perhaps as early as the eleventh century; the Tutsi came much later from the north, perhaps as late as the end of the sixteenth century. The Hutu were traditionally farmers and the Tutsi were traditionally cattle keepers who are said to have disdained manual labor. The Tutsi adopted the language and many customs of the Hutu, but became the aristocrats. In the early days of settlement, a Tutsi who gave a cow to a Hutu became the master of the Hutu and his children, thus beginning a long period of patronage that was similar to European feudalism and that continued in Burundi until the 1950s. A Hutu certainly could acquire independent wealth, and a Tutsi could lead a peasant's life, but the division of wealth was established, at least in the eyes of the outside world.

The European occupation of Burundi did not change this apparent unequal division of wealth. Many modern politicians and scholars say that ruling through the Tutsi was natural for the Europeans because of the Europeans' racist beliefs that the Tutsi, who were, on the average, taller and lighter-skinned, were also more intelligent. But the *ganwa* held most of the political and all of the royal power; the **Germans** and later the **Belgians** ruled through those already in power. How much of this perpetuation of the ethnic division was conscious on the part of the Europeans is not completely clear. Early documents and books do, in fact, make a point of mentioning the physical differences between the groups. In one of the most cited, *Die Barundi*, Hans Meyer spends several pages on it as well as many pages on the mental characteristics of the two groups. He describes the Hutu as "like all Bantu . . . by nature intelligent and [with] a lively and sanguine temperament. . . . In spite of their impulsive behavior, the Bahutu are incapable of any strong exertion of will. They are conservative out of inertia and indifference." Later, he says of the Tutsi: "Gradually one discovers the secret of the tremendous superiority of the relatively few Batussi [*sic*] over the one-and-a-half-million Bahutu: they are greatly superior to them in intelligence, calmness, composure, cruelty, cunning, racial pride, solidarity, and political talent." (English translation by Helmut Handzik) One fact of the colonial period was that, in the later years of outside rule, as nationalism began to emerge, fearing unity between Hutu and Tutsi, Belgian rulers banned any political party that crossed ethnic lines and encouraged the political parties primarily based on ethnicity.

At the current stage of history, however, these old outside opinions of the two groups are not as relevant as the two groups view each other. That view, unfortunately, is very negative and has been very negative since the country's independence in 1962. In fact, there has been a series of brutal civil wars and massacres, usually springing from the ethnic inequality and mutual dislike and fear. The facts are that, from independence until 1993, there was only one Hutu head of state (briefly); all of the political leaders came from the minority population, as did most members of the national **army**. The facts also include that the first Hutu president (elected in the first democratic election) was assassinated just a few months after taking office in a coup attempt by the army. Serious ethnic civil wars, each killing many hundreds of thousands of people, occurred in 1965, 1972, 1988, and 1993, with the last one continuing through 1994 and 1995 as a series of attacks by the army on villages and by Hutu militia on the army. The world took more notice of the small country following the 1972 massacre, which is said to have eliminated the vast majority of Hutu intellectuals and emerging political leaders. It also was the massacre that saw the death of Burundi's last monarch, **Ntare V**. The world again began to take notice of the country during the latest extended period of unrest that corresponded to an ethnic civil war in neighboring **Rwanda** as well. The Organization of African Unity continues to examine the ethnic concerns in the region, but also continues to recommend preparation for the worst.

One of the most respected and prolific of all Burundi scholars, René Lemarchand, says, "Nowhere in Africa has so much violence killed so many people on so many occasions in so small a space as in Burundi during the years following independence (1994, xi)." Even before the most recent series of massacres, another important Burundi scholar, Catharine Watson says, "The Hutu burn with the idea that they have always been oppressed. The Tutsi are haunted by the idea that they are the Palestinians of East Africa, about to be hounded from Burundi, already driven from Rwanda (1989, 51)."

Hutura (ku- (kwi-)). Because of the many years of **Tutsi** domination and, some say, the resulting **Hutu** self-hatred in Burundi, a phenomenon has been observed whereby Hutu undergo this "shedding off" of their ethnicity. *Kwihutura* literally means "to de-hutuize oneself."

-I-

Ibare (ci-, ivy-). If the *mwami* had a residence in the territory of a chief or subchief, this residence was immune from local jurisdiction. Literally, *icibare* means an area reserved for a child, and *icibare c'umwami* means a royal privilege.

Ica (kw-). This is the act of murder and there were a great many surrounding punishments in the traditional society, some of which remain viable today. The assassination of a *mwami*, a prince or a chief carried the death penalty, not only for the murderer, but for all members of his immediate family. The murderer himself was castrated after having been crucified. Most murders of ordinary Barundi (regardless of ethnicity) were avenged by individual families, but the punishment was symbolically pronounced by the *mwami*. The death penalty was the usual pronouncement; the family or the clan usually decided on the method.

Igitshutshu. Traditional beliefs of Burundi state that all people and animals possess the same principal life force, which is projected into physical existence. This universal soul, *igitshutshu*, disappears when an animal dies, but is transformed into a spirit of the dead when a human dies.

Ijenda. Shortly before the aborted Hutu revolt in 1972, the southern **Tutsi**, known as the **Bururi** group, who had been traditionally kept out of the political system, were on the verge of a violent clash with Tutsi from central and northern Burundi. The group in this conflict that had the northern location was the Ijenda.

Ikiza. Literally meaning "catastrophe," this word is sometimes used to describe the residual fear and mutual ethnic suspicion that remain in Burundi even today and that prevent a peaceful coexistence of the citizens.

Imana. Probably at least 70 percent of Barundi have been converted to Christianity, but those (both **Hutu** and **Tutsi**) who have not still share traditional animistic religious beliefs in which Imana, a powerful spirit, is the creator. When he took corporeal form, Imana was always a white lamb with no markings; he was said to skip and gambol about. The term *imana* also refers to the force of good that causes such things as prosperity, joy, peace, and fertility and is the intangible life force of all things both organic and inorganic. Human beings animals, plants, stones, fire, and rivers all have *imana*, a soul. The traditional religion includes two important components in addition to the recognition of Imana: the presence of the spirits of one's ancestors and the existence of a life force that is in all beings. The ancestral spirits can be malicious and must be placated. These departed ancestors are called *ubuzima*, *mizimu*, *imizimu*, or *abasimu*, and they are among the causes of cattle epidemics, crop failure, and sickness because they are supposed to envy the things they had to leave behind. Their influence extends only over their own clan, and the descendents must consult a diviner to discover the reason for the ancestor's anger. These ancestors can often be placated if the family builds a *kararo*, a "little sleeping house" supplied with food and beer beside the grave.

There are no institutionalized public cults, idols, or priests dedicated to Imana (he is honored but not feared because he has no power to harm), but individuals perform informal ceremonies. For example, a woman may leave a pitcher of water for Imana before going to sleep at night with the hope that he will make her fertile. In fact, traditionally, no married woman who still had expectations of child-bearing would ever go to bed without seeing that there was water (*amazi y'Imana*) in the house, because Imana was supposed to create during the night. Creation was not thought to occur at the moment of conception only, but to continue for several nights; if Imana found no water, he might not be able to create correctly. A ritual performed only by **Hutu** centers around the belief that the smooth stones in brooks and rivers carry the power of Imana. Several stones (*inguru*) are collected and placed in a small hut built outside the *rugo*; the stones are given offerings of meat, milk, broken pots, pumpkin shells, and beer. The belief is that eventually they give birth to 20 or 30 additional stones, demonstrating spiritual fertility. There are few if any creation myths or legends concerning Imana's relationship with humans, but within the oral tradition, stories tell of Imana's travels through the country. Another story tells of Imana's becoming visible in order to chase death. There is a saying in Kirundi that indicates the country's strong belief in a superior being: *Imana Y'i Burundi* ("Burundi is Imana's country"). Both the Barundi and the Banyarwanda have many praise names for Imana; among some of the more common ones are Rurema, the Creator (*-rema*, "create"), Rugaba, the Giver (*-gaba*, "give, rule"), Rugiravyose, the

Doer-of-all (*-gira*, "do"; *-vyose*, "all"), and Inchanyi, the Fire-Lighter (*-chana*, "light or blow up a fire").

An oral tradition explains why Imana no longer lives among humans as he once did. He used to talk to humans, causing the development of children until one day he created a disabled child. The parents were very angry and began looking for an opportunity to kill Imana with a knife. Of course, Imana saw all of this and said, "If they are going to behave like that I will depart to my own place and not show myself any more. Then I can create as I please, and if they are not satisfied, they can just grumble!" As a result, the tradition tells us, he never shows himself any more, but some are lucky enough to see him in his occasional unguarded moments.

There are many Kirundi words that have derived from the name Imana. For example, *ivyamana* means divine attributes or the attributes of a soothsayer; *igihamana* (plural: *ibihamana*) means a godsend or good luck; *indoramana* means theology or theological; *ikimana* is a false god or idol; *ikiremamana* (plural: *ibiremamana*) is a congenital defect or malformation; *ubuyobokamana* is faith and service to Imana; and *bumana* is a natural state.

Imfura. According to anthropologist **Ethel Albert**, this implies "speaking well" and is one of the primary characteristics of good breeding and aristocracy. She states that, among the upper classes, the ideals of oratorical ability are most stressed and that aristocratic boys are given formal education in speech-making from about the age of ten. This education includes the composition of impromptu speeches appropriate in relations with superiors in status or age, formulas for petitioning a superior for a gift, composition of praise poems (see *(ama-)zina*), self-defensive rhetoric intended to deflect an accusation or the anger of a superior, and formulas for addressing social inferiors, for funeral orations, for making judgments in disputes, or for serving as an intermediary.

Inama Kaminuza. During the early days of independence, **UPRONA** divided into two factions, and the breach was never fully healed. In September 1964, this summit conference was held in Kitega, and the impasse between the two factions was made clear. About 20 **Hutu** and **Tutsi** from each wing of the party came together to, according to a report from the conference, "debate in common the means to achieve national unity. . . . and the total reconciliation of the UPRONA leaders." To that end, they gave priority to "the constitution of a single Executive Committee."

Inanjonaki. She was the mother of **Ntare I** Rushatsi, the first king of Burundi. According to some oral traditions, Ntare's father is unknown; according to others, his name was **Rufuko**, but little more is said about him.

Inararibonye. By 1961, many of the old **UPRONA** chiefs had severed their ties with the party in order to set up their own political organizations. **Biha**, who never forgave **Rwagasore** for his political views or his popularity, founded the Inararibonye party in 1961. In Kirundi, the name refers to the Elders and is often associated with a legend about Mwami Mwezi **Gisabo**. After killing a lion, the Mwami removed the skin and wore it as a cape. As the sun became hotter, the skin began to shrink and to choke him. At this time, the Inararibonye arrived and took the Mwami to a nearby lake, immersing him in the water and freeing him from the lion skin.

Inaryangombe (also Inakiranga, Njanja, and Kajumbu). She was **Kiranga**'s mother. According to Zuure, to explain the independent and rebellious spirit that Kiranga exhibited, she once lamented:

> Tell me, people from here.
> I gave birth to an imbecile.
> He is a bad subject.
> I tell him this:
> Rwogamabenge [her name for Kiranga] do not go far
>   away
> You will die there.
> He does not listen, he goes.

Stop, do not go into the bush alone.
He does not listen, he goes.

Inder Frage. In the early part of this century, the **Germans** considered the many non-African, non-European merchants in Ruanda-Urundi to be a problem. They referred to this problem as the *Inder Frage* or "Indian Question" (by "Indian" was meant all Asians). This was controlled through the governor's ordinance of March 1905: ". . . until further notice entrance to the sultanates of Ruanda and Urundi is permitted only from the military station of Usumbura, and only with written permission from the district officer. . . ."

Inkinzo. As one of the radical **Tutsi** political parties that became vocal after the death of President **Ndadaye** and the ensuing massacres, this party stated that the **Frodebu** government should be tried for crimes against humanity. Among these crimes, they listed the spread of killings on the hillsides and the refusal of government officials to leave foreign embassies, an act that was described as caring more for their own safety than that of the population at large.

Intagohekas. Following the death of President **Ntayamira** and the subsequent shakiness of the coalition government, "those who never sleep," an extremist **Hutu** militia group, were known to chase **Tutsi** from the hills in the countryside (mostly Hutu) and to attack refugee camps where tens of thousands of displaced Tutsi live.

Inyenzi. Literally translated as "cockroaches" this secret terrorist organization comprised Tutsi exiles from **Rwanda**. They made three attempts to invade Rwanda in November and December 1963; the second (December 20) coincided with the break-up of a conference between the Rwanda and Burundi governments on the dissolution of their customs and monetary union. This conference had been acrimonious at times, and the Rwanda government suspected that the Burundi government gave the Inyenzi free rein to invade at the end of the conference. The Burundi authorities denied this.

Iyerezi (mu-, ba-). There were, traditionally, many types of ceremonial dances, the most highly admired dancers being the **Twa**. Men and women never danced together; rather, dancing was primarily for entertaining in the court. At the courts of kings and chiefs, there was always a carefully selected troupe of dancers chosen from the young warriors. These were the *abiyerezi*.

-J-

Jambo (i-, ma-). Verbal ability has long been highly regarded in Burundi society, making the oral tradition a strong one. This general term refers to speech or eloquence. Because the kingdom of Burundi was historically less centralized than **Rwanda**, fewer poems, songs, and stories chronicle the history of the country; nevertheless, the richness of the oral arts exists. Criteria for classification of such arts vary depending on whether one is primarily concerned with content or form, but many historians have distinguished four large categories, each containing several smaller groups. First is the narrative genre. Included in this group are the *imigani* (*mu-*) (plural forms will be given here, followed by the singular prefix in parentheses if relevant), which include fairy tales, fables, legends, and myths. Next are the *ibitito* or *ibitiko* (*gi-*), dramatic stories interspersed with song. Last are the *ibiganiro* or *ibiyago* (*ki-*), dialogue stories and chronicles.

The second large category contains the puzzles and proverbs; these include *ibisokozo* or *ibisokoranyo* (*gi-*), or riddles, *imigani* (*mu-*), proverbs, and *imyigovyoro* (*mu-*), truisms or adages. The third category comprises musical and lyrical stories. Among them are ***uguhoza umwana*** or lullabies, *ugucura intimba* or laments, *imvyino* or wedding songs, and *ibimpwiri* (ki-) or rounds sung by men and accompanied by hand-clapping. Within this third category are two smaller groupings including *ugukeza umuvyeyi*, which are songs praising motherhood, and songs that are specialized according to the musical instrument that accompanies them. Examples of these are the *inanga*, songs accompanied by the zither. The fourth, and perhaps largest category, comprises the *amazina*, which are discussed at length under their own entry, and the *ibicuba* (*gi-*) or praises of pastoralism.

Jeunesse Nationaliste Rwagasore (JNR). T h e origins of the JNR (initially known as the Union Culturelle de la Jeunesse Africaine du Burundi (UCJAB)) go back to 1959. The statutes of the original organization said: "Our movement aims at leading humanity towards a greater fraternity, a greater mutual understanding, a greater peace and happiness. . . . Its goals are to orient our youth towards a more mature form of nationalism, through appropriate civic training; to inculcate in our future generations of leaders a sense of mutual understanding . . . and to affirm the ideal of equality among all citizens." Shortly before independence, the government wanted to use it as a "parallel structure" for maintaining peace and order in the African quarters of Bujumbura. It became the youth division of the **UPRONA** party around the time of independence. Under the leadership of Prime **Nyongabo** and François **Bangemu**, the JNR took on an activist role, which remained its primary characteristic. In January 1962 the JNR launched a series of armed raids against some trade union leaders belonging to the **Parti du Peuple**. Included in these raids was arson against four houses in the Kamenge neighborhood of Bujumbura, during the course of which four prominent Hutu leaders were killed, including Severin Ndinzurwaha, permanent secretary of the Christian trade union organization, Mouvement Populaire Chrétien, and Jean Nduwabika, president of the union and secretary general of the **Parti du Peuple**. This prompted the Mwami to dissolve the association and incarcerate its leaders. In 1966, the JNR reformed, still in open defiance of the Mwami's instructions.

Jeunesse Rwagasore Révolutionnaire (JRR). O n February 10, 1967, Radio Bujumbura reported that all of the country's youth organizations had merged into this one large group.

Jiji (mu-, ba-). This was a very high-level **Hutu** family that had ties with *ganwa* and the court of the *mwami*. Their alternate name was Abarangaranga, "people of Kiranga," and they came from Nkoma in southeastern Burundi. Their roles in the court were many and varied; for example, they served as singers at the weddings of princes. Additionally, it was from this clan that guardians of the royal drum (**Karyenda**) and the wives of **Kiranga** (**Mukakiranga**) were chosen, and it was also often from this group that sub-chiefs in the countryside were chosen.

-K-

Ka (in-, in-). *Inka* (cattle) have been central to many aspects of Burundi society for almost as long as the society has existed. Cows were the basis of the patron-client relationships that dominated the precolonial social and economic structure of the country. An exchange of cattle usually confirmed important agreements. For example, they were traditionally the preferred form of bride wealth. Cows were not generally a source of food, but were regarded almost as living gold, the most highly prized form of wealth and a symbol of prestige; in fact, they were traditionally used for almost anything people in the modern world would use money, for example, repayment of a loan or salary. There is a popular saying in Burundi that is translated as "Down with the franc, long live the cow, source of all life." Because cows are dedicated to **Imana**, they are afforded respect through prayer, attentive care, and tabus. For example, Barundi never boil or even heat milk, because doing so could cause the cow to have a sore udder and stop giving milk; milk may not be drunk on the same day that peas or peanuts are eaten; if a person has an open wound, he or she cannot watch a cow give birth, because this would cause the wound to become worse. Myths, legends, and epics that abound illustrate the ways in which cattle and people share their lives. Even in postcolonial days, traditional greetings such as "*Amashyo*" ("May you have herds") and the response "*Amashongore*" ("I wish you herds of females") can sometimes be heard. "Darling, your eyes are like those of a cow" is considered a sincere compliment.

Kabura, Celestin. One of the approximately 5 percent **Hutu** soldiers in the Burundi **army**, he has been quoted speaking out against the military. In 1995, he said that the Hutu politicians do not trust the army and, as a result, they insist on keeping some of the very few Hutu soldiers as bodyguards. "When someone kills a Hutu, soldiers go laughing. They don't bother catching them." Kabura also said that some Tutsi soldiers supply Tutsi militias with grenades and bayonets.

Kageorgis, Jean. An unemployed Greek mercenary, he was the hired assassin of **Rwagasore**. Although his role in the assassination was not questioned, and he was sentenced to death for it, it was also clear from the beginning that it was a much bigger conspiracy and that he was nothing but a hired killer; the murder was masterminded by Joseph **Biroli** and Jean **Ntitendereza**, the leaders of the **PDC** and the sons of Chief **Baranyanka**.

Kamakare (mu-, ba-). These female counselors to the royal court were aides in charge of milking, among other duties, during the reign of **Gisabo**.

Kamana, Jean Paul. Imprisoned in Uganda since November 1994, he is accused of directing the assassination of President **Ndadaye**, which he has denied. He claims that he only told the soldiers to negotiate with the president and that mutinous soldiers held their guns on him as he tried to reach the room where the president was being held. He has not been charged with any crime in Uganda, and Burundi and Uganda do not have an extradition treaty. Several human rights organizations, including Human Rights Watch/Africa submitted a report in July 1994 stating, "The direct commander of the assassination of the president was Lt. Kamana." As a prisoner, he has complained about inaction by UNHCR. An officer in that organization has said that these alleged putschists are a dilemma for them because many want to be resettled in a third country, but UNHCR does not want to get involved with the protection of criminals. Kamana has also complained about unfair imprisonment and boredom; in answer to his second complaint, the Red Cross has given him a Scrabble game. He has continued to maintain that he was framed. According to an article by Catharine Watson and Alan Zarembo, he said, "The mutinous soldiers came to my residence and put me into a jeep and took me to the palace. But I told them to stop firing. That created an atmosphere of mistrust between me and them, so they locked me up in a room in the tank barracks. I was in that room when Ndadaye was killed." An international inquiry of the events of October 1993 reported that Kamana addressed a large group of excited troops on a barracks basketball court and announced that Ndadaye would be killed.

Kamatari. He was the brother of **Mwambutsa IV** and a descendent of the **Bataga**.

Kamenge. This suburb of Bujumbura has a history of violence in the ongoing struggle between **Hutu** and **Tutsi**. The people of the area (primarily Hutu) have more than once been the victims of attacks by Tutsi political groups and **army** personnel. In January 1962, the president of the **JNR**, Prime **Nyongabo**, held a meeting in Kamenge and, shortly after, launched a series of armed attacks against some Hutu. In this suburb, four houses were set on fire, and during what later became called the "Kamenge incidents," four prominent Hutu were killed. The riots that followed understandably created an even more explosive atmosphere in the country that helped to strengthen ethnic division within **UPRONA**. In the following two years, a group of Hutu students began to plot against the government in retaliation for these incidents. Lemarchand writes of a letter to the organizers, written by one of the students (who had been imprisoned); in part the letter said, "If we falter, we shall be the ones to be sent to the gallows." He went on to say "Do you really want to see 85 percent of the population thrown back into slavery . . . ?" Following these incidents, many sanctions were set against the JNR, which was eventually dissolved by the Mwami. The organization resurfaced in 1966.

Following the attempted coup and the assassination of President **Ndadaye** in 1993, Kamenge, called by some the "last Hutu stronghold," once again emerged as a location of violence. Several incidents occurred involving the mostly Tutsi army and Hutu militia groups in the area; the one involving the highest death toll as well as the most concern from the OAU and the **UN** occurred in June 1995. During a three-day period, army personnel surrounded the suburb where Hutu militia were alleged to be; at a time reported to be 13 hours before the time given to civilians as a deadline to evacuate, the army entered the neighborhood, leaving between 25 and 40 people (mostly children and elderly) dead. Another series of repercussions resulted from this attack, one of which left nine dead in Musaga, a Tutsi neighborhood.

Kamyi (mu-, ba-). There are two different historical roles attributed to these people of honor in the court of the *mwami.* Some sources say they were tutors to the royal children as well as something similar to court protocol officers. The more common description of their role was that of royal milkers. These were young **Tutsi** males, chosen from very noble families, usually of the Banyakarana clan. A young milker spent a lot of time being initiated into the rites of the court; he did not have direct contact with the royal cows until he reached the age of 15. The milkers were required to remain celibate; any sexual contact rendered them ineligible for royal service.

Kandeke, Jean. In late 1962, when the **JNR** made threats of violence against Hutu trade unionists and politicians, Kandeke was among the victims. At that time he was a supporter of the **Parti du Peuple** (PP) and was in charge of a local cooperative. The threats were sometimes only that, but Kandeke was almost bludgeoned to death by a group of JNR militants.

Kanugunu. Considered by many to be the most powerful and energetic of **Ntare** I's descendants (he was his great-grandson), this chief was also the most influential of all the **Batare** during the reign of Mwezi **Gisabo**. In his attempt to follow Ntare's policy, Gisabo waged long wars against his opponents in all areas of the country. During these wars, Kanugunu was killed, apparently with the assistance of the **German** troops, thus deepening the long hatred between the **Bezi** and the Batare.

Kanyenkiko, Anatole. In early 1995, a coalition government comprising at least 13 political parties and led by President **Ntibantunganya** was in office, apparently struggling to keep peace following the deaths of two presidents, **Ndadaye** and **Ntaryamira**. The leader of the strongest opposition party, Charles Mukasi, threatened to topple the fragile government, but said he did not want to use violence to achieve his goal. In February, his party, **UPRONA**, virtually shut down Bujumbura in a general strike to press for the resignation of Prime Minister Kanyenkiko; some hardliners in UPRONA considered him to be too sympathetic to Ntibantunganya's government. Kanyenkiko said that he would not resign until the two major parties agreed on his successor, but Mukasi said the strike would continue until Kanyenkiko's government collapsed. Kanyenkiko finally did resign about a week after the beginning of the strike, and was replaced by Prime Minister **Nduwayo**. Kanyenkilo said in a statement read on state radio that he had quit in the interest of the country and "to avoid problems such as steering Burundi in the same path as **Rwanda**."

Karani (mu-, ba-). The general term refers to assistants, secretaries, or scribes, and they were traditionally those responsible for the historical record-keeping of the chiefdoms and the court. The secretary of a chiefdom was called *umukarani w'igihugu c'umuganwa*, and the secretary to the mwami was called *yari umukarani w'umwami*.

Karibwami, Pontien. He was the president of Parliament during the brief tenure of President **Ndadaye** in 1993. Like the president and other members of the government at that time, Karibwami had also been a refugee following the 1972 massacres. He was killed during the 1993 coup attempt during which President Ndadaye was also killed.

Karyenda. Literally, this is the royal or sacred drum, a symbol of the office of kingship and, in turn, a symbol of social and political unity. Traditionally, when the king killed the enemies of the kingdom, the victims' genitals were hung from the drum. The traditional royal court had many rituals and ceremonies that included and even centered around the Karyenda. The symbolic wife of Karyenda is **Mukakaryenda**. Karyenda is one of the three main pillars of the monarchy, along with **Kiranga** and cattle.

Kashirahamwe, Pascal. A brother-in-law of **Micombero** and a member of the "**Family Corporation**," Kashirahamwe was president of the Banque Commerciale. As such, he dominated the economics of Burundi during his office.

Keba (mu-, ba-). In the oral tradition of the society, stories and proverbs were invented and repeated about these personal rivals or competitors.

Kevvi (mu-, ba-). Under the *ubugabire* system of patronage, these were the very important court cooks, who had the complete trust of the *mwami*. They also were responsible for carving and serving meat in royal households.

Kilima. Although Chief Kilima's real identity is obscure, it is clear that he was one of **Gisabo**'s most formidable rivals. According to legend (some begun by Kilima himself) he was the descendant of one of Ntare II's sons named Nyanamusango, who had lived with the Bafulero in the Congo for a time. One of Nyanamusango's sons, Njitshi, married a Bafulero girl named Naabakile, who bore Kilima.

In later years, Kilima allied himself with a group of chiefs of the Ruzizi valley and established his claims over the northwestern region of Burundi by finding followers among the **Hutu** and murdering all existing **Tutsi** there; he became known as "Batutsi-killer." Note that, if these legends are to be believed, Kilima and Gisabo were closely related by blood; this rivalry would then show clearly the long-standing hatred between **Bezi** and **Batare**, including fratricidal strife between Gisabo and his elder brothers. Kilima's territory continued to grow during the **German** occupation and with the coming of the **Belgians**. Later, Kilima's four sons, Ruhabira, Rusimbi, Kalibwami, and Rwasha, were each given extensive tracts of land by the Belgian administration. One oral tradition states that Kilima, who had been a rival claimant to the throne, was killed by Gisabo; Kilima's head was then displayed in the royal kraal. However, Gisabo died in 1908, and Kilima probably died later.

Kimyi (mu-, ba-). Under the *ubugabire* system of patronage, there were many individuals in the personal service of the *mwami*. Among the members of the court were the *bakimyi*, people who possessed supernatural powers and were responsible for milking the royal herd of cows.

Kinigi, Silvie. After the first democratic election in June 1993, which resulted in the election of the first **Hutu** president, Kinigi (a **Tutsi** married to a Hutu) was appointed prime minister. She lived through the original violence in October of that year, being granted asylum at the French embassy. At that time, she said, "It's very difficult to say who has power now. The **army** does not seem to want to lose it. I have no military, no police force, and no control of the media. I have nothing." She said she believed that the coup leaders panicked when they realized they were faced with a popular uprising by Burundians who had overwhelmingly voted for President **Ndadaye**. She reported that 60 percent of the army was still loyal to her and that the coup had been organized by officers mainly from Burure Province. She also appealed for international military intervention, saying that there was no guarantee of the security of civilian governments at that stage and that she could not "approve of my government entering into negotiations with people who assassinated our leaders." Several days after the attempted coup, Kinigi took control of the country again and ordered troops back to the barracks, promising to punish those taking part in the coup. Several months later, in April 1994, following the death of Burundi's next president along with the president of **Rwanda**, Kinigi said, "There is now an open war between the army and these Hutu mercenaries [Hutu militants arming peasants in the countryside]." She reported that the only hope was that Burundians would become exhausted by the fighting. She, like many moderate residents of the country, also saw the problems of 1993 and 1994 as resulting from democracy being thrust on the country too abruptly: "We entered into democracy without having the means of dealing with it. The process was too rapid. There was no time to form political leaders. So parties formed on the simple criteria of ethnicity. With Rwanda, we have in common inexperience in democracy and ineptness in managing power."

Kiranga. An early Kirundi-English dictionary written for a missionary group defines this as an "evil spirit worshipped by Barundi; similar to Satan." This definition, while often repeated in later descriptions, does not do justice to the spirit of Kiranga. Also known as Rikiranga or Ryangombe, he is, in the traditional religion, the powerful leader of all ancestral spirits and the hero spirit. Barundi traditionally believed that Kiranga could prevent **Imana** from helping people, so he must be placated in order to leave a clear channel for Imana's blessings to flow through. There is little or no prayer directly to Imana; most of the worship is to Kiranga. Oral traditions say that he came from **Rwanda** during the time of the clan state. It is believed that he was killed by a buffalo while hunting, and then all of his friends committed suicide near his body; Imana gave them a special place to lead lives of pleasure. Young men perform rituals, chants, and dances to honor him. During the *kubandwa*, a grain harvest festival, these young men paint themselves and decorate small spirit huts. One of the groups personifies Kiranga, who appears carrying a sacred spear. There are priests who are the human abodes of Kiranga's spirit and who act as mediators between spirits and people. The priests' positions are usually attained through heredity and inherited talent, but occasionally a man may be seized by the spirit and given the power of mediation. When an offering is made, the priests may speak to the spirits, delivering prophesies. Although the sect has some features of a cult (members traditionally believed that nonmembers would burn in an eternal fire), it is one area that has abolished ethnic differences as a consideration. Kiranga's initiates of varying degrees of rank call themselves *abana b'Imana*, "the children of Imana."

The worship of Kiranga is thought to have originated in the long-disputed area around the current border between Rwanda and Burundi sometime before the early seventeenth century. In Burundi, based on oral tradition as well as historical probability, Kiranga almost certainly predated the reign of **Ntare I**, although some legends have the two arriving simultaneously and establishing a mutually dependent relationship. Indeed, there was an ambivalent relationship between Kiranga's followers and the court influenced by two factors: that the religious system was in place before the beginning of the dynasty and that there simply were now two royal figures. A Burundi proverb even proclaimed "Kiranga is the king of all beings, living or not." Rodegem, through the recording of Burundi texts, suggested that Kiranga respected the *mwami* and the *mwami* feared Kiranga and was wary of opposing his decisions. Over time, kings devised myths proclaiming their priority over Kiranga.

Kirundi. The national language of Burundi is very closely related to and mutually intelligible with the language of neighboring **Rwanda**, Kinyarwanda. Both are members of the Bantu subgroup of the Niger-Congo linguistic family; speakers of the two languages comprise the third-largest group speaking any African language. The two larger groups speak Swahili and Lingala; the Kirundi/Kinyarwanda speakers differ from these two groups in that the languages are not *lingua francas* throughout large areas, but rather still function in their original areas.

Kirundi, as is characteristic of the Bantu subgroup, is a complex language from a Romance or Germanic perspective. Typical of Bantu languages is a system of gender categories, numbering between 13 and 19; these categories then determine prefixes on all classes of words. Additionally, Kirundi is a tonal language, another difficulty for speakers of atonal Western languages. All verbs, for example, fall into one of two tone classes, distinguishable by the presence or absence of a high tone. In 1948, Malcolm Guthrie classified Kirundi and Kinyarwanda as group D60, significant primarily because it separated the languages from those of Uganda and **Tanzania** while connecting them with many of the languages of **Zaire**. Guthrie himself said that there was little linguistic significance this grouping and that it was really a geographic consideration. Nevertheless, little separation of this type had previously been done, and it was a useful exercise. In 1953, a **Belgian** linguist, A. Meeussen, criticized this grouping, and his new studies under the Tervuren School produced a narrower regrouping. Many of the specific characteristics of Kirundi are discussed in the notes beginning this section.

Kirundi and Kinyarwanda are unusual languages in that they are spoken by all Barundi and Banyarwanda. Unlike most other African nations where linguistic divisions reflect ethnic ones, both major ethnic groups (as well as the **Twa**) in both countries speak the national languages. As the language is clearly Bantu in origin, it was most likely the language of the **Hutu** at the time of the **Tutsi** migration into the region. This—the adopting of the regional language by the dominating group—is also an unusual situation. The existence of these languages as universally known has created two other situations considered unusual in the region. First, although Swahili, the *lingua franca* for much of East Africa, is widely understood in the trade centers, it has made the use of Swahili as the vernacular largely unnecessary. Additionally, perhaps because of the common language among the people, the ethnic groups are far more difficult to distinguish than those of, for example, Tanzania.

The groups intermarry, share histories, and share a great many spiritual beliefs and rituals.

Although Kirundi is the national language and, with minor regional variations, is spoken and understood throughout the country, French, the language introduced by the Belgian administrators and missionaries, is also widely used in official documents, newspapers, and broadcasting. Swahili, the *lingua franca* of much of East Africa, is widely understood in Bujumbura.

Koro (mu-, mi-). This was a tribute owed to the *mwami* or chief. It was paid in either labor or cash.

Korora (gu-, verb). Traditionally, there appear to be no formal laws against artificial abortion, but it was often treated as a criminal offense. The practice (*gukorora*) was seldom mentioned publicly, but apparently, if an unmarried woman was pregnant, on rare occasions she might induce abortion by intense massage and herbal treatments.

Kura (gu-, verb). In traditional Burundi society, there were few rituals associated with maturation. There were, for example, no rites associated with circumcision or clitoridectomy. Additionally, sexual taboos were not considered significant before *gukura*, the transition from childhood to puberty between the ages of 12 and 15.

Kuru (bu-, im-). This is translated as "senior person," "seniority," or "superiority" and is a guiding principle of all behavior. Caste order is known to all interlocutors in a context; thus, the order in which individuals speak in a group depends on their seniority. According to **Ethel Albert**, "the senior person will speak first; the next in order of rank opens his speech with a statement to the effect of 'Yes, I agree with the previous speaker; he is correct, he is older and knows best, etc.' Then, depending on circumstances and issues, the second speaker will by degrees or at once express his own views, and these may well be diametrically opposed to those previously expressed.

No umbrage is taken, the required formula of acknowledgment of the superior having been used."

Kutsi (mu-, ba-). In traditional society, cows were so important to the culture that these people were special servants whose only job was to collect cow dung from the enclosures.

Kuvamukiriri. In traditional Burundi society, when a child has grown hair, is learning to walk, and the danger of infant death is decreasing, the *kuvamukiriri* (naming ceremony) takes place. Generally, names relate to attributes of **Imana**, familiar incidents, or events occurring around the time of birth. The Barundi are creative with names; some examples might be Kaimana ("Little Imana"), Mbonimana ("Gift of Imana"), or Keschimana ("Ornament of Imana"). A couple's 11th child is often named Misage ("to go too far"); the 12th is often named Ijana ("hundredth or many"), and the 13th is often named with a prayer to Imana to stop the overabundance of gifts: Niboyo ("cease"). If a couple has lost several children during infancy or before, they sometimes guard a new child with names that mean such things as "mouse excrement" or "prostitute" in the hope that the name will be unattractive to malevolent spirits.

Kwahukana (verb: ahukana). Divorce was not very common in traditional society, and it almost always involved the denouncement of the woman or her abandonment of the home. First, the parents of the couple tried to bring about a reconciliation. There were, however, a number of situations where the two partners mutually agreed to a divorce. There were also specific laws governing those faults of either partner that were grounds for the other demanding a divorce. The faults attributed to the wife included sterility (although the husband often simply chose polygamy as an alternative to divorce; polyandry was less often an option for women, but it was not unheard of), laziness or dirtiness, incurable illness, use of witchcraft against the husband, his parents, or his cattle, repeated adultery, incompatible personality, and refusal of conjugal relations. Faults attributed to the husband as possible grounds for divorce included insufficiency of the bride price (determined by the wife's father), insufficient feeding of the wife, grave public insult of the wife (although this would not include adultery as the traditional society was, if not always practically, polygamous), incurable or contagious disease, and sexual impotence. In cases of legal divorce, children below the age of puberty stayed with their mother with an allowance from their father; then they became part of the paternal clan.

Kwano (in-, in-). This is the bride price or the matrimonial price. Generally, in traditional Burundi society, cows served as gifts in the marriage contract (from the groom to the bride's family). There was no true marriage unless the matrimonial pledge was given; this exchange of gifts represented fertility in the coming marriage. The matrimonial price, of course, varied according to the class of the parties involved. The price for a princess could be as many as 15 cows. For a wealthy, but non-*ganwa* **Tutsi** woman, the price was usually a pregnant cow and a heifer or, if that was not possible, a healthy cow and a heifer. Poorer Tutsi women brought, at least in principle, one pregnant cow. Among the **Hutu**, the traditional price was one cow or two bulls if possible.

Kwashiorkor. This malnutrition condition was quite prevalent in young children because of the Barundi diet, which included little protein. When the children are weaned, they change to a predominantly carbohydrate diet. Kwashiorkor resulted in the deaths of many children, as well as a high rate of liver disorders among the survivors of the disease.

Kwirukana (verb: irukana). This condition of marital separation was usually the step before an official divorce was pronounced and was quite different from the situation of *intabwa*. The wife was free to either return to her family or search for better fortune elsewhere. The husband could always ask for his wife to return to their compound; in some situations, he could demand it.

Kwishongora (verb: ishongora). Supposedly strictly to be performed by men, these traditional songs are long, lyrical, rhythmic declamations, full of trills and requiring a clear, fairly high-pitched voice.

-L-

"Light on the Events of Ntega and Marangara." One of a series of ethnic massacres began in August 1988. The origins of the killings are not completely clear, but many **Hutu** said that they had been expecting violence since a coup in September of the previous year during which the **army** removed Jean-Baptiste **Bagaza** as president and replaced him with Pierre **Buyoya**. However, many **Tutsi** accused Hutu extremists of having planned an uprising for a long time. Western diplomats said that neither explanation was correct; they claimed that President Buyoya was a sincere moderate and that the uprising had not been planned by the government. Instead, they said that it was a local situation that had gotten out of hand. The government said that Hutu dissidents entered the country from **Rwanda** and incited the Hutu villagers to violence. This version said that the Hutu were "high on hemp" and bloodthirsty. It also said the rebels killed other Hutu who did not want to participate.

It is the official government theory that was circulated by the Ministry of Information in a 43-page booklet called "Light on the Events of Ntega and Marangara." Some of the things claimed in the book include: "It should be noted that the tactic of the drugged rebels was not only to kill with spears, arrows, stones, and machetes, but also to take a certain number of prisoners, notably girls who they forced to follow them after killing their parents. . . . These girls were used for various tasks before being raped. . . . Many were chained up and they drowned in the Akanyaru River. Because the delirious mob was setting fires and carrying out unheard of acts of violence, it was necessary to call the forces of order. . . . The army, therefore, did what it could to stop the carnage. They used their weapons not against civilians, but against the rebels. . . . Some innocent victims of all ethnicities were hurt by bullets. . . . The terrorists killed both ethnicities."

In any case, it is true that the killings centered around the communes of Ntega and Marangara in the already tense northern part of the country. Other nearby provinces were also affected. In Kirundo province where Marangara is located there had been unrest the previous year when Hutu found out that the ethnicity of students was being listed in school records; they feared that these records would keep their children from secondary school. When a local Hutu representative to the National Legislature brought the subject up in Bujumbura, he disappeared.

By 1988 in Marangara, the Hutu were not happy with four particular Tutsi civil servants in the area, who they said discriminated against them. On August 5, a small uprising took placeduring which the villagers demanded that the four be removed and then panicked when three military vehicles arrived. On August 6, the Hutu felled trees across roads and destroyed bridges in order to block the army. The villagers feared a repeat of the 1972 massacres and began to arm themselves. The Tutsi provincial governor met with the local population and claimed that the Hutu had been very frightened but vague as to why they were frightened. The Hutu claimed that they had been quite specific, asking for the removal of the four civil servants and asking the governor to act against "Tutsi plotters."

About a week later a wealthy Tutsi coffee merchant (alleged to have been involved in the 1972 killings) refused to pay money he owed to some Hutu; he killed five of them. The Hutu then mobilized, surrounding the merchant's house for hours and eventually killing him and his family. The events that followed remain unclear. Some church and aid groups said that the army arrived right away to arrest the merchant's killers and immediately began to kill Hutu. A nun said that the Hutu turned on the Tutsi, killing many whole families and that the army did not arrive for two days. All agree, however, that once the army arrived, the Hutu were on the run. The estimated total dead was between 5,000 and 13,000. Some sources claimed as many as 24,000 dead, and some as many as 23,000 unaccounted for. Western diplomats said that the lower number of deaths is closer to correct because most of the people fled the dangerous areas quickly.

After the massacres, the government allowed journalists to enter the area. Catharine Watson reported that the journalists saw no evidence of hemp use, prisoners, or rebel tracts. They reported evidence of bayonet wounds and other atrocities against Hutu women and children.

Lito (ki-, bi-). This is a type of elegy traditionally sung by young women and accompanied by very melancholy and sentimental music. These songs, it is said, were quite popular as evening entertainment for families having several daughters.

Lyango (mu-, **no plural**). This patrilineage was the primary grouping around which competition among the **Hutu** centered during the communal elections of 1960. Although the smallest grouping, it remained the dominant form of political organization in the northern part of the country until independence.

-M-

Macoonco. While a fairly minor historical figure, Macoonco's story is one that points to the difficulty of depending upon oral traditions for historical fact. According to **Vansina**, it is culturally permissible to alter any tale to make it more entertaining and satisfying for the audience, regardless of other documented facts, should they exist. Macoonco rebelled against **Gisabo** and was captured by **German** officials and imprisoned in Usumbura. He died in prison, but it is here that the facts become obscured. The popular folk tale says that one day he saw from the prison window two messengers from the **Mwami** walking down from the hills. He was certain that they had been sent to request his death, so he committed suicide in his cell; in fact, the story goes, they had come to ask for a reprieve for him. German records tell a different story: Macoonco attacked a

German officer in an escape attempt and was killed by other guards. There is no evidence of any messengers from Gisabo, nor is this likely, but the original storyteller apparently thought the suicide was a more satisfying story, and so it remains the "truth." Vansina discusses at length the idea of historical truth and its relativity. He says that Barundi have the idea that as soon as something is accepted as historical truth, they do not think about whether or not it really happened as tradition describes it; analysis is unnecessary, and often historical or logical discrepancies are dismissed by saying such things as perhaps things could have happened differently in former times.

Mali Proposal. During an emergency meeting of the OAU council of ministers in 1964, both Ghana and Mali proposed discussions that included the so-called "Congo problem." The Mali proposal resulted in an ad hoc commission, chaired by President Kenyatta of Kenya, mandated to help the efforts of the Zairian government in the restoration of national reconciliation and to seek all possible means to bring about normal relations between territories formerly attached to the Congo and its neighbors, "especially the Kingdom of Burundi and the People's Republic of the Congo (Brazzaville)."

Manirarira, Marc. As the minister of foreign affairs, he was the representative of the Burundi government who announce at a Nairobi news conference that neither the **United States** nor **China** had been implicated in the assassination of Prime Minister **Ngendandumwe** even though diplomatic relations with China had been temporarily suspended. He said that relations would be resumed "as soon as the confusion is lifted."

Masumbuko, Pie. Following the assassination of Pierre **Ngendandumwe**, Masumbuko acted briefly as prime minister. In 1963, three prominent citizens had been arrested and accused of participating in a conspiracy to undermine the security of the state. Masumbuko was among them; he also had the distinction at that time of being the only African physician in Burundi.

Matana (Tutsi). Within the **Tutsi** ethnic group were many factions, usually based on location. Often, conflict among these groups was more important to the dynamics of Burundi politics than was conflict between Tutsi and **Hutu**, and the seats of power constantly changed. At one point (from around the end of **Micombero**'s presidency to the mid-1980s), the Matana were one of the primary groups in conflict with the **Rutovu**. Their leader was Artémon **Simbananiye**, who was foreign affairs minister from 1972 to 1974.

Maus, Albert. A **Belgian** settler and formerly a Resident of **Rwanda** and a member of the Conseil du Vice-Government Géneral, he was one of the key individuals associated with the **Parti du Peuple (PP)**. He was known to give generously of his time and financial resources to the **Hutu** cause, and he acted as an intermediary between the PP and the administration. He was said to be pathologically anti-Tutsi and committed suicide upon learning of the **UPRONA** victory in 1961.

Mayugi, Nicolas. He was the first **Hutu** president of **UPRONA**, serving in this capacity from 1991 to 1995. Before this, he held the position of minister of higher education and research (from 1988 to 1991); prior to that, he taught at the Institut Pédagogique of Bujumbura.

Mazrui, Ali A. While director of the Center for Afro-American and African Studies at the University of Michigan, Ann Arbor, Professor Mazrui expressed an intriguing scenario concerning what might have been the fates of Burundi's **Hutu** and **Tutsi**. He suggested that had Burundi been handed over to the British to be administered with **Tanzania** (then Tanganyika) after World War I, relations between the two groups would not have led to the level of violence that they have known for the last 30 years or more because they would have been part of a larger country. He hypothesized that, because of the shared language and many cultural attributes, they might even have become allies against other groups in Tanzania. Of one thing Professor Mazrui was certain: neither of the groups would have achieved sole control of the armed forces.

Mbanzabugabo. After the death of his father (**Kanugunu**), this chief held his ground against **Gisabo** during the latter's continuing campaign to control all parts of the country (the policy that was supported by the **German** Residents). Mbanzabugabo's role in Burundi politics continued for a very long time; he was the father of André **Muhirwa**, who was to become Burundi's first prime minister in October 1961.

Mbwire gito canje. Entitled "Listen my son . . . " this pamphlet was the 1961 product of Paul **Mirerekano**. The title of the booklet comes from the proverb (found in Rodegem), *Mbwire gito canje gito c'uwundi yumvireho*, which has been more narrowly translated as "I am addressing my good-for-nothing son, but let others also learn a lesson." It was written in the form of a political manifesto and became an important document to **UPRONA** supporters. It gives an indication of what the monarchy meant to the Barundi at the time just before independence, and it also shows that Mirerekano's views on political issues were closely connected with his conception of the role of the *mwami*. He begins with, "Let the Owner of the Drum, the Mwami of Burundi, reign. Let *mwami*-ship be strong. Let it strengthen public order and the union of all Barundi in peace and justice!" The pamphlet went on to discuss such things as avoiding the example of neighboring countries and remembering the importance of devoting one's energies "around the drum." Other points of the pamphlet include: "Remember the beautiful customs of the realm. . . . Too many people have forgotten the customs and traditions of the past, and therefore no longer know the proper behaviour to adopt towards others. . . . The Barundi who are mindful of the established order know that to solicit each other's assistance is the basis of love and unity among men."

Mirerekano seeks, according to Lemarchand, to justify tradition on the basis of its longevity, "arguing that men must, on principle, obey their habitual social and political impulses." However, Lemarchand also charitably points out that Mirerekano's ideas are not purely reactionary, but, rather, a sign of his own personal commitment to the monarchy in times when the monarchy was not being directly challenged, but when so many changes were occurring.

Meeussen, A. See **Kirundi**.

Melady, Thomas. The **U.S.** ambassador to Burundi and Uganda from November 1969 to June 1972 publicly criticized the lack of **UN** action over massacres in the two African countries. In a letter published in the *New York Times* in early 1975, Ambassador Melady wrote: "I now know the clear moral injustices of South African apartheid from personal experience and have condemned it in two books. But what about other similar evils? I was present in Burundi in 1972 when most of the at least 90,000 **Hutu** were killed in what was a selective genocide. Why did the UN General Assembly not speak about this horror?" Melady is the author of *Burundi: The Tragic Years*, which describes the 1972 massacre. In it, he expresses surprise, indicating that there had been no signs of impending violence prior to 1970.

Micombero, Michel. Micombero was recalled from the Military Academy in Brussels where he had been training from 1960 to 1962 when Burundi attained independence. He was appointed captain and head of the police from 1962 to 1965. From 1965 to 1966, he was chief of the secretaries of state, appointed by Mwami **Mwambutsa**. Mwambutsa fled the country following the attempted coup in 1965 and left Micombero in control while Prime Minister **Biha** was recovering from the wounds he received during the coup. In July of the following year, Mwambutsa was ousted as king (in his absence) by his son Charles **Ndizeye**, who claimed that he was forced to assume power to prevent further deterioration of the situation in the country following his unsuccessful attempts to persuade his father to return.

Micombero denied the allegations that the ousting of Mwambutsa was the first step toward turning Burundi into a republic. He said that the Mwami's allegations that the crown prince was a puppet in the hands of extremists were groundless. Micombero further said that his intention was to redefine the role of the crown, returning to the principles in the 1962 constitution, which meant that the Mwami would still reign but would not have as much power to actually rule. On July 11, 1966, the new Mwami, **Ntate V**, asked Micombero to form a new government. One day after accepting the task, Prime Minister Micombero presented a 14-member cabinet with five posts held by **army** personnel, while he retained the posts of the ministers of defense and civil administration. In short, the country had undergone a peaceful military coup.

In November 1966, Micombero and other military leaders deposed the monarch and proclaimed Burundi a republic, naming himself the first president and continuing to hold the posts of prime minister and minister of defense. He replaced the eight provincial governors with army officers and established a **National Revolutionary Council** of 12 military officers, which he said would rule until a new government could be formed and would also draft a new constitution, the old one having been suspended by the last Mwami when he assumed power and dismissed Prime Minister **Biha**. This, of course, was a major turning point in the history of Burundi in ways that were both obvious and more subtle. Although conflicting factions continued to be central to Burundi politics, their dynamics shifted because Micombero represented a new generation. He was from the Bururi region, but was of mixed **Tutsi-Hima** origins and from a family that did not rank high in traditional prestige; he was far removed from the **Bezi-Batare** conflicts that were so prominent before and around the time of independence. Regional affiliations, however, became increasingly important. Micombero also stated that Burundi's international obligations would be honored and expressed hope for improved relations with **Rwanda**, **Tanzania**, and

Zaire.

The National Revolutionary Council first announced in December 1966 that Micombero's term as president would be seven years, at the same time promoting him to colonel. Shortly after this announcement, Micombero announced thatall governmental directives would be issued as presidential decrees after consultation with the attorney general.

During the following two years, Micombero continued to make many changes in his cabinet, constantly reshuffling, sometimes removing ministers without replacing them, and seldom explaining any of these actions. He did, however, give a reason for dismissing the commander of the army, Albert Shibura, and replacing him with Thomas Ndabemeye; he said there was reason to believe that "a small group of irresponsible men" had tried to "take advantage of the Republic." He also decreed during 1967 that the police should be integrated into the national army.

In November 1970, Micombero delivered a state of the nation address in which he spoke of the need to improve the lot of the Burundi peasant. This was thought to be a bid for **Hutu** support, although he did not directly refer to ethnic tensions. Indeed, around that time, he did free many Hutu political prisoners in an attempt to reconcile the rift between the ethnic groups. In his address, he also promised that there would be a national referendum and a new constitution the following year. Also during 1970 and into 1971, tensions between the **Bururi Tutsi** and other Tutsi came to the fore again when rumors spread of a coup attempt by a group of nonsouthern Tutsi. In 1971, the chief politicians of this group were arrested, brought to trial for treason, and many sentenced to death. However, in early 1972, the Tutsi were so strongly divided that Micombero feared an intra-Tutsi civil war and commuted the death sentences.

Micombero dismissed his entire government as well as the executive secretary of the ruling **UPRONA** party in April of 1972. This corresponded to the return of Mwami **Ntare** (Charles) to Burundi, and within hours the government radio station announced that "imperialist stooges and traitors who support the monarchy tried to overthrow the Republican rule and its constitution." The radio reported riots in Bujumbura, which included deaths and fighting in Gitega, where Ntare was under house arrest. During the riots, an attempt was made to rescue him, and he was killed. Further fighting in the southern regions was reported. This was the beginning of the largest bloodbath in Burundi's history, ending with anywhere from 100,000 to 200,000 dead, most of them Hutu. Western diplomats and government officials called it genocide. The degree to which Micombero was personally responsible for the killings remains unclear.

Micombero had promised a new order when he took power, but under his government, Burundi slipped even further into economic and political stagnation. The tensions among Tutsi from different regions continued, and the massacres of 1972 confirmed that discrimination against the Hutu had become endemic, in spite of the initial attempts by Micombero to resolve the ethnic tensions. In November 1976, two years after Micombero had himself elected to a second seven-year term as president, he was deposed in another bloodless military coup led by Colonel Jean-Baptiste **Bagaza**, a member of Micombero's so-called "**Family Corporation**." Micombero was placed under house arrest, and Burundi's only political party, UPRONA, was dissolved. The armed forces' broadcast announced that no one had been hurt and the country was calm. Micombero sought asylum in Somalia, where he died of a heart attack in 1983. President Mohammed Siad Barre of Somalia declared a three-day period of mourning for him.

Milner-Orts Agreement. This agreement of May 30, 1919 partitioned East Africa; it constituted the official proposal of the British and **Belgian** governments that part of German East Africa be administered by Britain and part—Ruanda-Urundi—by Belgium.

Minani, Jean. Shortly after the 1993 coup attempt, Health Minister Minani proclaimed a government in exile and accused the **Tutsi**-dominated Burundi **army** of committing genocide against the **Hutu** group since the coup. He also claimed that the military was rounding up villagers, protecting the Tutsi and killing the Hutu. Understandably, the November 1994 election of Minani, a Hutu, to the National Assembly created a great deal of controversy. Members of **UPRONA** accused him of inciting Hutu against Tutsi after the coup attempt and President **Ndadaye**'s murder. UPRONA also claimed that, while on a visit to **Rwanda** earlier in 1994, Minani had urged the people of Burundi by broadcast to oppose the coup plotters. He became the president of the **Frodebu** party.

Mirerekano, Paul and Muhirwa, André. The histories of these two men are so closely intertwined that a fuller picture can be given if they are described together. Upon the death of **Rwagasore**, much of the racial harmony and cohesion that he had engineered was lost. **UPRONA** divided into factions competing for control of the party. Two of the most powerful factions were led by Mirerekano and Muhirwa. Muhirwa was a **Tutsi ganwa** of the **Batare** clan and Rwagasore's successor as prime minister; Mirerekano was a **Hutu**. Each had supported Rwagasore, but each also claimed to be his rightful successor, and the political conflict expanded into a racial one.

In addition to their ethnic backgrounds, the two men differed in other respects. For example, Mirerekano was said to possess a simplicity of manners and to have retained a sturdy and simple outlook of a Hutu peasant his entire life. He was described as a merchant and a mystic with a sense of moral rectitude. He was a strong supporter of the crown. Muhirwa, politically shrewd as well as aristocratic, treated Mirerekano with contempt; his views were described as tinged with Tutsi chauvinism. Muhirwa was a Murare and the son of Mbanzabugabo, an enemy of Mwami **Mwezi IV**. After the death of his father in 1930, he and his brothers were exiled by the **Belgian** Residency; they returned to Burundi in 1931 after spending a year and a half in **Tanzania**. Muhirwa attended the Groupe Scolaire at Astrida and graduated in 1942; in 1944, he received a small chiefdom (Buhumuza) many miles from his original home. In 1953, he married the Mwami's daughter and was reinstated to the chiefdom of his ancestors.

Even before independence, the trust authorities tried to prevent the two men, as well as Rwagasore, from engaging in political activities. Mirerekano, once the national treasurer of UPRONA, was exiled in 1960 and not permitted back into the country until 1961. What they had in common, therefore, was their conviction; each considered himself the rightful heir to Rwagasore, and neither was willing to concede the UPRONA presidency. Mirerekano pointed out that he had been appointed interim president by Rwagasore upon his return; Muhirwa responded that, since he had taken Rwagasore's place as prime minister, he was also entitled to Rwagasore's seat in the party. Their two factions became known as **Casablanca** (led by Muhirwa) and **Monrovia** (led by Mirerekano), the former having an anti-Western orientation, the latter a more neutral one. Less than a month after independence, Mirerekano called a mass meeting of the rank and file of UPRONA at Rwagasore stadium in Bujumbura to renew his bid for the chairmanship of the party. He denounced the attitude of the Muhirwa government during the **Kamenge** incidents, implying that they had been planned by people high in the government. He also reminded the people how Rwagasore's view of the meaning of independence had been betrayed by his successor (Muhirwa's government). As the story is told, the audience seemed to be showing signs of restiveness, and authorities summoned a unit of gendarmerie (mostly Hutu) to the stadium to arrest Mirerekano and disperse the crowd. Instead, however, many of the gendarmes rallied around Mirerekano and acted as his personal bodyguard, while others did nothing but watch.

After the stadium incident, the Mwami announced that a new executive committee of UPRONA would be elected by the rank and file of the party. The elections, however, were held in **Muramvya** and were mostly attended by Muhirwa's supporters; this was because only a small minority of Hutu were given the official passes necessary to travel in order to vote. The resulting executive committee consisted of Joseph **Bamina** (a Hutu) as president and Mirerekano and Muhirwa as two out of three vice presidents. Mirerekano refused to attend any meetings of the new committee and organized a separate UPRONA wing.

Muhirwa resigned as prime minister in June 1963. This began a new phase of Burundi politics marked by a stronger participation of the court in government affairs. He was a suspect in the assassination of Prime Minister **Ngendendumwe**. In September 1966, a tract circulated in Bujumbura that demanded the execution of Muhirwa and other antiroyalty proponents. The execution did not occur, but he was imprisoned after **Micombero** overthrew the monarchy, then released in November 1967. He then received a position with the port authority of Bujumbura, but, even in this seemingly innocuous post, remained feared and hated by Hutu leaders.

In May 1964, Mirerekano was implicated in a plot against the **Nyamoya** government and fled to **Rwanda**. He returned to Burundi in early 1965. During his exile, however, he continued to write to the Mwami about the dismissal of the Nyamoya government and the expulsion of the Chinese from Burundi. There is evidence that he was also in contact with the U.S. Central Intelligence Agency during this time. Other evidence suggests that Mirerekano did not actually write all of the letters attributed to him, particularly letters conveyed through the Catholic Church, because Mirerekano did not write well in languages other than **Kirundi,** and the letters were written mostly in French. After his exile, still very popular with the Hutu, Mirerekano was elected vice-president of the National Assembly. His popularity and his ability to raise the ethnic consciousness of the Hutu had been a concern of Tutsi **army** officers and government officials; they had agreed to sentence him in absentia to 20 years in prison, but had changed their minds when he won the majority of the votes in Bujumbura. In October 1965 a group of Hutu army and gendarmerie officers tried to take over the royal palace while another group wounded Prime Minister **Biha**. After this incident, almost every Hutu leader was arrested. Mirerekano was among those sentenced to death. The sentence was not carried out.

Mission for Protection of Democratic Institutions in Burundi (MIPROBU). In early 1994, MIPROBU, which consisted of 47 officers from the Organization of African Unity (OAU), were sent to Burundi to discuss with the Burundian military how to protect existing democratic institutions. Both the military and the opposition parties agreed to convene.

Monrovia. See **Casablanca and Monrovia**.

Mpotsa. Located in the center of Burundi, south of the province of Muramvya, the hills of Mpotsa were the ancient home of both the queen-mother and the sacred royal drums.

Muhirwa, André. See **Mirerekano, Paul**.

Mukakaryenda. Sometimes referred to as Madame Tambour in writings about Burundi, she was the symbolic wife of **Karyenda**, the sacred dynastic drum. The role was occupied by a young girl charged with maintaining the drum; her sacred role required her to be a virgin.

Mukakiranga. Frequently, throughout the central African area, main divinities had human wives who were dedicated solely to them and not allowed to marry mortal men while they were in the spirit's service. The most important of these women was known as Mukakiranga, the official wife of **Kiranga**. According to Van Der Burgt, the master, Kiranga, owned two herds of cattle, each guarded by an *ngabe*, or sacred bull. Kiranga also had a sacred mountain administered by a virgin who was designated as his wife. This priestess came from the **Abajiji** clan, had great authority, and was exempt from paying any dues to the *mwami*, but she was condemned to permanent virginity and was watched constantly to prevent her from straying. If she did, she was put to death along with all members of her family. She assumed her position at the same time that the *mwami* did; if he died, she was forced to poison herself; if she died before the *mwami*, she was replaced by another young girl. Gorju said that Mukakiranga and the *mwami* were equals holding Burundi in common. The *mwami* was the visible chief, and Kiranga incarnated himself in his wife. Through kubandwa (see **bandwa**), she became Kiranga in person.

Mukasi, Charles. In 1993, just after **Ndadaye**'s assassination, Mukasi allegedly broadcast messages from **Rwanda** telling **Hutu** to kill **Tutsi**. After the appointment of Jean **Minani** (as Speaker of the National Assembly in November 1994), **UPRONA** strongly protested. Mukasi, head of UPRONA, was quoted as saying: "We cannot have a person with such a background as a Speaker. Following this appointment and a three-week standoff that virtually shut down the capital, UPRONA withdrew from the assembly. Minani eventually stepped down. In early 1995, when the president dismissed two UPRONA ministers who had skipped a cabinet meeting, Mukasi said in a news conference that the government "should be overthrown at all costs." A two-day strike at this time also shut Bujumbura down.

Mulele, Pierre. See **Mulelists**.

Mulelists. This group was named for Pierre **Mulele**, the main organizer of the Kwilu rebellion in **Zaire** (1964-1965), but the Mulelists were never actively involved in this rebellion in Zaire. Their role in Burundi remains unclear, but they are cited as having recruited **Hutu** and organized the initial stages of the 1972 massacre.

Muramvya. Located in the middle of Burundi, to the west, Muramvya was the home of the most ancient and the most important royal domains. The descendents of these ancient kings carried on the dynasties of Burundi into the modern age.

Musapfu. The Abasapfu clan was an antimonarchical group from **Bururi** that was held responsible for an attempted coup in 1967. The Abasapfu have an interesting origin, related by Lemarchand from Father M. Rodegem. He says that they are **Tutsi** of high-ranking status, originally from a **Hima** clan. For a reason that history has obliterated, one day Mwami **Ntare II** decided that all Abasapfu should be killed. He gave this task to the Abongera clan, who destroyed their cattle and crops and killed everyone they could find. One of the few survivors was a small boy who had remained hidden; he was taken to Mwami Ntare, who kept him at his court under his protection and named him Musapfu to commemorate his adventure.

Mutaga I (Seenyamwiiza). He is documented as the third monarch of Burundi, reigning from about 1735 to 1765

Mutaga II (ca.1893-1915). When **Gisabo** died in 1908, the lack of an adequate replacement for him created what the **Germans** considered a period of ongoing chaos in Burundi. His successor was his 15-year old son, Mutaga. Mutaga was a weak leader, certainly in part because of his extreme youth. The German Resident in Urundi wrote in 1911, "the Mwami himself has nothing to say except in his own village . . . in short, his political influence is non-existent; he exists because tradition says he must, but he is not the ruler of the country." Supposedly, the dominant influence on Mutaga was his mother, **Ndirikumutima**, but his mother's strongest rival, **Ntarrugera**, another prince of the royal blood, also influenced him considerably. The struggle between these two was probably the chaos described by the Germans, as Mutaga took on more of a leadership role as he matured. The Germans supported his authority, assuming that the situation would improve over time. It did not immediately improve, however, because the young Mwami died at the end of 1915. The circumstances surrounding his death are somewhat mysterious. According to Pierre Ryckmans, considered a reliable source by many historians, Mutaga died because of a love affair. As Ryckmans told the story, one of Mutaga's wives was having an affair with his brother, Prince Bangura. Mutaga eventually became suspicious and kept a close watch over the two alleged lovers. One day, finding them together, Mutaga stabbed Bangura in the chest with his spear. Bangura, in trying to defend himself, stabbed Mutaga in the abdomen. Both died, Mutaga only a few days after Bangura. According to official German documents, Mutaga and his brother were victims of malaria.

Mutwenzi. This name means "the dawn." In the traditional royal court, she was a sister of the *mwami*, who participated in the *umuganuro* ceremony. She also participated in a ritual sexual union with the *mwami* at dawn on the day of his enthronement.

Muyenzi, Gonzalve. A **Tutsi** born in **Rwanda** and employed by the **U.S.** embassy from 1962 to 1965, he was the confessed killer of Prime Minister **Ngendandumwe**. The new prime minister quickly reported that there was no evidence that the United States had been involved, but that "Tutsi extremists" were responsible.

Mwambutsa I. He is documented as the fourth monarch of Burundi, reigning from about 1765 to 1795.

Mwambutsa IV (Bangiricenge) (1913-1977). That he ascended to the throne at the age of two explains the extremely long reign of Mwami Mwambutsa (1915-1966). One of the last acts of the **German** government was Mwambutsa's installation upon the death of his father, **Mutaga IV**; because of the new Mwami's age, a regency was established to rule on his behalf until he reached the age of majority. The years of his reign spanned and exceeded the **Belgian** occupation of Burundi.

Following independence, the importance of the role of the Mwami fluctuated, but the court remained generally strong via the support of **UPRONA** and its nationalist underpinnings. In fact, much of the nationalistic popularity of Louis **Rwagasore**, both as the de facto head of UPRONA in its early days and the first prime minister-designate, was probably because he was Mwambutsa's son. The crown was never identified with either of the main ethnic groups, although many of its ritualistic aspects seem to be more closely traced to the **Hutu** than the **Tutsi**.

During the Belgian occupation, Mwambutsa was often criticized by his own people as being too attracted to the European people and culture. He was often portrayed as a hard-drinking womanizer who was often in serious debt. The Europeans criticized him for being unqualified for his job. Each side, of course, had motives for their criticism other than the behavior and leadership of the Mwami. Many Barundi were hoping for more backing of the pro-**Batare** factions from the Belgian Resident.

Mwambutsa, himself, was not consistent in his royal leadership, but from 1962 to 1965, the crown acted as the main stabilizing force in the country against rising criticism from both ethnic groups. The Mwami was himself often a symbol of national unity. At times, he maintained supreme authority over the constitution, often overruling decisions of the elected government. However, he spent part of the post-independence years in Europe, often claiming poor health; history sometimes portrays him as having been uncomfortable with his power and frightened of what he saw happening in Burundi, causing these many trips out of the country. An abortive coup in 1965 caused the near collapse of the entire governmental system that was built around the crown, as well as the liquidation of most of the Hutu leadership. Following this attempted coup, he again left the country, and for the last time, as it happened, conferring substantial powers on his son, Charles **Ndizeye**. It was unclear at the time whether this was a form of abdication, but he was, in fact, deposed in exile by Ndizeye, who was to rule under the dynastic name of **Ntare V**. Mwambutsa voiced sharp disapproval of the move, but remained where he was. After the ethnic massacres of 1972, during which Ntare V was killed, Mwambutsa offered to return to Burundi as Mwami; his offer was not accepted.

Mwami **(Plural,** *bami)* This is the **Kirundi** word for king. Much of the power of the *bami* and the other native authorities was abolished beginning in 1917. For example, domestic slavery was eliminated in 1923, and the triple hierarchy of the chief of crops, the chief of pastures, and the chief of armed units was replaced by a single authority. The *bami* are intriguing in the cultural context as they are closely associated with both a political and religious function. Each *mwami* was the medium between the people and supernatural forces. The word (actually, *mu/ba-aami*) is related to the verb, *ku-aama*, "to be fertile." They are also intriguing because they point out the cyclical nature of Burundi history. There are four dynastic names of *bami*, and the names themselves form a cycle: Mwambutsa, Ntare, Mwezi, and Mutaga. Traditionally, each king in the cycle has an ideal character, and every fourth generation each ideal type reappears. Ntare is the conqueror who founded the dynasty and is expected to continue to found dynasties; Mwezi is the ruler who must maintain his power in the face of rebels and who lives a long life; Mutaga is traditionally a good king but very unlucky; Mwambutsa's purpose is to prepare the way for a new Ntare. The Burundi history is static on these points concerning the *bami*, and the traditional tales reveal some of the historical background of many modern-day conflicts. For example, under the reign of Mwezi II, a series of uprisings occurred from members the family of *abatare*, the collective noun meaning those who could become Ntare. Traditionally, each uprising is described as a separate incident with no mention of any interconnections. The **Bezi-Batare** conflict was to live on for many generations.

Mwezi I. He is documented as the second monarch of Burundi, reigning from about 1705 to 1735.

Mwezi II. See **Mwezi IV**.

Mwezi IV (1845-1908). Born **Gisabo** (sometimes documented as Kisabo or Kissabo), he was Mwami of Burundi from 1860 until his death. He is sometimes documented as Mwezi II, and that he was indeed the second Mwezi in the cycle of the monarchy is just as possible. At that time, Urundi was not a centralized state, and Mwezi's reign was a constant struggle against district chiefs. Although Gisabo tried to wield absolute power according to the traditions of the Barundi, he was, in fact, quite limited in his power and regarded the **German** intrusion as a threat to his already precarious position. Captain von Bethe's (the head of the German military station in Usumbura) initial contacts with Gisabo in 1899 were friendly; Gisabo eagerly assured von Bethe that he and his people would cooperate and submit to German authority. What Gisabo actually hoped, however, was to defeat his enemies and establish his own absolute sovereignty with no German interference. Unfortunately, Gisabo was defeated more often than he was victorious, and his authority diminished rather than increased.

Another German captain (von Beringe) described events in Urundi in a long political report in July 1902. He was convinced that Gisabo was an enemy of Europeans and that most of the chiefs in Urundi were enemies of Gisabo. Beringe requested permission for an "Urundi expedition" of three months, during which time he wanted to gain Gisabo's submission to German rule once and for all. He recommended war against Gisabo. G. A. Götzen, the governor of German East Africa, believed in peaceful rather than punitive actions in Urundi, but was, at first, unable to stop Beringe, who executed his campaign against Gisabo. In June 1903, Beringe notified his government that the expedition had been a success and that Gisabo had submitted to German rule after losing 200 men in the fighting. Götzen was furious, believing that the military station had never been seriously threatened by Gisabo, and set out to try and repair the damage.

In April 1904, Götzen ordered Usumbura to regard all chiefs as subordinate to Gisabo, on the condition that Gisabo would continue to recognize German sovereignty. The chiefs to whom Beringe had granted independence consequently renewed their hostilities against both Gisabo and the Germans. One of the chiefs, Machoncho, to whom Beringe had granted independence, attempted to kill Beringe's replacement, Grawert, who shot the chief in self-defense.

By 1906, the German military had achieved a great deal in Ruanda-Urundi. The sovereignty of Gisabo over Urundi had been restored; Bering's "divide-and-rule" policy had been corrected to Götzen's original policy of "indirect rule." By

1908, Gisabo, with Grawert's help, had brought the remaining district chiefs under his control, thus stabilizing the central government of Urundi more than ever before. This German control over Urundi that had taken so many years to achieve was destroyed by the 1908 death of Gisabo at the age of 63. His death was followed not by revolution, as the Germans feared, but by what the Germans regarded as chaos. The new king (**Mutaga II**) was quite young and had no influence at all, the Rundi government being dominated by the king's numerous older relatives.

After his explorations in Africa, Sir Richard Burton said that Gisabo was able to assemble a considerable number of warriors who could strike fear in the hearts of his neighbors. Years later, after Gisabo's death, Hans Meyer said that he had been without doubt the most important sovereign in all of East and Central Africa.

Mwungere. Various functions of the traditional court were constant, and those who were in the position took on a new name. The guardian of the royal cattle (*umwungere*) took on Mwungere as his given name.

-N-

Nahimana, Antoine. A member of the conspiracy to kill **Rwagasore**, Nahimana was sentenced to death by the Court of First Instance. That sentence was commuted to 20 years of penal servitude by the Court of Appeal of Bujumbura. However, a law enacted in September 1962 established a Supreme Court with retroactive competence, which changed the decision of the court of appeal and court of first instance on the grounds that there had been no jury. At this time, the case was reheard by the court of first instance, which sentenced Nahimana, along with four co-conspirators, to death. In early 1963, the court of appeal confirmed the judgment; on January 14, all five were publicly hanged in Kitega. A British representative of Amnesty International said the three judges at the retrial did not understand the complex legal system inherited from the

Belgians and that the jurors were "completely in the dark about the whole proceedings."

Nandabunga. Mwezi **Gisabo**'s daughter was an unusually famous person in Burundi because she accomplished what few if any other women did. She received the chiefdom of Buyenzi-Bweru (in Ngozi), which she commanded by herself under the rightful title of **Muganwa**. She was married twice; little is known of her first husband, but her second husband was a non-ganwa **Tutsi** named Munyakarama and did not share in the administration of the chiefdom.

National Council for the Defense of Democracy. A former minister of the interior, Leonard **Nyangoma**, has led this group, which is known to be one of the extremist groups involved in the ethnic killings following President Ndadaye's assassination. Nyangoma claims responsibility for attacks on military and police posts.

National Revolutionary Council of Military Personnel. See **Conseil National de la Révolution**.

Ndadaye, Melchior. After the 1972 massacres, Ndadaye spent 11 years in exile in **Rwanda**. Upon his return to Burundi in 1983, he worked for nine years on underground political activities and spent two months in prison in 1988 after calling for greater democracy at a meeting following the Ntega and Maragara massacres. A new constitution, paving the way for multiparty government, was approved by over 90 percent of the electorate in March 1993. That constitution disallowed political organizations that advocated "tribalism, divisionalism, or violence," and stipulated that parties must represent both the **Hutu** and **Tutsi** ethnic groups. In Burundi's first democratic, multi-party election in June 1993, Ndadaye was the clear winner for his **Frodebu** party, surpassing the incumbent **Buyoya** by a two-to-one margin. At the time of election, Ndadaye, a 40-year-old banker, was the first Murundi president to be elected who was a civilian and a Hutu. His opponents tried to portray him as inexperienced with no political ideas except ethnic retribution, but, in fact, he was an intellectual who had previously formed two political parties: a workers' party in Rwanda (UBU) in 1975 and Frodebu in 1986. Some members of his Frodebu party compared him to Martin Luther King; he taught that justice would not occur unless members of his party showed respect for others as well; he was said to have preached nonviolence and nonsectarianism. In the week following his election victory, Ndadaye announced an amnesty for about 500 political prisoners that was seen as a conciliatory gesture to both Tutsi and militant Hutu. Under this amnesty, hundreds of Hutu prisoners accused of taking part in ethnic clashes of November 1991 were to be released, as was a group of Tutsi soldiers who took part in a March 1992 coup attempt intended to counter Buyoya's attempts at reforms.

Ndadaye also tried to create a broad-based government, naming nine Tutsi among his twenty-three ministers, including Silvie **Kinigi**, the first woman prime minister. Additionally, he tried to integrate the Tutsi control in the security forces and find ways to repatriate hundreds of thousands of mostly Hutu refugees living in other countries. In the September-October 1993 issue of *Africa Report*, Catharine Watson wrote that an **army** coup against the new administration was highly unlikely: "An army coup would set the country on fire. Frodebu enjoys rapturous support. If Ndadaye or his term were harmed, every Tutsi family in Burundi would be in danger." In spite of this prediction, however, on October 21, 1993, one hundred days after the election, Ndadaye was killed in a coup attempt. His last words are reported to have been, "Be careful of what you are about to do; it is very, very dangerous." Four days later, the coup leaders were calling for negotiations to return power to civilians, but, once again in the history of independent Burundi, the coup and assassination led to months of further ethnic bloodshed. This part of Watson's prediction proved true.

Relief agencies reported that the fighting begun during the coup attempt may have forced as many as one million people to flee to neighboring countries. The **United States** suspended its $16-million aid program to Burundi after the coup and later rejected an appeal to send troops there as part of a **UN** peacekeeping mission. Instead, the United States joined other members of the Security Council in asking UN Secretary General Boutros Boutros-Ghali to send a fact-finding team, which did arrive in Burundi in March 1994.

Ndabemeye, Charles. He was chief of staff under President **Micombero** and present at a meeting with members of the government when Rumonge was attacked in the early stages of the massacre of 1972.

Ndenzako, Leon. When **U.S.** ambassador to Burundi, Donald **Dumont**, and two other embassy officials were ordered to leave Burundi under accusations of conspiracy against the government, the United States retaliated and expelled the Burundian ambassador, Leon Ndenzako, from Washington the next day. The ambassador was summoned to the State Department and was handed a note containing a strong protest about the expulsions in Bujumbura.

Ndikumwami, Richard. Head of intelligence under President **Ndadaye**, he had, like the president, been a refugee following the 1972 massacres.

Ndimanya, Ignace. When three prominent citizens were accused of participating in a conspiracy to undermine the security of the state in 1963, Ndimanya, the former minister of public works, was among them. The two others were Thaddée **Siryuyumunsi** and Pie **Masumbuko**.

Ndinzurwaha, Severin. During the initial **Kamenge** incidents of 1962, four prominent **Hutu** lost their lives in the violence. Ndinzurwaha, who was then permanent secretary of the Syndicats Chrétiens and national secretary of the teachers' association, was among them.

Ndirikumutima. When **Mwezi Gisabo** died in 1908, Burundi politics was in confusion and turmoil. His 15-year-old son succeeded him as **Mutaga II**, but the new Mwami's youth prevented him from exercising the power necessary to stop some of his father's rivals from reclaiming parts of the territory as their own. Ndirikumutima was the queen mother and fought hard for her son. When Mutaga died very young and was succeeded by his infant son, who ruled as **Mwambutsa IV**, Ndirikumutima remained in charge of his regency. One of the **Belgian** governors said of her that she was:

> an old woman, with all the vices typical of her age, and endowed with a keen intelligence, she also displays a stubborn obstinacy. Nothing can possibly pry her loose from her blissful inertia. Once the wife of King Mwezi, who never cared much for contacts with the whites, she represents with indomitable tenacity the spirit of the old autocracy. She feels that the established order is the ideal and that everything we do can only upset this order. Her life's sole and constant preoccupation is to plunder other people's patrimony for the benefit of her sons. . . .

Ndizeye, Charles. See **Ntare V.**

Nduwabike, Jean. In 1962 when young **Tutsi** militants affiliated with the **JNR** made threats against **Hutu** trade unionists and politicians, Nduhabike was among them. At the time, he was the president of the Syndicats Chrétiens. Later that year, when he was also national secretary of the **Parti du Peuple** (PP), he was killed in one of the Kamenge incidents.

Nduwayo, Antoine. He became the prime minister under the coalition government of President **Ntibantunganya** in February 1995. This appointment followed the resignation (caused by a general strike called for by **UPRONA**) of Prime Minister Anatole Kanyenkiko. Ntibantunganya is Hutu, and Nduwayo is Tutsi; this ethnic mix, while theoretically necessary in the volatile atmosphere following the 1993 assassination of President **Ndadaye**, is potentially explosive in its own right. The president and prime minister do not agree on many governmental policies, but represent the interests of their separate parties.

Upon his appointment, Nduwayo called for the restoration of peace, cautioning that nothing could be achieved before that goal was attained. In March 1995, Nduwayo appointed seven new government ministers. During that same month, Nduwayo and Ntibantunganya worked together to sign an agreement brokered by the French mission to pursue stability, protect lives, and encourage the return of about two million refugees living in camps.

However, in June, Nduwayo was a central figure in orchestrating an **army** operation in the Bujumbura suburb of **Kamenge** against members of the Hutu militia. He urged civilians to evacuate, but many were killed in this and other violent operations; he reported that these deaths were inevitable, because the Hutu guerrillas had been shielding themselves with civilians. At the first Independence Day celebration that occurred during his term of office (July 1, 1995), the prime minister and the president celebrated separately—the president in Gitega, which has a majority Hutu population, and the prime minister in Bujumbura, which has become almost completely Tutsi. This was seen to emphasize the separation of the two ethnic groups.

Nduwumwe. He was the son of Mwami **Mwezi Gisabo** and one of the principle chiefs of Burundi during his father's reign. It was he who gave assurance to the regency of the country during the early part of Mwami **Mwambutsa**'s reign, when the Mwami was still a child. Nduwumwe was also among the leading experts concerning the secrecies of the royalty.

Nettoyage. Literally translated as "cleaning or mopping up," this French term has been used to describe the actions of the Burundi **army** during Hutu uprisings throughout the history of the country. It has come to mean "ethnic cleansing" in Burundi.

Ngendandumwe, Pierre. In March 1963, as tensions between the **Monrovia** and **Casablanca** groups were increasing, Prime Minister **Muhirwa** ordered the arrest of three Monrovia leaders, alleging conspiracy against the state. Mwami **Mwambutsa IV** intervened, releasing the three men, and the Muhirwa government was dissolved three months later. Ngendandumwe, a 31-year-old **Hutu** loyal to the Monrovia group, was named new prime minister. The change in government marked a change in the general political workings of Burundi; from this time until the abolition of the monarchy and the forming of a republic, the prime minister and his cabinet were answerable only to the Mwami, who became the chief initiator as well as the executor of all legislation in the parliament.

It was somewhat ironic that Ngendandumwe led the government during this time of strong intervention by the court. In 1959, he had written in a report that the "*bami* and the chiefs" were the ones to emerge as "the great beneficiaries of the decree of July 1952 [establishing the hierarchy of subchieftaincy, chieftaincy, territorial, and country councils]." He went on to say that "the present tragedy in Ruanda-Urundi does not consist only in the fact of white colonisation but also in the paradox that in spite of representing a minority, the near totality of chief, subchief and judge are in the hands of the **Tutsi**."

Having a Hutu prime minister and the strong intervention of the court did little to calm the tensions between the two tribal groups or the factions of **UPRONA**. In what have been described as "Byzantine practices," Tutsi extremists brought about the downfall of the Ngendandumwe government by maneuvering the Monrovia regime into recognizing the People's Republic of **China**; this was contrary to the preferences of the **Belgian** and **U.S.** embassies, of course, but it was also contrary to those of the Mwami. In March 1964, the Mwami dismissed four Hutu ministers who court officials said held views "which did not fit in with the peaceful coexistence of the country's two tribal groups." At this point Ngendandumwe resigned as prime minister, and **Nyamoya** took over.

In January of the following year, 1964, the Mwami withdrew support from Nyamoya and, once again, asked Ngendandumwe to form a new government. Just three days after doing so, as he was leaving from a hospital visit to his wife, who had just given birth, Ngendandumwe was shot and killed. Tensions between the two groups grew even stronger following this act of violence, and relations became so bad that accommodation was not considered possible. Although China was not implicated in the assassination, diplomatic relations between Burundi and China were suspended.

In fact, the killers were a group of **Rwandan** Tutsi refugees. A week after the assassination, Burundi police announced that a Rwandan employed as an accounting clerk in the U.S. embassy had confessed to the murder. Acting Prime Minister Pie **Masumbuko** stressed that the United States was not involved. In February, another Rwandan named Butera (who also worked for the U.S. embassy) was arrested, and a ballistics expert reported that the bullet that had killed the prime minister came from a revolver found in his possession. Butera was the son of Rukeba, a well-known Rwandan guerrilla. Finally, in December 1967, Burundi's supreme court acquitted, for lack of evidence, all of the others who had been accused of being involved in the assassination. Among those acquitted were the accounting clerk, Gonzalve Muyenzi, and the former president of the **JNR**, Prime **Nyonabo**. The death of Ngendandumwe, a moderate Hutu, provoked yet another new crisis in Burundi politics. In May 1965, the first parliamentary elections since 1961 were held. UPRONA was challenged by the Hutu-supported **Popular Party**. The result was a parliament in which Hutu held 80 percent of the seats.

Ngeze, François. The minister of interior in **Buyoya**'s government, Ngeze was one of the rare **Hutu** who held any position of power from 1965 to 1993. He is mentioned as a reason to look more deeply into the Burundi situation; the general assumption of disadvantaged Hutu pitted against the majority and ruling **Tutsi** becomes somewhat more nuanced when it is known that such powerful Hutu exist, although rarely. After the coup of 1993, which resulted in the death of President **Ndadaye**, Ngeze was made head of the new ruling **Committee of National Salvation** and claimed that he had been forced to support the coup and assume a leadership role.

Ngunzu, Pierre. From the time of **Ntare**'s 1966 overthrow of **Mwambutsa**'s crown, many people who were prominent under the old monarchy lost their positions, their reputations, and often their lives. Once minister of education in the **Muhirwa** government, Ngunzu was placed under arrest along with other prominent citizens, but was released within 48 hours after the court intervened. This was probably an act intended to remind the government of the court's expected role.

Nicayenzi, Zénon. When the 1962 so-called "stadium incident" involving the surprising support of Paul **Mirerekano** by a group of gendarmes occurred, Nicayenzi, then commissaire in charge of the armed forces, put the **army** in a state of emergency. Only two months before this incident, Nicayenzi had talked about the union of **Hutu** and **Tutsi**, who he said were "intimately linked to each other" and free of the problems that plagued the two groups in **Rwanda**.

Nsanze, Terence. In November 1970, *Africa Report* printed an article titled "Burundi: Political and Ethnic Powderkeg." The article was anonymous, according to the magazines policy if the author so chooses. Nsanze, then the Burundi ambassador to the **UN**, wrote a strong protest based on a supposed lack of impartiality, compounded by the anonymity of the article. He accused the article of lacking "the most elemental academic integrity."

Ntamagara, Augustin. He was the leader of the **Fédération des Travailleurs du Burundi**, a vehemently pro-**Tutsi** and anti-Western group. In September 1966 he organized a meeting at a stadium during which he was reported to have said: "Let the people's enemies—Ndenzako, Nsengyumva and **Muhirwa**—have their heads chopped off, and their bodies thrown to the dogs." In October 1967, Ntamagara was one of many to be demoted to a position of negligible power in the new government.

Ntare I (Rushatsi). When the **Tutsi** first arrived in the area that is now **Rwanda** and Burundi, each individual's control was limited to small areas; a chief ruled only one or two hills. It was Rushatsi, the first Burundi monarch whose dynastic name was Ntare I, who consolidated a number of these smaller realms and established his rule over a larger area centering around what is now **Muramvya**. Oral historians place his reign from about 1675 to 1705. *Intare* is the skin of a lion and was a symbol of royalty; some legends suggest that the monarch's family name or surname before he adopted Ntare was Rufuko, but others tell that this is the name of his father.

Ntare II (Rugaamba). Often considered to be the first monarch of what would become modern Burundi, his reign was approximately from 1795 to 1852. During his rule, he expanded the established boundaries of the kingdom considerably to include areas that are now part of **Rwanda** and **Tanzania**. These territorial conquests added much to his fame and reputation as one of Burundi's most illustrious kings. Rugaamba, in order to consolidate his territory, spread the wealth from his victories to his sons, some of whom began to assert their independence from the reign of their father. This is considered to be the point in Burundi's history when the *ganwa* began playing an important and decisive role in the political system. From then on, the *bami* sought to evict relatives and followers of their predecessors and replace them with their own people. This included, of course, sons evicting their fathers' loyal supporters and was the beginning of the **Batare-Bezi** conflict that affected so much of Burundi's twentieth-century politics.

Ntare V (Charles Ndizeye) (1947-1972). The last king of Burundi, Ntare's dynastic order is sometimes documented as III or IV; III is most likely the correct number, based on the rotation of kings every four generations. Also, nothing of another Ntare III or Ntare IV has been documented.

After an abortive coup in October 1965, Mwami Mwambutsa left Burundi for Europe, passing many of the powers of the crown over to his son. In July 1966, Prince Charles announced over the radio that he was taking over the throne of Burundi from his father. Mwambutsa condemned the rebellion against his authority and accused extremist elements of manipulating his son. The 19-year-old prince said in his address that he wanted to bring an end to "four years of chaos and anarchy, of nepotism and corruption." He also said that he wanted to "bring about a revaluation of the Murundi personality in the context of a continuous and harmonious economic development." He dismissed Prime Minister **Biha**, suspended the constitution, and asked Michel **Micombero** to form a new government. In September, he was formally proclaimed Mwami of Burundi in coronation ceremonies held in the ancient capital of **Muramvya**. In his coronation speech, Ntare called on all Barundi to heal their ethnic divisions: "I shall reign in the name of all of you, and for you. My reign will seek to bring back understanding in all Burundi."

Initially, there was great enthusiasm over the coronation, but it was very short-lived. The new Mwami was too young to have mastered the arts of political intrigue, yet he made an effort to do so. This effort brought him into conflict with **Tutsi** politicians, some of whom abolished the monarchy entirely in November 1966 while Ntare was on a state visit to Kinshasa. This coup that ousted the final king of Burundi and proclaimed Burundi a republic was led by Micombero and two subsequent coup leaders, Jean-Baptiste **Bagaza** and Pierre **Buyoya**.

Charles went first to Europe, settling for a time in **Germany** and, eventually, to Uganda where he convinced President Idi Amin to aid him in his return to Burundi. Amin attempted to do so, extracting in March 1972 a written guarantee of Charles's safety from Micombero. One of Micombero's letters to Amin stated that, "Your Excellency can be assured that as soon as Mr. Charles Ndizeye returns to my country he will be considered as an ordinary citizen and that as such his life and his security will be assured."

Charles decided to take advantage of the promise of amnesty and was taken to Bujumbura on Amin's personal helicopter. When he arrived, he was transferred to a Burundi military helicopter and flown to a destination that was unknown at the time. He had been arrested and accused of plotting (or according to one Burundi radio report the day after his arrival, actually leading) an invasion assisted by West German mercenaries. A radio report the day after his arrival warned the people of Burundi to be on their guard against the threat "to which the republic almost fell victim . . . . Militants, we must not forget that this was not only an attack against our republic, it was Africa and the honor of Africa that was the target of these sworn enemies of the African continent."

The next two months were chaos in Burundi. The arrest of the former Mwami was the first in a chain of events that would become known as the massacre of 1972. The former mwami died about a month after his return to the country; the details of how or by whose hand are unclear although it was not a natural death. Some reports say that an attempt was made to rescue him from house arrest, and he was killed during the ensuing struggle. After a **Hutu** revolt that resulted in the deaths of many thousands of Tutsi, the Tutsi retaliated and slaughtered many tens of thousands of Hutu. Micombero retained power through all of this.

Ntarugera. An elder brother of Mwami **Mutaga**, he was one of the chiefs who took advantage of his position as **Mwezi Gisabo**'s son to acquire as much land as was possible. He eventually became known as one of the greatest and richest men in Burundi, and he was feared in Mutaga's court. Along with his mother, **Ndirikumutima**, he became a regent in the court of his infant nephew, **Mwambutsa**, and was highly thought of by the colonial governor. He died in 1921, but in 1947, Mwami Mwambutsa was quoted as blaming Ntarugera and his other uncles for his own lack of a European education and his resulting desire to send his own son away to school.

Ntaryamira, Cyprien. A founding member of **Frodebu**, he took over as president of Burundi following the assassination of President **Ndadaye** in the attempted coup of October 1993. He was appointed as head of state by the National Assembly, but the appointment was challenged in the Constitutional Court. The National Assembly had, shortly before, amended the constitution, thus allowing the assembly to elect a successor rather than hold general elections. Ntayamira was finally inaugurated in February 1994. His term of office was very short; in April 1994, the plane in which he and **Rwandan** President Habyarimana were travelling crashed near Kigali, the capital of Rwanda. The incident initiated months of civil war in Rwanda, where citizens were convinced that the plane had been shot down. In Burundi, a fragile peace remained; the majority of the citizens chose to consider it, at least publicly, as an unfortunate accident. Both of the presidents were **Hutu**.

Ntawumenyakarizi, Basile. One of the prominent **Hutu** who lost their lives in the earlier of the **Kamenge** incidents, he was a **Party du Peuple** (PP) militant as well as the principal of a secondary school.

Ntibantunganya, Sylvestre. He was appointed the minister of foreign affairs after the democratic presidential election of June 1993. Like President **Ndadaye**, he had been a refugee following the massacres of 1972. In the attempted coup during which Ndadaye was killed, Ntibantunganya's wife was also killed by soldiers sent to look for the foreign affairs minister. Following the death of Ndadaye's successor, Cyprien **Ntayamira**, in April 1994, Ntibantunganya was the popular choice for president, but he did not accept the office until late 1994. He remained the head of a weak and often explosive coalition government until the middle of 1996, and he has little power over the **army**, which is almost completely **Tutsi**; he is **Hutu** and appointed a Tutsi prime minister in an attempt to strike a balance among the various political parties.

Ntiruhama, Jean. The minister of interior in 1962, he was severely criticized by a group of **Hutu** deputies for his alleged collusion with the **JNR** leaders during the **Kamenge** riots. The accusations brought against him were sometimes vague and the evidence often scanty, but the belief that the government may have been at fault served to strengthen racial solidarities, especially among the Hutu parliamentarians. By the end of 1962, the Hutu parliamentary group, which represented about half of the total membership of the National Assembly, became known as the **Monrovia** group.

Ntitendereza, Jean. He was the son of **Baranyanka** and the brother of Joseph **Biroli**; he became one of the founders of the **Parti Démocrate Chrétien** (PDC). He was hanged in Gitega in 1962 for his involvement in the assassination of Prince **Rwagasore**.

Ntu (bu-). The qualities of an ideal male were clearly defined in traditional Burundi society. Above all else, he was *ubuntu*, an example of goodness, polite, refined, and knowledgeable about proper behavior in all circumstances. This root (with other prefixes) is also important: for example, *muntu* (plural: *bantu*) means "being," "an individual," or "to be human"; *ihwanyabantu* means "nationality"; *muryabantu* means "cannibal."

Nyabyuma (mu-, ba-). In the traditional society, these were the guardians of the relics and charms among the royal treasures.

Nyamoya, Albin. A **Tutsi** (but not *ganwa*) loyal to the **Casablanca** faction of **UPRONA** and a relative through marriage of Mwami **Mwambutsa II**, Nyamoya became prime minister upon the resignation of **Ngendandumwe** in April 1964. In his first address to the National Assembly, Nyamoya reaffirmed Burundi's "traditional policy of non-alignment and neutrality" and the government's desire to have friendly relations with all countries. He also assured the assembly that he would make inquiries into charges of corruption among some civil servants. Very quickly he had reason to repeat these promises. His term of office coincided with rebellions in **Zaire**, so the factor of **Chinese** intervention in the area was a major focus at the time. During his short time in office, Nyamoya tried to maintain relations with neighboring countries. For example, he affirmed that Bujumbura University would continue to admit students from Zaire even though Zaire had expelled Barundi students that year.

By June 1964, a great many refugees from Zaire were in Burundi. In fact, the government specified the number at 5,052: 5,000 civilians, 41 soldiers, and 11 politicians. Nyamoya denied accusations that the acceptance of the refugees was motivated by any considerations other than humanitarian ones. The Nyamoya government prohibited public meetings among the refugees as well as the formation of armed groups, the possession of weapons, and the circulation of what it called political propaganda. In spite of these precautions, Nyamoya contacted the chairman of the OAU ad hoc commission on Zaire as well as the secretaries general of the OAU and the UN, charging that Zairian military aircraft had bombed communities in Burundi twice.

In December 1964, a large cache of arms and ammunition was discovered near Kitega, and rumors of an impending coup sponsored by China quickly circulated. Very shortly after that, alleging errors and misjudgment on the part of Nyamoya, the Mwami withdrew his support from Nyamoya's government and again asked Ngendandumwe to form a new cabinet.

Nyangoma, Gervais. Following the legislative elections of May 1965, he was the directeur-général in the prime minister's office. He was believed to have participated in the planning and execution of the coup that occurred in October 1965. In fact, although there is no conclusive evidence, Nyangoma was said to be the most actively involved and is generally assumed to have been the one to conceive the idea of the coup against the monarchy.

Nyangoma, Leonard. See The **Popular Democratic Hutu Army**, The **National Council for the Defense of Democracy**, and **Front for the Defense of Democracy** (**FDD**)

Nyarurimbi (mu-, ba-). These were the supreme court judges in the *mwami*'s traditional court tribunal. Words related to it are *Abarimbi*, descendants of the original Karimbi clan, an important **Hutu** family, and *Umurimbi*, which is synonymous with *Umuhutu* in the country's historical poetry.

Nyenumugamba. In traditional Burundi society, the queen mother (*mugabekazi*) held a very important political and ceremonial role. If she died before or during the reign of the *mwami*, he could name an adoptive mother, usually a young woman, to fill the role; this was similar to the tradition of replacing **Mukakiranga** if she died before the *mwami* did. The ceremonial name for the substitute was Nyenumugamba. One had to be chosen because a *mwami* could not ascend the throne without a queen mother; it was said that *ubwami barabusangiye*, "The royal power must be shared."

Nyongabo, Prime. While a student at the Université Officielle in Lubumbashi, he was one of the founders of the **JNR**, later becoming the organization's national president. He was also known to have launched the 1962 **Kamenge** incidents, which prompted the Mwami to dissolve the organization. The leaders were imprisoned, but the organization was revived in 1966. Nyongabo later became the foreign minister in **Micombero**'s cabinet.

Nyovu (i-, i-). These are the collectively used uncultivated pastures for cattle found outside a group of family enclosures.

Nywana (ku-). In traditional Burundi society, members of different clans would occasionally develop strong friendships that led to the sharing of clan identities. This, the *ukunywana*, or blood brotherhood, was accomplished in a formal ceremony. The two individuals involved formalized the relationship by mixing and drinking the blood from skin incisions on their chests. As part of the ritual, they pledged eternal loyalty and mutual assistance, particularly in the accumulation of cattle.

Nzambimana, Edouard. One of the earliest appointments of **Bagaza** after the 1976 coup was that of Nzambimana as prime minister. In early 1978, Prime Minister Nzambimana announced that the country's military rulers were planning to hand over power to civilians in 1981, which would have been five years after the overthrow of Micombero and his government. He eventually lost his place on the **Central Committee** of **UPRONA** in 1984.

Nzikoruriho, Didace. Following **Buyoya's** complete and unhesitating acceptance of his defeat in the elections of June 1993, the **army** also upheld the election results. When a group of officers tried to move against the elected government in July, just a week before its swearing in, Lieutenant-Colonel Nzikoruriho, deputy chief of staff, dismissed it as "just some small boys gone astray."

Nzohabonayo, Sylvère. A member of **Micombero**'s "**Family Corporation**" (the brother of **Gakiza**, who was Madame Micombero's uncle), he was appointed director-general for judicial, administrative, and political affairs in the office of the presidency. In March 1974, he became the attorney general.

-O-

Office des Cités Africaines (OCA). In 1952, the Office des **Centres Extra-Coutumiers** changed its name to this. When the local and colonial governments were faced with an overpopulation problem as trade and industry brought more people to the urban centers, the Office for African Communities built about 2,500 housing units to accommodate about 15,000 people, set up work units, and erected many community buildings, all within five years. This housing development was divided into five neighborhoods, each with schools, athletic fields, and stores. The project became known as a highly successful experiment in urban housing.

Oko (bu(w)-, am-). In the traditional lineages, the *ubwoko* was the largest grouping—the clan or **patriclan**.

Oro (bu-). This word means "poverty" or "misery"; many names in Kirundi replace their subject or object morpheme with the *-bu-* from *ubworo*. For example, *Burahenda* is a woman who causes intoxication.

-P-

Parti Démocratique Chrétien (PDC). The elder sons of Chief **Baranyanka**, Joseph **Biroli** and Joseph **Ntitendereza**, launched this political party just prior to independence when they severed ties with **UPRONA**. The party's leaders were directly involved in the chain of events that led up to Prince **Rwagasore**'s death and were convicted of the conspiracy.

Parti Démocratique et Rural (PDR). Founded by a famous *ganwa* of Bezi origins, Pierre **Bigayimpunzi**, this was one of the political parties that emerged just prior to independence when many of the old **UPRONA** chiefs severed their ties with the party and set up their own political organizations.

Parti des Jeunes Travailleurs du Burundi (PDJTB). During the time just before independence, 23 political parties were registered. Among them were some based on ethnic interests and solidarity. This party was among those based on particular social class.

Parti du Peuple (PP). Founded in 1959, influenced by events in **Rwanda**, this party became the most known and outspoken of the **Hutu** parties by 1961. In 1965, Hutu candidates won the national elections with a total of 23 out of 33 seats in the National Assembly. Official reports, however, obscured the victory for the Hutu and the PP, only stating that **UPRONA** was victorious, and the PP won 10 of the seats, not that UPRONA was in disarray and not the cohesive party they wished to present to the country and the world.

Parti du Mouvement de l'Emancipation d'Hutu (PARMEHUTU). This was a movement in **Rwanda** begun in 1959 and committed to the **Hutu** cause. It would eventually have an effect on Burundi politics as they approached independence, causing an identification of the Burundi Hutu with those in Rwanda. This was perhaps not an accurate identification at the time, but one that would have much to do with emerging political parties and ethnic strife.

Parti de l'Union et du Progrès National (UPRONA). This political party spans the entire history of independent Burundi. It was founded in the late 1950s, and **Rwagasore**'s return to Burundi coincided with its foundation. In 1958, Rwagasore took control of UPRONA, and the party became a strong nationalistic force in the country. In the party's second manifesto, Rwagasore made it clear that, even though he was a *ganwa* and the son of Mwami **Mwambutsa**, and even thought the party sought to identify with the crown while trying to live up to the progressive intentions of its name, he endorsed the monarchy "only insofar as this regime and its dynasty favoured the genuine emancipation of the Murundi people."
In the same manifesto, it was noted "that the Burundi monarchy is *constitutional*, and wishes to see the constitution of the realm adapted to a *modern state*. UPRONA favours the democratisation of institutions . . . and will firmly and tenaciously combat all forms of social injustice, regardless of the system from which they may come: *feudalism*, *colonialism*, or *communism* . . . .

UPRONA favours the election of the chiefs and subchiefs by the population, and will combat with all its forces those who seek to destroy the *unity* of the country" [italics in the original text]. This outward show of nationalism was alarming to the **Belgians**, who considered the demands radical.

By the end of 1960, there were approximately 20 recognized political parties; UPRONA was the largest with its strongest challenge from the **PDC**. When communal elections were held in November and December 1960, Rwagasore was under house arrest and the PDC won 2,004 of the National Assembly seats to UPRONA's 545. However, the following year, after Rwagasore was released, there were general elections that were swept by UPRONA and that named Rwagasore as the country's first prime minister following independence. He was assassinated in 1961, and the party separated into factions based on old family and ethnic conflicts. That breach was not reconciled, and there was never again such a strong central political body in Burundi. UPRONA remained somewhat elitist and primarily **Tutsi**.

UPRONA remained the only viable political party until the 1990s when it was challenged by **Frodebu**. In June 1993, Frodebu's candidate, Melchior **Ndadaye**, won in the first democratic election since independence, taking the majority of the votes against incumbent Pierre **Buyoya**, UPRONA's candidate. The death of Ndadaye just a few months later in an attempted coup led to the most recent long period of ethnic unrest in an even longer series of such events. UPRONA remains a strong force in the political structure of Burundi, currently considered to be one of the opposition parties in a weak coalition government nominally run by Frodebu.

Parti pour la Libération du Peuple Hutu (Palipehutu). The Party for the Liberation of the Hutu People had its roots outside of Burundi; in 1980 it was begun in Mishamo, a refugee camp in **Tanzania**, by Rémi Gahutu, who died in 1990. It has since become known as the most radical and uncompromising of all Hutu opposition movements. In 1989, a Palipehutu document stated, "The myth of ethnic superiority was the source of a feudal ideology intended to maintain and protect the interests of the feudal monarchy. The feudal lords in turn used this ideology to humiliate and dehumanize the Hutu serfs." Since the fighting in 1990 and 1991 and the attempted coup in 1993, the Palipehutu has become quite active in Burundi; they are often accused of initiating attacks even if no proof exists; they are also accused of attempting to sabotage the reconciliation process. Very few points of agreement exist between the extremists in Palipehutu and the moderates in **Frodebu**.

Party for National Reconciliation (PARENA). This is described as a radical **Tutsi** party, partly because it is the only recognized party in Burundi that was not a part of the coalition government initiated by a power-sharing agreement signed in late 1994. It is led by former President Jean-Baptiste **Bagaza**.

Patriclan. This is the largest of the levels of kinship groups in traditional Burundi society. People in such a group recognize a common paternal descent line, but often are unable to identify a specific ancestor. Interestingly, in spite of their original ancestral differences, both **Tutsi** and **Hutu** may belong to the same patriclan.

People's Reconciliation Party (PRP). In 1992, prior to the first democratic election since Burundi's independence, this seemingly anachronistic party emerged. It was a royalist party advocating a parliamentary monarchy with a prime minister and a council of both Hutu and Tutsi. Its leader in Bujumbura, Jean Bosco **Yamuremye**, did not see this as anachronistic: "The King, who will act as an arbitrator, remains above ethnic categorization—a constitutional monarchy is the only way to insure national unity in Burundi."

Pfumu (mu-, ba-). These people were soothsayers, healers, magicians, clairvoyants, or oracles and were central to Burundi's ancient traditional society. In the tradition of **Imana**, clairvoyant individuals were considered benefactors to humanity; however, these people acted quite apart from Imana and were, instead, in close league with **Kiranga**. Besides being able to divine the future, the *bapfumu* could give charms and medicines as well as detect thieves and murderers.

Popular Democratic Hutu Army. Officials reported that after President **Ndadaye**'s assassination in 1993, armed groups left the districts of Kinama and **Kamenge** and reorganized into the self-declared Popular Democratic Hutu Army led by the former minister of interior and public security, Leonard Nyangoma. In September 1994, they reemerged in Kamenge.

-Q-

Quincunx. Although the word is English, one finds it often as a description of the pattern common to the basketwork of Burundi. It is an arrangement having five points or components, one at each corner and one in the center of a square or rectangle. Many baskets were decorated with strips of black or mauve fibers, dyed with mud from marshes, and arranged in these geometric patterns. Combinations of narrow fiber strips subtly represented the natural latticework of banana leaves, a common artistic theme because of the importance of the banana plant as a main source of beer, considered a necessity in many social relations.

-R-

Régnier (Resident). After the assassination of Prince **Rwagasore**, a Belgian lawyer known for his **UPRONA** sympathies produced a mimeographed pamphlet called "Le Livre Blanc sur le Procès des Assassins du Prince Rwagasore." (The White Book on the Process of the Assassination of Prince Rwagasore). In it, the principal commissaire at the residency is cited as saying that during a meeting in September 1961, the **Belgian** Resident (Régnier) said: "Rwagasore must be killed!" and "In **Rwanda** there would be no problem. . . . Of course, what I foresaw did happen—the **Front Commun** lost the elections, but nothing is lost if one gets rid of Rwagasore in time. . . . Once the deed is accomplished, the lake is not too far away."

Religion. Approximately 60 to 70 percent of the population of Burundi has adopted forms of Christianity. Most of these have joined the **Catholic Church**, but there is a small population of Protestants as well. A small population also follows Islam. However, many, if not most, Barundi (**Hutu** and **Tutsi** alike) maintain many of the traditional animistic beliefs. These beliefs include a creator, **Imana**, and a number of other spirits. Most important among these is **Kiranga**.

Renchard, George W. On June 7, 1968, President Lyndon Johnson appointed Renchard as **U.S.** ambassador to Burundi. The post had been vacant since January 1966, when Burundi expelled the U.S. ambassador, Donald Dumont, on suspicion of involvement with opposition conspirators.

Rimba (ki-, bi-). This term refers to the court of Mwezi **Gisabo**, which consisted of three principal parts. The *intangaro* was an enclosure divided into two parts: the first was for the queen's cattle and the second for the Mwami's cattle. The *inyubakwa* was the main palace, and the *ikigo* was the grazing pasture.

Rozi (mu-, ba-). In the traditional cults of **Kiranga**, these were the negative sorcerers, casters of bad spells, and general doers of evil. They were thought to cause death, sterility, and other ills. While magic and sorcery were an important aspect of traditional Burundi society, practitioners convicted of this form of black magic (*burozi*) were often sentenced to death by impalement or crucifixion.

Rufuko. See **Ntare I**.

Rugaamba. See **Ntare II**.

Rugo. Literally, these are fences or fenced circles scattered on the many *collines* in Burundi. Each houses a family unit.

Ruhuna, Archbishop Joachim. There was a great deal of tension between the Roman **Catholic Church** and the administration of President **Bagaza** that probably dated back to the early missionary work among the **Hutu**. A government spokesman denied press accounts that Archbishop Ruhuna of Gitega had been arrested in 1985 and further described as "slanders and lies" Amnesty International's allegations of that period that at least one priest had died due to harsh prison conditions.

Rukinzu. The Mwami's entourage traditionally included the royal drum (**Karyenda**), accompanied by six smaller drums, Rukinzu, the drummer guard, and five *amashakwe* (sing. *ishakwe*), the drummers who keep the cadence of the march.

Rushatsi. See **Ntare I**.

Rutovu (Tutsi). See **Matana** Tutsi.

Rwagasore, Prince Louis. Often cited as the person who brought Burundi politics toward independence, Prince Louis Rwagasore remains one of the most revered Barundi figures in history. As the son of Mwami **Mwambutsa**, he had many advantages in his life, but it was neither his princely nor even his *ganwa* status for which he is most remembered. The foundations of **UPRONA** coincided with Rwagasore's return to Burundi after he completed his studies at the Institut Universitaire des Territoires d'Outre-Mer in Antwerp. At this time, he was given the chiefdom of **Butanyerera** to administer, but this apparently did not satisfy his political ambitions; between 1958 and 1959, Rwagasore virtually took control of UPRONA, both anticipating the visit from the **Groupe de Travail** and helping to change the party into a clearly anti-**Belgian**, pro-independence party.

Many causes explain Rwagasore's popularity and ability to unite the growing elite among both of the major ethnic groups in Burundi. For one, as the son of Mwambutsa, he belonged to the **Bambutsa** clan; thus, he was able to be the acknowledged representative of the **Bezi** but stand outside of the **Bezi-Batare** conflict as a true national figure, while still having obvious ties to the still popular crown. It is said that this royal tie added some legitimacy to the UPRONA party, giving it a necessary edge over its opponents. He also had the advantage of a university education; although he was not known to be very intellectually sophisticated, his education did seem to give him a more progressive outlook, setting him off quite dramatically from many of the other chiefs. Additionally, he married a **Hutu** woman, which made him more sympathetic to the Hutu cause as well as more popular among the Hutu. Finally, he was simply a very energetic and charismatic figure and an inspiring public speaker.

Rwagasore was not popular among the Belgian administrators. The Belgians referred to the UPRONA leadership as "crypto-communists" and openly sided with their opposition in the **PDC**. In fact, in 1956, the Resident of Burundi wrote in his annual report that Rwagasore's attitude was typical of "progressive tendencies," which he said reflected those of the former students of the Group Scolaire of Astrida and the former seminarians. This administrator stated that these young men "do not always enjoy the sympathy of the administration, because they lack moderation." While thrown together in this category of young upstarts, Rwagasore actually enjoyed even less popularity from the Belgians than most of the others because of his uncompromising commitment to immediate independence. At one point he reported, "The Belgians accuse us of being Communists. At the same time, they accuse us of being monarchists and feudal. They must make up their minds as to what we really are." While his populist views were seen as communist by the administration, his antiadministration views enhanced his status as a nationalist leader among the Barundi.

With this prevailing atmosphere, in August 1960, a meeting was held in Brussels to discuss arrangements for the communal elections and plans for administrative reorganization. During this meeting, an addition to an earlier decree was made that stated that relatives of the *Mwami* within two degrees of relationship could not receive an electoral mandate, hold political office, or take official part in any political activity. As a result, Rwagasore's role in UPRONA remained strictly an advisory one through many internal changes of party leaders. He remained popular with the public in spite of these restrictions as well as the administration's efforts to discredit him, and he was finally placed under house arrest in late 1960 in an attempt to stem his influence. The arrest led to a defeat of UPRONA in communal elections in November 1960, but in September 1961, after his release, under **U.S.** supervision, general elections to elect a government to lead the country after independence were held. UPRONA won overwhelmingly, and Rwagasore was elected the prime minister of the country.

From the beginning, Rwagasore had understood the need to make UPRONA into a party for the masses. To this end, he tried to incorporate into the formal leadership of the party an even proportion of Hutu and Tutsi. In 1961, the **Central Committee** of the party comprised three Tutsi and four Hutu, this imbalance compensating for the fact that the president and vice-president of the party were both Tutsi. In spite of the feelings that much of Rwagasore's political success sprang from his relationship to the Mwami, the relationship between the two was not one of unconditional support; Rwagasore made these conditions clear from the start in the party's second manifest, which stated that the party was prepared to endorse a monarchic regime "only insofar as this regime and its dynasty favoured the genuine emancipation of the Murundi people." Rwagasore also made clear that the Mwami would stay in office only by surrendering power to the government. For his own part, the Mwami never showed a great deal of affection for UPRONA even to the extent of not helping in the political success of his son. Rwagasore was not a member of the "inner circle" of the king's men, many of whom went their own separate ways by forming their own preindependence political parties.

The most powerful of these opposition parties was the **PDC** (of the **Front Commun**), which was led by **Ntitendereza** and **Biroli**. According to testimony, the Belgian resident held a meeting in September 1961 that was attended by the European secretary of the PDC. During this meeting, Resident Régnier reportedly stated, "Rwagasore must be killed! . . . the Front Commun lost the elections, but nothing is lost if one gets rid of Rwagasore in time. . . . Once the deed is accomplished, the lake is not too far away." This feeling fed into the Bezi-Batare conflict nicely. On October 13, 1961, less than a year before independence, Rwagasore was assassinated by a hired Greek gunman. The assassination was found to be a conspiracy organized by the rival political faction; Ntidendereza, Biroli, and several other members of the Batare clan were implicated by the assassin, and all were eventually found guilty and executed in January 1963 with approximately 20,000 observers.

It is said by many that Rwagasore's death created a political vacuum that was to influence decades of Burundi politics to follow. Whether this can be verified or not is irrelevant; it is the belief of so many that it is an opinion deserving credence. Very soon after his death, UPRONA fell prey again to fundamental ethnic and ideological divisions with all measures of ethnic cohesion seeming to disappear. Although **Muhirwa** succeeded Rwagasore as prime minister, he and his followers did not enjoy the support of the Barundi as Rwagasore had. Even as much as four years later, when another prime minister, **Ngendandumwe**, was assassinated, many political analysts attributed the death to the crisis developed in the political vacuum left by Rwagasore's death. Even more than 30 years later, in 1994 and during another crisis in Burundi, some Barundi have expressed their belief that the country would have developed completely differently had Rwagasore lived. A Murundi ambassador to the United States said, when asked if one man could really have made so much difference, "Yes, definitely, if he had been allowed to live longer . . . our fathers and grandfathers do tell us that Rwagasore was something else—that had he lived longer, he would have brought about universal changes. I think [Burundi] would have been politically stable, or as politically stable as **Tanzania** next door. Rwagasore was a contemporary of Nyere [president of Tanzania], and they shared much of the ideological framework, the ideological thinking, which, in those days, was of course tending towards socialist thinking. . . . In Tanzania, you can have anything else; you can have political disturbances, but you cannot have any ethnic conflict. There are problems in Tanzania; the economy is bad, but never in Tanzania would you have killings, would you have internal massacres, and there you have real ethnic groups unlike in Burundi where you have pseudo ethnic groups, people sharing the same language, same culture, same values, same history, same everything."

Rwanda, Relations with. Of almost equal size and separated by the Akanyaru river, the two countries of Rwanda and Burundi compose the region that was known to many early explorers as the "Switzerland of Africa." But in spite of the joint administration of the two countries (as Ruanda-Urundi) under the **Germans** and **Belgians**, Rwanda and Burundi have always been separate entities with separate royal and political structures. In Rwanda, the historical rift was between **Hutu** and **Tutsi**; in Burundi, the conflict was historically more the *ganwa* against the Hutu and Tutsi together.

Meyer said of the two countries: "In Burundi the Tutsi are neither so pleasure-seeking, lazy, mendacious, violent and opportunist as in Rwanda; nor are the Hutu so servile and hypocritical toward the mighty and so impertinent toward the weak; nor is [sic] the king and his court so addicted to idleness, wastefulness, intrigue, and so eager to satisfy their depraved and cruel instincts" (1916, 14-15). He also said that "despite great differences in status [in Burundi], Tutsi and Hutu conduct friendly social intercourse" and "the Hutu who is better off considers himself socially on the same level as the ordinary Tutsi who has no property."

A great many current news articles about Burundi end by stating that the ethnic makeup of the country is the same as that in Rwanda, implying that the history and development of the two countries has been similar. As stated above, this is certainly not strictly the case, although one cannot deny the similar populations and the influence the countries have had on each other (see, for example, the **Rwandan Syndrome**).

Lemarchand says "The refugee problem in Burundi cannot be dissociated from its broader regional context. . . . For every outburst of anti-Tutsi violence in Rwanda, one can expect a similar explosion of anti-Hutu sentiment in Burundi, and vice versa" (1994, 175). When outside observers discuss the future of either country, the name of the other always comes up. Regardless of the precolonial and colonial histories of the two countries, it has become increasingly clear over the last three decades that they are connected, even if it is in what some call an unholy union. In 1962, they became (at least theoretically) independent not only from their Belgian colonizers, but also from each other. Since that time, in ethnic conflict after ethnic conflict, the conflicting ethnic groups of the two countries have drawn together, not only in the eyes of the outside world.

Rwandan Syndrome. Although many **Tutsi** did not feel that **Ndadaye** should have been killed, they did feel that the attempted coup of October 1993 was justified. According to Catherine Watson, many said that Ndadaye's government made serious errors in a short time by replacing too many Tutsi in the government with **Hutu**, bringing back Hutu refugees too quickly, and trying to bring Hutu, who they said were underqualified, into the military. This, they said, seemed like the "Rwandan Syndrome," a situation dreaded by Burundi Tutsi since the Hutu uprising in Rwanda in the 1950s. At that time, Hutu overthrew the Tutsi monarchy, killed and exiled hundreds of thousands of Tutsi, and marginalized those who remained. The Hutu maintained power in Rwanda until 1994.

Rwuba. The "Miscreator" is thought to be the adversary of **Imana**. His form is not specified; he is sometimes referred to with Class 3/4 agreements (as is Imana), and sometimes with Class 1/2 agreements (as with human beings). Rwuba is the most evil of spirits. He watches for his chance to do harm, and his primary goal is to spoil whatever Imana has made. The name, Rwuba, is connected to the verb *-ubagura*, which means "spoil" or "ruin."

Ryango (mu-, mi-). The **Tutsi** and **Hutu** traditionally had essentially the same kinship system, in which the smallest social unit was the local kin group of the male descent line, the *umuryango*, which included all married male members of a family and their wives, as well as unmarried children, both male and female. Each family subdivision had a designated chief, usually the eldest male or *umukuru*. *Umukuru w'umuryango* was the chief of the clan, *umukuru w'inzu* was the chief of a household or nuclear family. In addition to these family heads, there are many terms in **Kirundi** for family relationships. Often, and in this case it was clearly true, kinship terms reveal a great deal about a traditional society and the relationships of importance within it. Following are some Kirundi terms, some quite remote by Western standards, showing the vast intricacies of the clan system. A husband is *umugabo* and a wife is *umugore*, but the husband of two wives is *umugabo w'ihari*; the wives address each other as *umukeba wanje*. A son is *umuhungu*, his mother calls him *umuhungu wanje*, and his father's other wife calls him *umuhungu wa mukeba wanje*. A daughter is *umukobwa*, her mother calls her *umukobwa wanje*, and her father's other wife calls her *umukobwa w'wanje*. The language for siblings in a polygamous society is potentially vast, with all of the necessary permutations of relationship. For example, a male calls his brother from the same mother and father *mukuru wanje* if the brother is older and *uwo dusangiye data na mama* if the brother is younger; he calls his full sister *mushiki wanje mukuru* if she is older and *mushiki wanje* if she is younger. A female calls her full older brother *musaza wanje mukuru* and her younger brother *musaza wanje*; she calls her sisters *mukuru wanje* and *butoyi*. If the father is the same, but the children have different mothers, the forms of address are different. For example, a male calls his older half-brother *mwene data mukuru* and his younger half-brother *mwene data mutoya*; a female calls her older half-sister *mukuru wanje wo kwa data* and her younger half-sister *murumuna wanje wo kwa data*. If the children have the same mother and different fathers, the incidents of the word, *data*, change to *mama*. For example, a male would call his older half-brother *mwene mama mukuru*. These intricacies extend beyond the nuclear family as well. Each aunt, uncle, cousin, grandparent, and in-law has his or her own form of address. For example, a female would call her older male and female cousins on her father's side *mwene datawacu mukuru* and her younger male and female cousins on her mother's side *mwene mamawacu mutoya*. Paternal and maternal uncles are *sewabo* and *inarume*, respectively; paternal and maternal aunts are *senge* and *mama wacu*, respectively. The son of a man's brother is his *umuhungwacu*, and the son of a man's sister is his *umwishwa*; a paternal aunt refers to her nephews as *umusengezana wanje* and a maternal aunt refers to her nephews as *umuhungu wanje*. There is even a word for the second wife of a sister's husband: *mukebacu*.

-S-

Saba (ku-). Literally, this verb means "to solicit aid from someone" and was used often in **Mirerekano**'s booklet, **Mbire gito canje. . .** , apparently to impress on the reader the importance of traditional hierarchical relationships.

Saku (ru-, in-). The word, itself, means "curiosity" or "to be very curious," but its root is important in the oral tradition of Burundi. **Amazina** *y'insaku* is the name of the form that presents and stresses clan rivalries; *izina ry'urusaku* is the name of the form that expresses hatred, animosity, and ill will.

Semasaka. Literally, the "father or master of sorghum," he was, in traditional society, the chief of the royal herds. The last Semasaka, under the reign of **Mwambutsa**, died in 1935; when **Ntare** became Mwami in 1966, another Semasaka was sought, but the reign ended before the office was filled.

Sendegeya, Pierre Claver. A third candidate in Burundi's first democratic presidential election in June 1993, Sendegeya was a member of the **People's Reconciliation Party** (PRP). He received 1.44 percent of the vote after **Ndadaye**'s 64.7 percent and **Buyoya**'s 32.47 percent.

Sentare. This tribunal of the *mwami* functioned to arbitrate services and activities on a colline (see **chanyo**) where there were no local regulations to cover the matter. The name is attributed to **Ntare I**, during whose reign the *Sentare* were the governmental administrators.

Shebuja (mu-, ba-). This is the general term designating one's patron or protector. It was of crucial importance during the period of Burundi's history that relied on a system of patronage.

Shegu (gi-, bi-). At the core of the initiation rite into the cult of **Kiranga**, infants receive the name of an ancient companion of the spirit. These companions are *bishegu*; this is also the word for the politically connected mediums of the court; they were considered extremely powerful and were often sent to exact payment from one against whom the *mwami* held a grudge. **Vansina** relates a story revealing the power of the *ibishegu*. Ndivyariye, a regent of **Mwezi II**, was ousted after many years in office. The *mwami* had him strangled, wrapped in mats, and transported to the countryside. But the porters transporting his body met with thieves along the way and were forced to abandon the assumed body. The regent, who was not yet dead, dressed as a medium and assumed the name of Baruubahuka. Under this disguise, he returned to the court and was accepted as a medium dressed as Ndivyariye, rather than the other way around. The story concludes by telling that people "did not touch him and he left to live in Bweru."

Kiranga was considered the king of *bishegu* in some traditions. He had a large entourage including members of his family and other trusted individuals. Among them were, of course, **Inaryangombe** and **Mukakiranga**. In addition, there were Serutwa, Kiranga's son and the carrier of his lance; Kagoro, Kiranga's daughter; Nabirungu, the leader of the pages and hunters; Sakitema (also known as Inamukozi and Inamurimyi), the woman in charge of the cultivation of the land; Kisiga, head of the lance carriers other than Kiranga's; Rubamba, Kiranga's chief sorcerer; and Zura, the one who prepares the dead for burial and attempts to rid them of evil spirits and bad destinies. There are many other lesser *bishegu* as well.

Shigantahe (mu-, ba-). In traditional society, these were advisors at every level of the political hierarchy. They were also recognized elders and judges with whom the highest ideal of public speaking was associated. According to **Ethel Albert**, he was expected to be "intelligent, in complete command of the arts of logic, a fine speaker—i.e., he speaks slowly and with dignity, in well-chosen words and figures of speech; he is attentive to all that is said; and he is an able analyst of logic and the vagaries of the human psyche. Initiation as *umushigantahe* comes late—usually not before age 45. It is restricted to men of means who can pay for the costly initiation party and who have demonstrated their ability, usually in a long apprenticeship." Although their function was essentially judicial, the *bashigantahe* wielded considerable political influence and enjoyed considerable esteem in the society. There were three categories of *bashigantahe*. At the lowest level were the *bashigantahe bo ku mugina*, entrusted with the task of settling disputes among families or individuals on a colline. At the **ganwa** level, disputes were handled by the *bashigantahe bo ku nama*; highest up in the hierarchy and attached to the royal court were the *bashigantahe bo mu rulimbi*. The *bashigantahe* of the *ganwa* were held in higher esteem than ordinary chiefs, and those attached to the court were more influential than the *ganwa*. Because the *bashigantahe* were selected on their own merits and skills, a **Hutu** could qualify for the office and thus achieve higher status than many ordinary **Tutsi**. Later, when the government became more centralized, the *bashigantahe* were the deputies to the National Assembly. Around the end of the monarchy, they were still considered to be the elders whose support was politically necessary.

Shitsi (mu-, ba-). These traditional spiritual mediums could contact a living person, however distant, and make him or her answer, often with the intent of forcing a confession of some offense. In **Rwanda**, the *bashitsi* were even more powerful, also able to invoke the dead.

Shoreke (in-). Under the *ubugabire* system of patronage, these were female attendants and servants who were in the constant company of the *mwami*.

Sibomana, Adrien. Attempts at mending ethnic divisions continued throughout President **Buyoya**'s administration. In October 1988, the president created a consultative commission on national unity to investigate the massacres earlier that year with 12 **Hutu** and 12 **Tutsi** members. Also in October, and more importantly, he re-created the position of prime minister and filled it with Sibomana, a Hutu and former provincial governor. More Hutu were brought into the ruling council so that they eventually became the majority. Sibomana became a member of the legislature in 1994 under the administration of President **Ntibantunganya**.

Sigo **and** *Kange (gi-, bi-).* These are nature spirits that were once human forms and now inhabit the incorporeal world. They are said to keep to themselves in desolate places. Along with the *bisigo*, they make up the group of nature spirits. The three are supposed to dwell in desolate places such as rock outcroppings, steep valleys, and large expanses of water. Traditionally, anyone refusing to be initiated into **Kiranga**'s cult was threatened with the alternative of becoming one of these spirits, a terrifying prospect. The spirits are malicious and have been said to seize people who intrude on their domains; the results are thought to be seizures, severe stomach pain, and even strokes.

Simbananiye, Artemon. In 1965 as minister of justice, Simbananiye organized a selective genocide of **Hutu** intellectuals after the aborted coup. He was one of the leaders of the repression again in 1972 and was a chief architect of the strategy of promoting southern **Tutsi** into positions of power. In 1974, influenced by his **Family Corporation** and others, President **Micombero** removed Simbananiye from the important post of foreign minister he then held. He was appointed minister of education, but the national university was withheld from his jurisdiction. During the following year, the struggle for power between the family corporation and the **Matana** group of Tutsi led by Simbananiye. In 1976, Simbananiye's power began to rise, and he enjoyed renewed access to Micombero. In May of that year, Simbananiye won a major victory when Micombero placed the university under the Matana leader's jurisdiction. The members of the family corporation, as well as many development-minded Tutsi considered this a major setback.

Siryuyumunsi, Thaddée. In 1963, under the leadership of the National Assembly president, Siruyumunsi, the **Monrovia** group delivered a series of attacks against the policy of the government during the **Kamenge** incidents. They managed to apply enough pressure on the Mwami to have the minister of interior removed from office, but the effect of this was short-lived. Apparently in an attempt to ward off any further trouble, **Muhirwa** accused Siryuyumunsi and two other prominent citizens of conspiring against the security of the state and ordered their arrest. Mwami **Mwambutsa**, who was in Switzerland at the time for medical treatment, instructed the government to put the men under house arrest rather than in prison. At one time, Siryuyumunsi had been a member of the Crown Council. The men were later released, and in February 1964, the National Assembly (almost all **Hutu**, but still under his presidency; he was a **Hima**) began to protest the interventions of the court. In April 1964, Siryuyumunsi led a National Assembly delegation on an official visit to Peking.

Sizi (mu-, ba-). Many people were traditionally employed in the entourage of the *mwami*. These were the court poets and songwriters.

Smbiyara, Cyprien. Once secretary-general of **UPRONA**, **Micombero** replaced him in 1968 with Gilles **Bimazubute**, who also was named secretary of the interior and secretary of civil service.

Sozi (mu-, mi-). This is another word for "hill," important in the culture of Burundi because of the terrain of the country. See also *chanyo*.

-T-

Tabishi (i-, ma-). In some situations, divorce settlements were paid to estranged wives from 1940 to 1952. Often, these payments were made out of the returned bride wealth, but alternative arrangements could also be made. The practice ended when the local **Belgian** official ruled that payment of *matabishi* "smacked of concubinage and prostitution."

Tabwa (in-, in-). In cases of abandonment (physical or emotional) in traditional marriages, there were specific guidelines for either member of the couple to separate. If the wife was left in this condition of *intabwa*, she was able to live until her death in her husband's home. If the wife committed adultery, she was not strongly renounced if she had children, but her husband could then separate from her. Both members could remain in the compound, but the husband would not spend the night with her again. All cattle came under the jurisdiction of the husband, including all milk and butter. She might, if the husband consented, continue to cultivate small parcels of farmland.

Tanzania, Relations with. In spite of their proximity, the two countries have not historically had a lot of contact. In the 1960s, there were a few border skirmishes, but these never came to much beyond mutual protests and subsequent apologies. The apologies were made by the Burundi government; Tanzania remained important to overland trade and import for Burundi.

When ethnic unrest and massacres began in Burundi, Tanzania became a safe haven for many **Hutu**. In fact, the **Palipehutu** is a product of the refugee diaspora; its founder, Rémi Gahutu, was a spokesman for Hutu interests, and, in 1980, began the party in a Tanzanian refugee camp. Since then, many bands of Hutu refugees have entered Burundi from Tanzania and attacked a military camp in Makamba.

Tegatega (mu-, ba-). This is one who rids others of evil spirits and malevolent spells in the religion of the traditional society.

Teka (i-, ma-). One of the qualities of the ideal male in traditional Burundi society is *iteka*, a respect for all human life.

Ten-Year Economic Plan. In response to the conclusion of the visiting missions of 1948 and 1951, **Belgium** instituted a series of economic and administrative reforms embodied in a comprehensive ten-year Economic Plan for Ruanda-Urundi. Proposals for administrative reforms involved several significant changes in the organization of the indigenous political structure and began a limited degree of representative government. The ten-year plan was based on extensive research into the existing economic situation and an analysis of the immediate and long-range needs of the territory. Proposals included in the plan were economic development projects, the expansion of education and health programs, and a consideration of the problems of population. Before this plan, Ruanda-Urundi had few if any professional schools; within the framework of the plan, the government added two large professional schools for crafts, one in Usumbura and one in Kigali, and promoted and encouraged the organization of about 30 handicraft schools and sections in the missions of the more rural parts of the countries.

Terekera (gu-). Beer (usually made from banana, sorghum, millet, or honey) is a necessity for all socially significant communal gatherings, and this word means to offer as a gift or to offer a gift to the the spirits. The use of beer is not restricted to special ceremonies where large quantities would be consumed. It is an everyday adjunct to social interaction and is involved in large part with friendships, marriages, funerals, and contracts. Sometimes, in addition to being a gift, beer is used as a medium of exchange. It is offered as an expression of homage as well as for amusement and simple refreshment. It is usually drunk through a straw from a large drinking pot. The type of pot used indicates the status of the drinker. All adults (especially males) are beer drinkers; to refuse beer when it is offered is an insult, and, traditionally, drunkenness was often considered the mark of a prosperous person.

Terekerezi (mu-, ba-). Also known as *baheza*, these priests of pythons were charged with keeping the royal pythons healthy and fertile. The priests were protected by the king because some oral traditions report that the python carries the spirit of dead kings.

Tererezi (mu-, ba-). This is the general term for the family, friends, neighbors, and allies with whom relations are maintained through the regular exchange of beer and other gifts.

Tezi (in-, in-). This specific type of illness or malady was attributed in traditional society to the influence of bad spirits or evil spells.

Tima (mu-, mi-). According to the traditional religious belief, each individual is made up of this, the heart or the center of emotion and spirit. The counterpart of this soul or conscience is the *ubwenge*, or the intelligence.

Timbo (mu-, ba-). This is the general term for one who is a specialist of the royal drum, covering both the making and the playing of it. A related and similar term is *munyuka* (plural, *banyuka*).

Tongo (i-, ma-). Consisting of less than two-and-a-half acres, these small family homesteads usually consisted of at least a hut, a corral for livestock, and a farming area for seasonal crops and bananas.

Toni (mu-, ba-). These were traditionally the favored confidants of the king or chief; they were entrusted with the confidential missions initiated by the leader.

Tore (in-, in-). Most commonly known today for their internationally famous dancing, these young men, dressed in leopard skins, elaborate headdresses, and bells on their ankles, were at one time part of the royal **army**.

Tung Chi-ping. In May 1964, the day after his arrival in Burundi, this Chinese embassy staff member asked for political asylum at the **U.S.** embassy in Bujumbura. Several weeks later, the *People's Daily* (**China**) reported the "kidnapping of Tung Chi-ping, staff member of the Chinese embassy in Burundi, by the U.S. embassy" as "another crime U.S. imperialism has perpetrated in its long series of hostile acts toward the Chinese people. . . ." In July, the U.S. embassy disclosed that Tung had disappeared. American efforts to arrange for his departure from Bujumbura had been blocked for two months by the Burundi government. Burundi Radio denounced Tung's disappearance as "an unfriendly act which could damage relations between Burundi and the United States. A U.S. embassy spokesman stated that Tung, who had voluntarily entered the embassy, had also left "by his own choice."

Tung believed that he had been sent to Bujumbura because French-speaking Chinese were in short supply; he was assigned as the assistant cultural attaché to serve as interpreter to the attaché, who did not speak French. Tung also believed that his political reliability was doubted.

Tungane (bu-). It was considered essential that the traditional ideal male in Burundi possessed *ubutungane*, sincerity in personal relationships. Advantageous uses of rhetorical skill in business negotiations were also acceptable and, some report, even considered proper although insincere.

Turire (gi-, bi-). Literally, this is a pitcher of beer or honey. In traditional Burundi society, closely tied to the patron-client relationship probably because of its highly personal character, was the custom of gift-giving, *igiturire*. The Barundi have a saying: "To ask for a gift is to honor; to give a gift is to like."

Tutsi. See **Hutu and Tutsi**.

Twa. This is the third and least discussed ethnic group that comprises the population of Burundi; their population is estimated at about 1 percent. The Twa are a Pygmy group widely believed to be the original inhabitants of the area that is now Burundi and **Rwanda**. As early as the nineteenth century, these groups, known as part of the Forest People, were declining in population. Apparently one of the first aspects of their culture to disappear was their language, and by the early twentieth century, most of the surviving Pygmy groups spoke the language of their agricultural neighbors. Many of the country's indigenous crafts, particularly basketry, are still the jurisdiction of the Twa.

Tware (mu-, ba-). This was the general term for a local leader or subchief, an important post prior to a central government. *Umutware w'intara* was a district subchief; *umutware w'umosozi* was a chief of a colline or hill; *umutware w'umukenke* was the chief of pastureland from whom others secured their land; *umutware w'inka* was the chief of cattle; *umutware w'ingabo* was the military chief; and *umutware n'uwugaba inka* was the charitable chief who gave cattle to others. The word later evolved from a political to more of a military sense.

- U -

Ujusohor. Traditionally, most children were born in the family home. When it was about time for a child to be born, the mother called in many of her female neighbors, often including some who were experienced midwives. Immediately after the birth, the child was washed in cold water and rubbed with butter. To protect the infant from harmful spirits, the placenta was buried under the bed, and the mother kept the umbilical cord as an amulet. After six days of seclusion, the child was presented to the family or clan in the *ujusohor* ceremony; the mother was honored with a crown of maternity, and she and the child were greeted by the family with gifts. Birth begins the cycles of life and is known as *ukusohore* in **Kirundi**. The other major cycles of life are *kutera imbuto* (marriage) and *igicaniro* (death).

Umugambwe wa'Bakozi Uburundi (UBU). This was a **Rwanda**-based refugee organization born in the late 1970s. The name means "Party of Burundi Laborers," and this underground group, led by Melchior **Ndadaye**, was the beginning of the **Frodebu** party.

Union Culturelle de la Jeunesse Africaine du Burundi (UCJAB). See **Jeunesse Nationaliste Rwagasore (JNR)).**

Union des Démocrates Barundi (UDB). Like the **Palipehutu**, this was a **Hutu** movement that came about in the exiled Barundi population following the 1972 massacres. It lacked the wide international scope of the Palipehutu, however.

Union des Femmes Burundaises (Union of Burundi Women) (UFB). Founded in 1967, this women's organization was in charge of promoting feminine life or, what has been called in Burundi, "*animation féminine.*"

Union Nationale du Burundi (UNB). Just before independence, old princely rivalries were reasserted. At the same time, many new political factions arose, often with new and sometimes revolutionary goals. In the middle of 1961, there were 23 officially registered political parties; some, such as the UNB, were confined to specific regions of the country and were very short-lived.

Union Nationale de Étudiants Burundi (National Union of Burundi Students) (UNEBA). Established by many young Barundi who were educated in Europe, this youth organization was dissolved along with the **JNR** in 1967 and made part of the **JRR**. It was considered a radical student organization with a very pro-**Tutsi** orientation and played a large role in gathering support against the Crown in the mid-1960s. Its leader was Gilles **Bimazubute**.

United Nations (UN). During the years leading up to independence, the UN and the **Belgian** authorities were pitted against each other in the growing tensions within Burundi. In the struggle between **UPRONA** and the **PDC**, many of the final decisions were made by the UN Trusteeship Council in New York. UN resolutions called on the Belgian government to dismiss the interim government (with the PDC in superior numbers to UPRONA) and hold legislative elections. Since independence, the UN has granted aid and technical assistance to Burundi. Their primary role in the country and the region, however, has been through the **UN Office of High Commissioner for Refugees**.

United Nations Office of High Commissioner for Refugees (UNHCR). UNHCR began its involvement in the region around the time of independence, first concerned with **Tutsi** refugees following the 1959 uprising in **Rwanda**. Since then, the Tutsi refugees from Rwanda and the **Hutu** refugees from Burundi have continued to make the region a concern to the UNHCR. The refugees from both countries have fled to **Zaire**, **Tanzania**, Uganda, and various European countries, as well as Rwandans to Burundi and Barundi to Rwanda. The host countries, particularly Zaire, have had difficulties in both the resettlement and repatriation of the displaced people. There have also been a number of uprisings against the two countries developed by refugees while in exile.

UNHCR reported in 1991 that the Burundi Hutu refugee population had reached approximately 240,000. Many are the result of the 1972 massacre, but there are increasing numbers from 1988, 1991, and 1993. A tripartite agreement of the UNHCR, Burundi, and Tanzania led to the repatriation of many refugees in 1991; this group has been named as responsible for much of the violence in the country later that year. As of the end of 1995, the primary immediate concern was with Rwandan refugees in Burundi and Zaire, but there is no denying the effect this has on Burundi, Barundi refugees, and Burundi's relations with its neighbors.

United States (U.S.), Relations with. There has actually been very little in the way of a relationship between the United States and Burundi. The United States has been an importer of Burundi coffee and has offered some financial aid and technical assistance. There was a brief period of time in the early to middle 1960s when the U.S. government saw Burundi as a major concern in East-West relations because of Burundi's relationship with **China**. However, this was short lived, and the United States has, for over 30 years, paid little attention to Burundi and its human rights violations. Following the 1972 massacre, Senators Ted Kennedy and John Tunney called for international action to deal with the "situation" in Burundi. In 1995, President Bill Clinton urged Burundi to "say no to violence and extremism." Also in 1995, former President Jimmy Carter, former **Tanzanian** President Nyere, and South African

Archbishop Desmond Tutu served as mediators between factions in Burundi and **Rwanda**.

- V -

Van der Burgt, Johannes-Michael. This Dutch priest founded a Catholic mission in Burundi, arriving in the country in 1896 and leaving in 1908. He travelled the country extensively, making a number of relief maps of the area. Most notably, however, was his work on a French-Kirundi dictionary, which came out in 1903. Critics have noted its many digressions, calling them useless, but all note the importance of this monumental task, which included precise information about the history and anthropology of the country in addition to the language.

Vansina, Jan. A historian of oral tradition, Professor Vansina claimed in 1961 that Burundi had no equivalent of the wealth of traditional genres pertaining to the monarchy of **Rwanda**. He further claimed that, because of the circumstances that brought them to power, the *ganwa* were naturally afraid of the verdict of history, leading to a Burundi that was "characteristically prejudiced against history." Vansina pointed out that the field of oral traditions is not completely barren in Burundi; folktales and legends fill the gaps of history, but lack the supplementary memory of court historians of Rwanda, whose task was to hand down the traditions of the realm as royal ordinance prescribed. In spite of these differences with Rwanda, Burundi's oral tradition has been well studied by Vansina. One of the problems is that traditions are not transmitted by specialists, trained for the task or endorsed by any central body. A result of this lack of specialization is that the approximately 40 primary traditions could potentially be told by almost 9,000 informants, making the task of the researcher nearly impossible.

Voix de la Révolution (Voice of the Revolution). During the **Micombero** administration, the government disseminated information to the public through the national radio station, Voix de la Révolution and the official newspaper, *Unité et Révolution*. Through an agreement between Burundi and the Soviet Union, international news service was supplied to *Unité et Révolution* through TASS, the Soviet news agency, as well as through the French press agency, Agence France Presse. **UPRONA** also periodically sent political teams to all parts of the country to explain official policy and mobilize the population. The radio station continued to be the official government news outlet through several later administrations.

Vurati (mu-, ba-). These are the royal rainmakers, traditionally very important during the sorghum and other fertility festivals, such as the *muganuro*. They were traditionally said to own the rain, so could also prevent rain if they wanted to. They were greatly feared because they were thought to be able to send out a thunderbolt to kill anyone who angered them.

Vyeyi (bu- no plural). Another of the qualities that traditionally exists in the ideal Burundi male is this type of parental devotion. This is the basis of respectful relationships between parents and their children. It represents the dignity and respect of a parent and that which is due to a parent. The root with the prefixes designating humans (*umuvyeyi, abavyeyi*) means "parent(s)." The word *imvyeye* means "cow who has recently calved."

Vyino (ru-, im-). These group songs were popular at reunions of clans. They had refrains comprising short musical phrases with strong beats; the singing was often accompanied by dancing. Sometimes, a soloist improvised couplets in the *imvyino*; these were closely related to the present moment or events and were often used to bring news to the group.

Vyivare (i-). These were the royal domains within the traditional system. Of interest is that often there were **Hutu** chiefs who held office in these domains. These chiefs had some advantages, because they were not subject to the *baganwa* and the problems involved in the dynastic families; therefore, they could act as independent chiefs. The Hutu chiefs were dismissed by the administration in 1931.

-W-

White Fathers (Pères Blancs). Although this is the most used name of the **Catholic Church** missionary group, their formal title is the Roman Catholic Order of the Missionaries of Africa. The first mission schools in Burundi are said to have been established in about 1900 by the White Fathers. Traditional education before this time was informal in that it primarily focused on providing the children with skills necessary in fulfilling their social and economic responsibilities and becoming productive members of society. The immediate family and the kinship group shared the responsibility for the training of children.

White Sisters (Soeurs Blanches). This group of European nuns came to Ruanda-Urundi during the period from 1898-1922 when the **White Fathers** and other missionary groups were becoming well-established in the territory. They devoted themselves primarily to teaching women and girls, giving medical care in local dispensaries, and organizing a novitiate for members of the population who wanted to become nuns.

Women. See **Action Sociale**, **Foyers Sociaux**, (umu)**ganuro**, and **Union des Femmes Burundaises**.

-Y-

Yamuremye, Jean Bosco. See **People's Reconciliation Party (PRP))**.

Yangayanga (mu-, ba-). These travelling merchants traditionally traversed the country, trading bracelets and other trinkets for cattle. They were very important to the economy of Burundi before the period of European colonization. They were business agents.

Youth. Since independence, the youth of Burundi have emerged in leadership roles. Many of these people were young **Tutsi** who had been educated in **Catholic** mission schools. Young men, especially during precolonial and colonial times, were trained in oratory skills for leadership roles.

Youth organizations have long played an important role in the politics of Burundi (see, for example, **Jeunesse Nationaliste Rwagasore, Jeunesse Rwagasore Révolutionnaire**, and **Union Nationale de Étudiants Burundi**). Today, in spite of some attempts by the government to encourage constructive organizations, many of the **Hutu** and Tutsi very young men and boys are militia members. In the case of the Hutu, this is perhaps not surprising; many older educated and military Hutu have been killed over the years in various massacres.

Yoya (ka-, tu-). A newborn infant of either gender was traditionally called *akayoya* or *uruyoya* until the age of two months. The various ages of an individual's life continue to have their own names in **Kirundi**. Children of both genders are called *igitwengerabarezi* until the age of three months, *igitambambuga* until the age of one year, *umucuko* until the age of two years, and *ingimbi* until the age of ten years. Boys are called *umwana agimbutse* until the age of 15 years, and girls are called the same thing, but only until that age of 12. After this approximate age of puberty, the names describing an individual's life vary for males and females. A male is *igikwerere* until the age of 20, *umugabo* until the age of 25, *umusore ashitse* until 30, *umuhumure* until 55, *umukambwe* until 60, and *umutama* until 70. A female is *umuyabaga* until 14, *inkumi* until 16, *inkumi sezegeri* until 18, and *igitamba* until 20. After this age, it was traditional to refer to women with respect to their child bearing: from the first child, a woman is *avyaye rimwe* (one); from the second, she is *avyaye kabili* (two), etc. After her child-bearing years, she is *umutamakazi* until age 50 and *nyogokuru* beyond that.

- Z -

Zaire, Relations with. Although Ruanda-Urundi and Zaire (Belgian Congo) were both colonized and administered by the **Germans** and then the **Belgians**, this country has been, for the most part, separate both politically and culturally. However, in 1963-64, repercussions of the Congo Rebellion in Zaire were felt in Burundi when the **Chinese** embassy in Bujumbura became a major source of arms and equipment for the Armée de Libération Nationale (ALN) in Zaire. Zairian militia groups have also been accused of supporting other uprisings in Burundi and **Rwanda**.

As the postcolonial years passed, Zaire became a country of refuge for displaced Barundi, beginning particularly during and after the 1972 massacre. Today, many refugee camps exist in Zaire; in November 1995, Zaire's President Mobutu, who had threatened to expel all Burundi and Rwandan refugees from the uprisings over the last two years in both countries, relaxed his deadline. He is thought to be sympathetic to **Hutu** militia members if not to the rest of the refugees. Having threatened to expel the refugees by December 31, 1995, Mobutu instead asked that the **United Nations High Commissioner for Refugees** do more to encourage repatriation.

Zimu (mu-, mi-). This is the general traditional name for the spirits of the dead, not particularly benevolent or evil. When Barundi died, their deaths were not considered final. Their bodies decomposed and became dust, but their souls remained and entered other beings. Other derivations of this word are *ubuzimu*, or reincarnation, and *kuzima*, or to disappear or become extinct.

Zina (i-, ma-). Literally, this means "names," figuratively, "praise names." In Burundi, the ability to speak well and eloquently is thought to be highly significant both practically and aesthetically. Among the upper classes, speaking well (see *(im)fura*) is a sign of good breeding, and the ideals of oratorical ability are highly stressed. From the age of about ten, aristocratic boys learn speech making, including the composition of these *amazina*, or praise poems.

According to **Ethel Albert**, who researched these speech patterns extensively, the form of these poems is fixed, but the contents are created on an impromptu basis. The naturally alliterative character of **Kirundi** (as is the case with Bantu languages in general) is reinforced by conscious selection of assonant words in the construction of praise names and figures of speech. There are slight modifications in wording and number of verses as authors repeat their increasing store of *amazina* on appropriate occasions. Each composer must demonstrate his own abilities, so nobody borrows the *amazina* of others except to learn the art of composition.

An interesting aspect of them is that they have a great deal of latitude in terms of truth. **Vansina** tells a story of a teenage boy who recited the *amazina* verses he had composed in praise of himself; they included the names of enemies he had killed with his lance and his bow, but the boy freely admitted that he had never actually killed anyone. The boy further explained that the purpose of the poem was to boast of heroic deeds, and it did not matter if the deeds were completely imaginary. Again the question of depending on oral traditions for historical facts arises; it is reasonable that the historian might have some doubts. As these grow over the years of a person's life, an elderly man with a long history of bravery, for example, might fill three or four hours with his chanted recitation.

These compositions are primarily for the upper caste; however, there are also farmer's *amazina*, which praise things of interest to the agricultural life. There have even been recorded cases of cow thieves composing *amazina* in self-praise: because the punishment for stealing cattle was immediate crucifixion if the thief was caught in the act, and because precautions against stealing were elaborate, a cow thief who lived to tell the tale was considered to have earned the right to his *amazina*. The *amazina* are divided into four main groups. *Amazina y'ubuhizi* (or *amazina y'urugambo*) are the heroic stories; *amazina y'inka* are pastoral stories;

amazina y'uruhigi are comical odes; and *amazina y'isuka* are the stories of community farming.

Ziro (mu-, mi-). This term was employed for a gamut of tabus, the violation of which could bring grave consequences to the perpetrator. These could include hindrances to marriage, prohibitions of mating for both humans and cattle, and dietary prohibitions, among others.

Bibliography

This bibliography is an attempt to list as many sources on Burundi as possible, but it is by no means complete. Since Burundi's independence in 1962, there have been slightly more sources in English than there were before, but this is not to say that there are many. Most of the primary sources describing the history, culture, and language of the country are in French. Sadly, many of the English sources have emerged only because of Burundi's several periods of civil unrest in the country's postcolonial period. Some of these include articles in *Africa Report*, *Issue*, and *Africa Today*, as well as occasional articles in such general news magazines as *Time*, *Newsweek*, *The Nation*, the *New York Times*, and the *New Yorker*. Other useful sources of secondary material in English on Burundi include AP and Reuters news releases. These can be accessed electronically on reuters@clarinet.com and also on ap@clarinet.comvia clari.world.african news.

There are very few comprehensive bibliographies on Burundi and very few collections of primary materials. Some useful sources, however, include the Africa Library in Brussels and the Museum for Central Africa in Tervuren (Belgium). In North America, there is the Hoover Institution at Stanford in which part of the Derscheid Collection is available. This collection is probably still one of the best known of primary collections on Burundi. Fortunately, the modern researcher has the advantage of highly efficient inter-library loan systems throughout the world.

There have been several general histories of Burundi written in English, and some of these have been especially useful in the forming of this dictionary and bibliography. Listed in this bibliography are numerous books and articles by two prolific researchers, René Lemarchand and Warren

Weinstein. Professor Lemarchand's *Rwanda and Burundi* (1970), is an excellent source of information on the details of history and culture of the two countries until that time; it also includes a limited but useful bibliography. A quarter of a century later, Professor Lemarchand is still examining the intricacies of the country and its motivations; *Burundi: Ethnocide as Discourse and Practice* (1994) gives the reader an interesting perspective for the current unrest in Burundi and also provides another useful bibliography. Professor Weinstein's *Historical Dictionary of Burundi* (1976), probably provides the most comprehensive bibliography in English on Burundi to date. Additionally, Weinstein's books and articles spanning the last 20 years provide insight into Burundi's international relations.

Sources on Burundi's economy remain scarce, as do sources specifically dealing with the language and literature of the country. A few researchers are prominent in these narrrower areas: Jan Vansina for cultural anthropology and oral literary history, and Ethel Albert, F. Rodegem, A. A. Trouwborst, R. Bourgeois, and Jean-Pierre Chrétien for sociology, cultural anthropology, and literary and language history.

This bibliography is divided into 14 sections in an attempt to make it useful to readers with different purposes; other researchers might divide the sources differently, but these are the categories that seemed to naturally emerge as the dictionary was being formed. The first two sections include the general history of Burundi specifically and regional history because so much of Burundi's development is tied in with other countries in the region, as well as being similar in some ways to development in other African countries. The next three sections of the bibliography divide Burundi's history temporally: precolonial history, which includes some works on the early exploration of the region; colonial history, which includes works on both the German and Belgian occupations of the region; and postcolonial history, which covers Burundi's general history and political affairs up to the present time. The sixth section covers economics and development. Section seven is on linguistics and covers language issues under the current definition of the field: all issues of language, including its discourse structure and influence on social aspects of a people. The eighth and ninth sections cover verbal, musical, and visual arts, and general sociology. The tenth section is on religion and includes works on traditional as well as imported religion. The remaining sections include international relations, education, geography, geology, and agriculture, and health and medicine.

1. General History

Botte, Roger. "Burundi: De Quoi Vivait l'État." *Cahiers d'Etudes Africaines* 22, nos. 3-4 (1988): 277-317.

Bourgeois, R. *Banyarwanda et Barundi* 3 vols. Brussels: Académie Royale des Sciences Coloniales, 1954-1957.

Camus, C. "Le Ruanda et l'Urundi." *Congo* 6 no. 1 (1924): 105-11.

Chrétien, Jean-Pierre. "Le Burundi." *Documentation Française*, no. 3364 (1967).

Derkinderen, G. *Atlas du congo Belge et du Ruanda-Urundi*. Paris: Elsevier, 1956.

Gann, L. H., and P. Duignan. *The Rulers of Belgian Africa 1884-1914*. Princeton: Princeton University Press, 1979.

Gildea, R. Y., and A. Taylor. "Rwanda and Burundi." *Focus* 13, no. 6 (February 1963).

Hakizimana, Deo. *Burundi: Le Non-dit*. Geneva: Editions Remesha, 1992.

Jamoulle, A. "Le Ruanda-Urundi." *Expansion Belge* 8 (1927): 18-23.

Laurenty, Jean-Sebastien. *Les Cordophones de Congo Belge et du Ruanda-Urundi*. Tervuren: Musée du Congo Belge, 1968.

Legum, Colin. *Congo Disaster*. Baltimore: Penguin, 1961.

Lemarchand, René. *Rwanda and Burundi*. New York: Praeger, 1970.

Louis, William Roger. *Ruanda-Urundi, 1884-1919*. Oxford: Clarendon Press, 1963.

Maes, J. "Ruanda-Urundi." *Afrika* 2 (1947): 1037-47.
Maquet, J. J. "Ruanda-Urundi, Lands of the Mountains of the Moon." In *The Belgian Congo from Wilderness to Civilization*. Brussels: Les Beaux Arts, 1956.
Marzorati, A. "The Belgian Congo and Ruanda-Urundi." *Civilisations* 1 (1951): 149-54.
McDonald, Gordon C., et al. *Area Handbook for Burundi*. Washington, D.C.: American University, 1969.
Meyer, Hans. *Die Barundi*. Leipzig: Otto Spamer, 1916. English translation: *The Barundi*. Translated by Helmut Handzik. Human Relations Area Files, 1954. French translation: *Les Barundi*. Paris: Société Française d'Histoire d'Outre-Mer, 1984.
Mulago, Vincent. "L'Union Vitale Bantu ou le Principe de la Cohésion et de la Communauté chez les Bashi, les Nabyarwanda et les Barundi." *Annali Lateranensi*, 20 (1956): 61-263.
Mworoha, Émile. *Histoire du Burundi*. Paris: Hatier, 1987.
Nahayo, Simon. "Contribution à la Bibliographie des Ouvrages Relatifs au Burundi." *Geneva Africa* 10, nos. 1-2 (1971):92-9 and 100-111; 11, no. 1 (1972): 94-104.
Rodegem, F. M. *Documentation Bibliographique sur le Burundi*. Bologna: Editrice Missionaria Italiana, 1978.
Roucek, Joseph. "Rwanda and Burundi." *African Trade and Development* 4 (1962): 12-15.
Rozier, R. *Le Burund, Pays de la Vache et du Tambour*. Paris: Presses du Palais Royal, 1972.
Sandrart, Georges. *Ruanda-Urundi*. Brussels: Dessart, 1953.
Schumacher, P. "Urundi." *Aequatoria* 12, no. 4 (1949): 129-32.
Sohier, J. *Répertoire Géneral de la Jurisprudence et de la Doctrine Coutumière du Congo et du Ruanda-Urundi*. Brussels: Ferdinand Larcier, 1957.
Steinhart, Edward. "Vassal and Fief in Three Lacustrine Kingdoms." *Cahiers d'Études Africaines* 7, no. 4 (1967): 606-23.

Straunard, S. A. "Le Ruanda-Urundi." *Revue Nationale* 191 (1949): 193.
Traveller's Guide to the Belgian Congo and Ruanda-Urundi. Brussels: Tourist Bureau for the Belgian Congo and Ruanda-Urundi, 1956.
Verger, Pierre. *Congo Belge et Ruanda-Urundi.* Paris: P. Harmann, 1952.
Weinstein, Warren. *Historical Dictionary of Burundi.* Metuchen, N. J.: Scarecrow Press, 1976.
Weinstein, Warren, and Robert Schrire. *Political Conflict and Ethnic Strategies: A Case Study of Burundi.* Syracuse, N. Y.: Maxwell School of Citizenship, 1976.
Whitaker, P., and J. Silvey. "A Visit to the Congo, Rwanda and Burundi." *Makerere Journal*, no. 9 (1964): 71-82.

2. Regional History

Barns, A. *The Wonderland of the Eastern Congo.* New York: Putnam, 1922.
Burkitt, M.C. "Prehistory in the Congo." *Nature* 155 (1945): 585.
Cervenka, Z. *Land-locked Countries of Africa.* Uppsala: Scandinavian Institute of African Studies, 1973.
_____. *The Unfinished Quest for Unity.* New York: Africana, 1977.
Chrétien, Jean-Pierre. "Echanges et hiérarchies dans les Royaumes des Grands Lacs de l'Est Africain." *Annales* 29, no. 6 (1974): 1327-37.
_____, ed. *Histoire Rurale de l'Afrique des Grands Lacs.* Paris: Diffusion Karthala, 1983.
Clark, J. Desmond et. al. *The Cambridge History of Africa.* Vol. 1-8. Cambridge: Cambridge University Press, 1975.
Cole, S. *The Prehistory of East Africa.* New York: New American Library, 1963.
Currie, D. P. *Federalism and the New Nations of Africa.* Chicago: University of Chicago Press, 1964.

Davidson, Basil. *Can Africa Survive?* Boston: Little, Brown, 1974.

Decalo, Samuel. *Coups and Army Rule in Africa.* New Haven: Yale University Press, 1975.

Emerson, Rupert. "Nation-Building in Africa." In *Nation-Building,* edited by K. Deutsch and W. Folz. New York: Atherton, 1963.

Forde, C. D., ed. *African Worlds.* London: Oxford University Press, 1954.

Foster, F. Blanche. *East Central Africa: Kenya, Uganda, Tanzania, Rwanda, and Burundi.* New York: Watts, 1981.

Frederick, A., Duke of Mecklenburg. *In the Heart of Africa.* London: Cassel, 1910.

Gabel, C., and N. R. Bennett, eds. *Reconstruction of African Culture History.* Boston: Boston University Press, 1967.

Gann, L. H., and P. Duignan, eds. *Colonialism in Africa 1870-1960.* Cambridge: Cambridge University Press, 1975.

Gluckman, Max. *Order and Rebellion in Tribal Africa.* London: Cohen & West, 1963.

Gourevitch, Philip. "Letter from Rwanda: After the Genocide." *The New Yorker,* 18 December (1995): 78-94.

Gray, Richard, and David Birmingham, eds. *Pre-Colonial African Trade.* London: Oxford University Press, 1970.

Hodgkin, Thomas. *Nationalism in Colonial Africa.* London: Oxford University Press, 1958.

Hunter, G. *The New Societies of Tropical Africa.* London: Oxford University Press, 1962.

_____. *The Best of Both Worlds? A Challenge on Development Policies in Africa.* London: Oxford University Press, 1967.

Hunton, W. Alphaeus. *Decision in Africa: Sources of Current Conflict.* New York: International Publishers, 1960.

Ilunga, A. "Crise Politique: Concept et Application à l'Afrique." *Cahiers Économic et Sociaux* 3, no. 3 (1965): 321-38.

Legum, Colin et. al. *Africa in the 1980s: A Continent in Crisis.* New York: McGraw-Hill, 1979.

Lemarchand, René, ed. *African Kingdoms in Perspective: Political Change and Modernization in Monarchical Settings.* London: F. Cass, 1977.

Leys, C., and C. Pratt, eds. *A New Deal in Central Africa.* New York: Praeger, 1960.

Lystad, Robert A., ed. *The African World: A Survey of Social Research.* New York: Praeger, 1965.

Maquet, J. J. *Aide Mémoire d'Ethnologie Africaine.* Brussels: Institut Royal Colonial Belge, 1954.

_____. *The Premise of Inequality in Ruanda.* Oxford: Oxford University Press, 1961.

_____. Institutionalisation Féodale des Relations de Dépendance dans Quatre Cultures Interlacustres. *Cahiers d'Études Africaines*, vol. 9, no. 35 (1968): 402-14.

_____. *Africanite.* New York: Oxford University Press, 1972.

Martin, Jane J. *Africa.* Guildford, Conn.: Dushkin, 1985.

Mazrui, Ali A. *The African Condition: A Political Diagnosis.* Cambridge: Cambridge University Press, 1980.

Moraes, Frank. *The Importance of Being Black.* New York: Macmillan, 1958.

Murphy, E. Jefferson. *History of African Civilization.* New York: Delta, 1972.

Parkin, D. J. *Town and Country in Central and Eastern Africa.* London: Oxford University Press, 1975.

Phillipson, David. *African Archaeology.* Cambridge: Cambridge University Press, 1993.

Posnansky, M., ed. *Prelude to East African History.* London: Oxford University Press, 1966.

Suret-Canale, J. *Afrique Noire, Occidentale et Centrale.* New York: Pica Press (translated from the 1961 edition), 1971.

Taylor, Bayard. *The Lake Regions of Central Africa.* New York: Negro Universities Press, 1969.

Ungar, Sanford. *Africa: The People and Politics of an Emerging Continent*. New York: Simon & Schuster, 1986.

Van der Burgt. *Un Grand People de l'Afrique Equatoriale*. Holland: Bois le Duc, 1963.

Van Noten, Francis. *The Archaeology of Central Africa*. Graz, Austria: Akademische Druck, 1982.

Vansina, Jan. "The Use of Process Models in African History." In *The Historian in Tropical Africa*, edited by Jan Vansina et al. London: Oxford University Press, 1964 375-90.

Wakano, Katambo. *Coups d'Etat, Revolutions and Power Struggles in Post-Independence Africa*. Nairobi: Afriscript, 1985.

Wallerstein, I. *Africa: The Politics of Independence*. New York: Vintage, 1961.

Ziégler, Jean. *Le Pouvoir Africain: Elements d'une Sociologie Politique de l'Afrique Noire et de sa Diaspora aux Ameriques*. Paris: Editions du Seuil, 1971.

3. Precolonial History and Early Exploration

Bennett, Norman, ed. *Henry Stanley's Despatches to the New York Herald, 1871-1872, 1874-1877*. Boston: Boston University Press, 1970.

Bequaert, M. "Nouveaux Eléments d'Étude Concernant la Répartition des Pierres Trouvées dans le Congo Oriental et le Ruanda-Urundi." *Bulletin de la Société Royale Belge d'Anthropologie Préhistorique* (1954): 175-86.

Bloch, Marc. *Feudal Society*. London: Routledge and Kegan Paul, 1965.

Botte, Roger. "Burundi: la Relation Ubugabire dans la Tête de Ceux qui la Décrivent." *Cahiers d'Études Africaines* 9 (1969): 363-71.

Burton, Richard F. *The Nile Basin*, 2 vols. London: Tinsley, 1864.

_____. On Lake Tanganyika: Ptolemy's Western Lake-Reservoir of the Nile. *Journal of the Royal Geographic Society* (1865): 1-15.

Chrétien, Jean-Pierre. "Le Passage de l'Expédition d'Oscar Baumann au Burundi." *Cahiers d'Etudes Africaines* 8 (1968): 48-95.

_____. "Du Hirsute au Hamite: Les Variations du Cycle de Ntare Rushatsi du Burundi." *History in Africa* 8 (1981): 3-41.

Cohen, Daniel. *Henry Stanley and the Quest for the Source of the Nile*. New York: M. Evans, 1985.

Eisenstadt, S. N., and Lemarchand, René. *Political Clientelism, Patronage and Development*. London: Sage, 1981.

Ghislain, Jean. *Le Féodalité au Burundi*. Brussels: Académie Royale des Sciences d'Outre-Mer, 1970.

Grant, James A. *A Walk Across Africa: Domestic Scenes from my Nile Journal*. London: William Blackwood and Sons, 1864.

Guillet, Claude, and Pascal Ndayishinguje. *Légendes Historiques du Burundi: Les Multiples Visages du Roi Ntare*. Paris: Karthala, 1987.

d'Hertefelt, M., A. A. Trouwborst, and J. H. Scherer. *Les Anciens Royaumes de la Zone Interlacustre Méridionale: Ruanda, Burundi, Buha*. London: International African Institute, 1962.

Hiernaux, Jean, and E. Maquet. "Un Haut Fourneau Préhistorique au Buhune." *Zaire* 6 (1954): 615-19.

_____. "Cultures Préhistoriques de l'Âge des Métaux au Ruanda-Urundi et au Kivu." *Bulletin de l'Académie Royale Scientifique Coloniale* 6 (1956): 1126-49.

Leroy, F. J. "Archéologie Préhistorique au Burundi, Mugera, 1926." *Revue de l'Université Officielle de Bujumbura* 2, no. 7 (1966): 165-71.

Leroy, P. "Stanley et Livingstone en Urundi." *Lovania* 44 (1957): 23-4.

Nenquin, Jacques. *Contributions to the Study of the Prehistoric Cultures of Rwanda and Burundi*. Tervuren: Musée Royal de l'Afrique Centrale, 1967.

_____. "Notes on the Protohistoric Pottery Cultures in the Congo Ruanda-Burundi Region." In *Background to Evolution in Africa*, edited by W. W. Bishop and J. D. Clark. Chicago: University of Chicago Press, 1967.

Nsanze, Augustin. *Un Domaine Royal au Burundi: Mbuye.* Bujumbura: Université du Burundi Centre de Civilisation Burundaise, 1980.

Rotberg, Robert, ed. *Africa and Its Explorers: Motives, Methods, and Impact.* Cambridge: Harvard University Press, 1970.

Salée, A. "Un Atelier de Style Paléolithique dans l'Urundi." *Annales de la Société Scientifique* (1927): 76-7.

Speke, John Hanning. *Journal of the Discovery of the Source of the Nile.* London: Blackwood and Sons, 1863.

Stanley, Henry M. *How I Found Livingstone: Travels, Adventures and Discoveries in Central Africa.* New York: Scribner, Armstrong & Co., 1872.

_____. *My Kalula, Prince, King, and Slave: a Story of Central Africa.* 1874. Reprint, New York: Negro Universities Press, 1969.

_____. *Through the Dark Continent* . New York: Harper, 1878.

_____. *The Exploration Diaries of H. M. Stanley, from the Original Manuscripts.* New York: Vanguard, 1961.

Thomson, J. *To the Central African Lakes and Back* 2 vols. London: Sampson Low, 1881.

Trouwborst, Albert. Le Barundi. In *Les Anciens Royaumes de la Zone Interlacustre Méridionale: Rwanda, Burundi, Buha*, edited by J. Vansina. Tervueren: Musée de l'Afrique Centrale, 1962.

_____. "La Base Territoriale de l'État du Burundi Ancien." *Revue Universitaire du Burundi* 1, nos. 3-4 (1973): 245-55.

Van Grunderbeek, Marie-Claude. *Le Premier Age du Fer au Rwanda et au Burundi: Archeologie et Environnement.* Butare, Rwanda: Institut National de Recherche Scientifique, 1983.

Vansina, Jan. "Note sur la Chronologie du Burundi Ancien." *Académie Royale des Sciences d'Outre-Mer Bulletin des Séances* 3 (1967): 429-44.

Wauters, A. *Exploration du Dr. Baumann dans la Région Située entre le Lac Victoria et le Tanganyika.* Brussels: Le Mouvement Géographique, 1893.

_____. *Les Montagnes de la Lune: Exploration du Dr. Oscar Baumann.* Brussels: Le Mouvement Géographique, 1893.

Zangrie, L. "Quelques Traces Ethnologiques de l'Origine Égyptienne des Batutsi." *Jeune Afrique* 15 (1951): 9-15.

4. Colonial History

Anstey, Roger. *King Leopold's Legacy.* London: Oxford University Press, 1966.

Berlage, Jean. *Repertoire de la Presse du Congo Belge, 1884-1954, et du Ruanda-Urundi, 1920-1954.* Brussels: Commission Belge de Bibliographie, 1955.

Botte, Roger. "Rwanda and Burundi, 1889-1930: Chronology of a Slow Assassination." *International Journal of African Historical Studies* 18, no. 1 (1985): 53-91.

Bragard, Lucie. "Vers l'Indépendence du Ruanda-Urundi." *Les Dossiers de l'Action Sociale Catholique* 8 (1959): 643-76.

Brausch, E. J. *Belgian Administration in the Congo.* London:Oxford University Press, 1961.

Buhrer, J. *L'Afrique Orientale Allenmande et la Guerre 1914-1918.* Paris: Fournier, 1923.

Bustin, Edouard. *Lunda Under Belgian Rule: The Politics of Ethnicity.* Cambridge: Harvard University Press, 1975.

Cauvin, Andre. *Bwana Kitoko: Un Livre Realise au cours du Voyage du Roi des Belges au Congo et dans le Ruanda-Urundi.* Brussels: Elsevier, 1956.

Chauleur, P. "Les Etapes de l'Indépendence du Ruanda-Urundi." *Etudes* 314 (September 1962): 225-31.

Comhaire, J. "Au Ruanda-Urundi: Faits, Programmes, Opinions." *Zaire* 10 (1952): 1051-68.

_____. "Evolution Générale du Ruanda-Urundi en 1953." *Zaire* 8 (1954): 1067-74.

_____. "Le Ruanda-Urundi en 1952." *Zaire* 8 (1954): 55-61.

Conseil Supérieur du Pays, Procès-Verbaux [transcript of proceedings]. June 10-13 (1958): 17ff.

Delacauw, A. "Droit Coutumier des Barundi." *Congo* 3, 332-57; 4 (1936): 481-522.

_____. "Emigration des Barundi." *Grands Lacs* 64, nos. 4-6 (1949): 41-44.

Durieux, André. *Institutions Politiques, Administratives et Judiciaares du Congo Belge et du Ruanda-Urundi.* Brussels: Editions Bieleveld, 1957.

Engels, A. "La Conquête du Ruanda-Urundi." *Bulletin de l'Institut Royal Colonial Belge* (1935): 359-60.

des Forges, Alison. The Impact of European Colonization on the Rwandese Social System. Paper presented at the annual meeting of the African Studies Association, Bloomington, Indiana, October 1966.

Gahama, Joseph. *Le Burundi sous Administration Belge.* Paris: Karthala, 1983.

Gelders, V. and J. Biroli. "Native Political Organization in Ruanda-Urundi." *Civilisations* 4 (1954): 125-32.

Gille, Albert. "Histoire du Muname." *Jeune Afrique* 4 (1948): 17-27.

Goebel, C. "Mwambutsa, Mwami de l'Urundi." *Revue Coloniale Belge* 115 (1950): 510-11.

Gorju, Mgr. *En Zigzags à Travres l'Urundi.* Namur: Missionaires d'Afrique (Pères Blancs), 1926.

Halewyck de Heusch, Michel. *Les Institutions Politiques et Administratives des Etats Africains soumis à l'Autorité de la Belgique.* Brussels: Bolyn, 1938.

Harroy, Jean-Paul. *Burundi: 1955-1962.* Brussels: Hayez, 1987.

d'Hertefelt, Marcel. "Le Ruanda et le Burundi vers l'Indépendence." *Archives Diplomatiques et Consulaires* 27, August-September (1962): 372-3.

Heyse, T. *Grandes Lignes du Régime des Terres au Congo Belge et au Ruanda-Urundi et Leurs Applications (1940-46)*. Brussels: Institut Royal Colonial Belge, 1947.

_____. *Congo Belge et Ruanda-Urundi: Notes de Droit Public et Commentaires de la Charte Coloniale*. 2 vols. Brussels: Van Campenhout, 1952-54.

"Les Institutions Féodales de l'Urundi." *Revue de l'Université de Bruxelles* 1 (1949): 101-12.

Jentgen, P. *Les Frontières du Ruanda-Urundi et le Régime Internationale de Tutelle*. Brussels: Académie Royale des Sciences d'Outre-Mer, 1957.

_____. "Ruanda-Urundi: The Mandate and International Trusteeship." *Geographical Review* 49, January (1959): 120-22.

Jesman, Czeslaw. "Ruanda-Urundi in Transition." *British Survey Main Services*, August (1961): 1-21.

Jewsiewicki, Bogumil. "The Formation of the Political Culture and Ethnicity in the Belgian Congo, 1920-1959." In *The Creation of Tribalism in Southern Africa*, edited by Leroy Vail. London: James Currey 1989.

Joye, P., and R. Lewin. *Les Trusts au Congo*. Brussels: Société Populaire d'Editions, 1961.

Lechat, Michel. *Le Burundi Politique*. Bujumbura: Service de l'Information du Ruanda-Urundi, 1961.

de Maire, Warzee G. "L'Acquisition de la Nationalité Belge au Ruanda-Urundi." *Journal de Tribunes d'Outre-Mer* 24 (1952): 75.

_____. "La Réforme de l'Organisation des Jurisdictions Indigènes du Ruanda-Urundi." *Journal de Tribunes d'Outre-Mer* 40 (1961): 141-2.

Malengreu, Guy. "Cassation: Incompétence pour les Décisions Rendues au Ruanda-Urundi." *Journal de Tribunes d'Outre-Mer* 31 (1953): 6-7.

Maquet, J. J. "Ruanda et Burundi Évolutions Divergeantes ou Parallèles?" *Afrique Contemporaine* 5, no. 25 (1960): 21-5.

_____. "Ruanda-Urundi: The Introduction of an Electoral System for Councils in a Caste Society." In

From Tribal Rule to Modern Government, edited by R. Apthorpe. Lusaka, 1960.

Maquet, J. J., and M. d'Hertefelt. *Élections en Société Féodale: Une Étude sur l'Introduction du Vote Populaire au Ruanda-Urundi*. Brussels: Académie Royale des Sciences Coloniales, 1959.

Maus, Albert. "Ruanda-Urundi: Terre d'Invasions." *Société Belge d'Etudes et Expansion* 178 (1957): 1023-27.

_____. "L'ONU au Ruanda-Urundi." *Eurafrica* 1-2 (1959): 12-14, 26-28.

_____. "Le Statut Politique du Ruanda-Urundi et la Situation des Bahutu." *Eurafrica* 3 (1959): 19.

Meyer, Roger. *Introduction au Congo Belge et au Ruanda-Urundi*. Brussels: Office of Publicity, 1955.

_____.*Introducing the Belgian Congo and Ruanda-Urundi*. Brussels: Office of Publicity, 1958.

Michiels, A., and N. Laude. *Congo Belge et Ruanda-Urundi*. Brussels: Universelle, 1958.

Moulaert, G. "La Conquête du Ruanda-Urundi." *Bulletin de l'Institut Royal Colonial Belge* (1935): 361-71.

Mungarulire, P. "Déplacement d'un Shebuja, Obligation de le Suivre." *Bulletin de Juridictions du Ruanda-Urundi* 1 (1946): 49-50.

Mworoha, Émile. *Peuples et Rois de l'Afrique des Lacs: Le Burundi et les Royaumes Voisins au XIXe Siècle*. Dakar: Les Nouvelles Editions Africaines, 1977.

_____. "La Cour du Roi Mwezi Gisabo (1852-1908) du Burundi à la fin du XIXe Siècle." *Études d'Histoire Africaine* 7 (1985): 39-58.

Neesen, V. "Le Premier Recensement par Échantillonnage au Ruanda-Urundi." *Zaire* 5 (1953): 469-88.

Neesen, V. "Quelques Donnés Démographiques sur la Population du Ruanda-Urundi." *Zaire* 7, no. 10 (1953): 1011-25.

Ntidendereza, Joseph. "Note à l'Occasion de la Visite du Groupe de Travail au Burundi." Mimeo, Kitega, 25 April 1959.

Orts, P. "Le Mandat de la Belgique sur le Ruanda-Urundi." *Bibliothèque Coloniale Internationale*. Proceedings,

The Hague Session (1927): 385-89.

_____. "Le Ruanda-Urundi Devant l'Organisation des Nations Unies." *Revue Coloniale Belge* 88 (1949): 333-56.

Papy, L. "Un Pays d'Afrique Centrale: Le Ruanda-Urundi d'Après le Travaux Récents." *Cahiers d'Outre-Mer* 24 (1953): 399-407.

Perraudin, J. "L'Oeuvre Civilisatrice de la Belgique au Ruanda-Urundi." *Grands Lacs* 121 (1949): 53-65.

Pétillon, L. "Le Ruanda-Urundi et le Conseil de Tutelle." *Revue Coloniale Belge* 106 (1950): 151-54.

Postiaux, H. "La Colonisation du Territoire du Ruanda-Urundi." *Les Cahiers Coloniaux de l'Institut Colonial de Marseilles*, nos. 551-2 (1929): 332.

Rousseau, R. "La Dernière Année de la Tutelle Belge au Rwanda-Burundi." *Vie Economique et Sociale* 33 (1962): 306-12.

Ryckmans, Pierre. "Le Probleme Politique au Ruanda-Urundi." *Congo* 1, no. 3 (1925): 407-13.

_____. "La Conquête Politique de l'Urundi." *Grands Lacs* (1936): 305.

_____. "Note sur les Institutions, Moeurs et Coutumes de l'Urundi." In *Rapport sur l'Administration Belge au Ruanda-Urundi*. Brussels Resident Report 1936, 34-58.

_____. "Le Ruanda-Urundi et l'ONU." *Revue Coloniale Belge* 76 (1948): 749-53.

_____. "Le Régime Juridique au Ruanda-Urundi." *Journal de Tribunes d'Outre-Mer* 59 (1955): 68-9.

Sandrart, George. "La Justice Indigène au Ruanda-Urundi." *Servir* 2 (1940): 26-8.

Sasserath, Jules S. *Le Ruanda-Urundi: Un Étrange Royaume Féodal au Coeur de l'Afrique.* Brussels: Germinal, 1948.

de Schlippe, P. *Vers un Progrès Social Planifié: Rapport d'une Mission au Ruanda-Urundi (20 Février-20 Mai 1957).* Usumbura: Vice-Gouvernement Général, 1958.

Sears, Mason. Trust Territory of Ruanda-Urundi. *U.S. Department of State Bulletin* 41, 3 August (1959): 180-81.

Sendanyoye, George. "Un Jugement Rendu dans une Colonie Voisine peut-il être Exécutoire au Ruanda-Urundi." *Bulletin de Juridictions du Ruanda-Urundi* 9 (1950): 476-8.

Simon, M. "L'Oeuvre Civilisatrice de la Belgique au Ruanda-Urundi." *Revue Coloniale Belge* 8 (1946): 9-11.

"Situation Actuelle dans le Ruanda-Urundi." *Congo* 1 (1929): 819-23.

Slade, Ruth. *King Leopold's Congo*. London: Oxford University Press, 1962.

Taquet, J. "Deux Questions Intéressant la Location des Terres Domaniales dans le Ruanda-Urundi." *Revue Juridique du Congo Belge*, October (1934): 192-8.

United Nations Report on Ruanda-Urundi. Trusteeship Council 26th Session, Supplement No. 3, Document T/1551. 14 April to 30 June 1960.

Vallotton, H. *Voyage au Congo Belge et au Ruanda-Urundi*. Brussels: Weissenbruch, 1955.

Van Bilsen, A. A. J. *Vers l'Independance du Congo et du Ruanda-Urundi*. Kinshasa: Presses Universitaires du Zaire, 1977.

Van der Kerken, Georges. "L'Evolution de la Politique Indigène au Congo Belge et au Ruanda-Urundi." *Revue de l'Institut de Sociologie* 1 (1953): 25-62.

Van der Linden. "La 'Palabre' du Ruanda-Urundi." *Revue Coloniale Belge* 70 (1948): 566-67.

Van der Stickelen, A. "Régime Juridique au Ruanda-Urundi." *Journal de Tribunes d'Outre-Mer* 57 (1955): 33-4.

Van Grieken-Taverniers, Madeleine. *La Colonisation Belge en Afrique Centrale: Guide des Archives Africaines du Ministere des Affaires Africaines, 1885-1962*. Brussels: Ministere des Affaires Etrangeres, du Commerce Exterieur et de la Cooperation au Developpement, 1981.

Vanhove, J. *Histoire du Ministère des Colonies.* Brussels: Académie Royale des Sciences d'Outre-Mer, 1968.

Vansina, Jan. "Notes sur l'Histoire du Burundi." *Aequatoria* 1 (1961): 1-10.

Verstappen, R. "Note sur les Dommages-Intérêts en Matière Répressive (Territoire de Ngoze, Urundi)." *Bulletin de Juridictions Indigène et du Droit Coutumier Congolais* 1 (1935-1936): 16-17.

5. Postcolonial History

Anjo, J. "L'Affaire Ngendendumwe." *Remarques Africaines* 306 (1968): 46-7.

Aupens, Bernard. "Burundi: Le Massacre Érigé en Politique." *Revue Française d'Etudes Politiques Africaines* 78 (1972): 7-11.

_____. "L'Engrenage de la Violence au Burundi." *Revue Française d'Études Politiques Africaines* 9 (July 1973): 48-69.

Bacamurwanko, J. "Burundi: Which Way Out?" Unpublished ms., Washington, D. C., 1994.

_____. "Crisis in Burundi: The Agony of the Text." Unpublished ms., Washington, D. C., 1994.

Batungwanayo, Charles. "Burundi, le Pourquoi d'un Génocide." *Remarques Africaines* 407 (1972): 19-21.

Batururimi, Elias." Ou Va le Pays?" *Remarques Africaines* 7, no. 252 (1965): 5-7.

_____. "Le Pari du Mwami Mwambutsa IV." *Remarques Africaines* 7, no. 247 (1965): 3-5.

Bernard, René. "The Constitutional Crisis in Burundi." *The Nationalist* (Dar es Salaam), 17 August 1966.

Bertenel, Paul. "Burundi: Pourquoi." *Jeune Afrique* 597 (1972): 18.

Bimazubute, Gilles. "L'Uprona: Du Parti Indépendantiste au Parti-État." *Le Réveil*, 7-13 June 1991.

Boyer, Allison. "Unity at Last?" *Africa Report*, March/April 1992 37-40.

Brooke, James. "In Burundi Minority Persists in Control of Nation." *New York Times*, 5 June 1987.

Buname, Emmanuel. "Burundi: Régime d'Opression." *Journal du Centre International des Etudiants Etrangers de Louvain* 4 (1971): 28-9.

"Le Burundi." *Bulletin d'Information de la Coopération au Dévéloppement* 11 (1966): 29-36.

"Le Burundi à la Recherche d'une Stabilité." *Présence Africaine* 47 (1963): 235.

"Burundi at Close Range." *Africa Report* (March 1965): 19-24.

"Burundi: Génocide ou Massacre?" *Jeune Afrique* 596 (1972): 16-17.

"Burundi: No End in Sight." *Africa Confidential* 13, no. 12 (1972): 1-2.

"Burundi: Sursis pour les Tutsis." *Jeune Afrique* 256 (1965): 24-25.

"Burundi: Time for International Action to End a Cycle of Mass Murder." *Amnesty International Bulletin*, 1994.

Cart, Henri-Philippe. "Conceptions des Rapports Politiques au Burundi." *Etudes Congolaises* 9 (1966): 1-22.

Celis, Georges. *La Philatelie de Transition: Du Congo Belge au Congo, du Ruanda-Urundi au Rwanda et au Burundi*. Brussels: G. Celis, 1983.

Ceulemans, Jacques. "Burundi: La Gestion Doulereuse de l'Indépendance." *Remarques Africaines* 8, no. 275 (1966): 520-22.

Chrétien, Jean-Pierre, and André Guichaoua. "Burundi, d'une République à l'Autre: Bilan et Enjeux." *Politique Africaine* 29 (1988): 87-100.

Christiansen, Hanne. *Refugees and Pioneers: History and Field Study of a Burundian Settlement in Tanzania*. Geneva: United Nations Research Institute for Social Development, 1985.

"Le Climat Politique au Burundi: L'Affaire Ngendendumwe." *Remarques Africaines* 8, no. 265 (1966): 221-26.

Coalition for Peace and Justice in Burundi. Response to Ambassador Bacamurwanko's Document "Burundi: Which Way Out, Perspective of the Crisis," 1994.

_____. Newsletter 1, no. 1, 1994.

Crucifix, L. *Résumé du Cours Pratique sur la Fonction Publique*. Bujumbura: Ecole Nationale d'Administration, 1967.

Dejemeppe, B. *Le Naufrage au Burundi*. Louvain: Ligue Belge pour la Défense des Droits de l'Homme, 1972.

Forscher, Romain. "Les Massacres au Burundi." *Esprit*, July-August (1972): 123-31.

Gahungu, Pierre. "Ou va le Royaume du Burundi?" *Remarques Africaines* 7, no. 248 (1965): 8-9.

Greenland, Jeremy. "Black Racism in Burundi." *New Blackfriars*, October 1973: 443-51.

Halberstam, D. "Rwanda and Burundi become Independent African States." *The New York Times*, 1 July 1962.

Hammer, Joshua. "Fears of Another Rwanda." *Newsweek*. 10 April 1995: 38-39.

Howe, Marvine. "Slaughter in Burundi." *New York Times*, 11 June 1972.

Hoyt, Michael. "Messages Concerning the Burundi Massacres to and from the American Embassy in Bujumbura." Melvill Herskovits Library, Northwestern University, Evanston 1972.

Hutu Students of Burundi. "Manifeste des Étudiants du Burundi." mimeo, 1969.

International Commission of Jurists Bulletin. "A Political Trial in Burundi." 16 (1963): 15.

International Commission of Jurists. "Events in Burundi." Press release, 1966.

International Labor Organization. "Les Violations de la Liberté Syndicale et des Droits de l'Homme au Burundi." Press release, 1966.

Kay, Reginald. *Burundi since the Genocide*. London: Minority Rights Group, 1987.

Kidwingira, Bonaventure. "Le Vrai Visage de l'UNEBA." *Remarques Africaines* 9, no. 285 (1967): 121-24.

Kiraranganiya, Boniface. *La Vérité sur le Burundi*. Sherbrooke, Canada: Editions Naaman, 1985.

Latham-Koening, A.L. "Ruanda-Urundi on the Threshold of Independence." *World Today* 18 (July 1962): 288-95.

Lemarchand, René. Social and Political Changes in Burundi. In *Five African States: Responses to Diversity*, edited by G. Carter. Ithaca: Cornell University Press, 1963.

_____. "Political Instability in Africa: The Case of Rwanda and Burundi." *Civilisations* 16 (1966): 1-29.

_____. "Social Change and Political Modernisation in Burundi." *The Journal of Modern African Studies* 4, no. 4 (1966): 14-24.

_____. "The Passing of Mwamiship in Burundi." *Africa Report*, January 1967: 14-24.

_____. *Selective Genocide in Burundi*. London: Minority Rights Group, 1973.

_____. "The Military in Former Belgian Africa." In *Political-Military Systems: Comparative Perspectives*, edited by C. M. Kelleher. Beverly Hills: Sage Publications 1974.

_____. "The Killing Fields Revisited." *Issue* 18, no. 1 (1989): 22-8.

_____. "Burundi: Ethnicity and the Genocidal State." In *State Violence and Ethnicity*, edited by Pierre van den Berghe. Niwot: University Press of Colorado, 1990.

_____. "Genocide au Burundi." *Le Monde*, 3-4 October 1992: 2.

_____. *Burundi: Ethnocide as Discourse and Practice*. New York: Woodrow Wilson Center Press, 1994.

_____. "Managing Transition Anarchies: Rwanda, Burundi, and South Africa in Comparative Perspective." *The Journal of Modern African Studies* 32, no. 4 (1994): 581-604.

Mabushi, C. "Le Succession Testamentaire en Droit Coutumier Burundais." *Revue Juridique et Politique* 26, no. 4 (1972): 625-36.

Madirisha, Juvénal. "Le Burundi, ses Leaders et l'UNEBA." *Remarques Africaines* 8, no. 277 (1966): 562-64.

_____. "L'UNEBA Devient une Milice Républicaine." *Remarques Africaines* 9, no. 290 (1967): 272-75.

"Manifeste des Étudiants Barundi en Belgique." *Remarques Africaines* 8, no. 261 (1966): 119-26.

Manirakiza, Marc. *La Fin de la Monarchie Burundaise, 1962-1966.* Brussels: Le Mat de Misaine, 1990.

_____. *Burundi: De la Révolution au Régionalisme, 1966-1976.* Brussels: Le Mat de Misaine, 1992.

Martin, David, and Réné Lemarchand. *Selective Genocide in Burundi.* London: Minority Rights Group, 1974.

Melady, Thomas Patrick. *Burundi: The Tragic Years.* Maryknoll: Orbis, 1974.

Morris, Roger et al. *Passing By: The United States and the Genocide in Burundi, 1972.* Washington, D. C.: Carnegie Endowment for International Peace, 1973.

Mpozagara, Gabriel. *La République du Burundi.* Paris: Éditions Berger-Levrault, 1971.

Munene, Mbenga. "Burundi: L'Oeuvre des Mercenaires." *Remarques Africaines* 419 (1973): 6.

Ncutinamagara, A. "La Responsabilité de l'État du Fait des Magistrats en Droit Burundais." *Revue Juridique et Politique* 27, no. 4 (1973): 831-38.

Ndabakwaje, Libère. "L'Histoire de l'UNEBA." *Remarques Congolaises et Africaines* 6, no. 8 (1964): 184-88.

Ndaje.* "L'Impérialisme, la Féodalité et la Persécution du Peuple au Burundi." *Remarques Africaines* 8, no. 268 (1966): 324-26. *Ndaje is a pseudonym for Hutu students of Burundi.

_____. "Le Masque de l'UNEBA." *Remarques Africaines* 8, no. 276 (1966): 551-54.

Nelan, Bruce. "A Recurring Nightmare." *Time.* 10 April 1995: 50-51.

Newbury, David. "Burundi without Peasants." *Journal of African History* 31, no. 3 (1990): 509-10.

Ngabissio, N. N. "Burundi Pourquoi?" *Jeune Afrique*, 17 June 1972: 18-20.

Nicayenzi, Zénon. "Note des Éveques sur le Danger qui Menace le Burundi." *Remarques Congolaises et Africaines* 6, no. 20 (1964): 470-72.

Niqueaux, Jacques. "Le Burundi à l'Épreuve." *Revue Nouvelle* 43, no. 2 (1966): 176-81.

_____. "Rwanda et Burundi, les Frères Ennemis aux Sources du Nil." *Revue Nouvelle* 43, no. 5 (1966): 466-81.

"Nouveaux Témoignages sur le Burundi." *Remarques Africaines* 15, nos. 430-31 (1973): 34.

Nsanze, Térence. "Burundi: Tableau Authentique des Faits et Événements Récents." *Remarques Africaines* 8, no. 268 (1966): 321-23.

_____. *L'Edification de la République du Burundi au Carrefour de l'Afrique.* Brussels: Remarques Africaines, 1970.

Nyangoma, Gervais. Letter to the editor. *The Reporter*, 9 April 1964: 8-9.

Nzeyimana, Laurent. "Burundi: Aux Nouveaux Hommes, au Nouveau Régime, de Nouvelles Institutions." *Remarques Africaines* 9, no. 283 (1967): 61-5.

Nzisabira, Benoit. "Le Multipartisme et la Politique de l'Unité Nationale au Burundi." *Le Réveil* June 1991: 31-38.

Nzohabanayo, C. "La Possession d'État de National au Burundi." *Revue Juridique et Politique* 25, no. 4 (1971): 445-70.

"Out of Africa: Burundi." *Africa Report* (June 1962): 8-9.

Pabenel, Jean-Pierre. "Statistiques Tribales au Burundi en 1986. *Politique Africaine* 32 (1988): 111-16.

Pereira, C. C. "Décentralisation et Développement National au Burundi." *Bulletin de l'Institut International d'Administration Publique* 21 (1972): 55-62.

Perlez, Jane. "The Bloody Hills of Burundi." *New York Times Magazine*, 6 November 1988, section 6: 90, 92-3, 98-9, 125.

"A Political Trial in Burundi." *Bulletin of the International Commission of Jurists* (July 1963): 5-15.

Ragoen, J. "Il n'y Aura pas de Printemps Burundais." *Zaire* 24 (15 May 1972): 8.

_____. "Rébellion au Burundi." *Zaire* 24, (29 May 1972): 26-9.

Republique du Burundi: IIe Republique Respect des Engagements. Bujumbura: Ministere de L'information, 1984.

Rodegem, F. M. "Burundi: La Face Cachée de la Rébellion." *Intermédiare* 4 (1973): 15-19.

Sabimbona, Simon. "Une République Révolutionnaire?" *Remarques Africaines* 9, no. 285 (1967): 127-29.

Sebiva, Gatti. "Burundi: Détente entre le Parlement et le Gouvernement." *Etudes Congolaises* 8, October (1963): 42-44.

Semahuna, Charles. "Aux Aveugles du Burundi." *Remarques Congolaises et Africaines* 6, no. 21 (1964): 498-99.

_____. "Communiqué de la Fédération des Travailleurs du Burundi." *Remarques Congolaises et Africaaines* 6, no. 10 (1964): 20-21.

Sharlet, Jeff. "Burundi Bleeds." *The Nation*. 24 January 1994: 41.

Sohier, J. P. "Le Prince Charles a mis en Question le Principe même de la Monarchie." *Le Monde*, 2 August 1966.

Soulik, S. "Interview du Colonel Michel Micombero." *Remarques Africaines* 305 (1968): 6-9.

Staub, Irvin. *The Roots of Evil: The Origins of Genocide and Other Group Violence*. Cambridge: Cambridge University Press, 1989.

Tannenwald, Paul. "Burundi: Le Prix de l'Ordre." *Revue Française d'Etudes Politiques Africaines* 58 (1970): 69-87.

Ugeux, E. Xavier. "Génocide au Burundi." *Remarques Africaines* 400 (1971): 3-6; 401 (1972): 11-12.

_____. "Parodie Judiciare au Burundi." *Remarques Africaines* 393 (1972): 9-10.

_____. "Après Sept ans de République: Le Bilan d'une Tragèdie." *Remarques Africaines* 429 (1973): 14-16.

Ugeux, E. Xavier and J. Wolf. "Une Interview Exclusive de Mwambutsa IV, Ancien Roi du Burundi." *Remarques Africaines* 403 (1973): 8-11.

_____. "Le Burundi veut Condamner Notre Directeur." *Remarques Africaines* 429 (1973): 12-14.

"The United Nations Findings on Rwanda and Burundi." *Africa Report* 9, no. 4 (1964): 7-8.

United States Senate House Committee on Foreign Affairs, Subcommittee on Human Rights and International Organizations. "Recent Violence in Burundi: What should be the U. S. Response?" 1988.

UPRONA. "Compte-rendu de la Conférence au Sommet de Kitéga du 8 Septembre au 6 Octobre." Bujumbura, 1964. Mimeographed.

Watson, Catharine. "After the Massacre." *Africa Report* January/February (1989): 51-55

_____. "Burundi." *Africa Report* September/ October (1993): 58-61.

_____. "Death of Democracy." *Africa Report*, January/February (1994): 26-31.

Webster, John.*The Constitutions of Burundi, Malagasy, and Rwanda*. Syracuse: Syracuse University Maxwell Graduate School of Public Affairs, 1964.

_____. *The Political Development of Rwanda and Burundi.* Syracuse: Syracuse University Program of Eastern African Studies, 1966.

Weinstein, Warren. "Burundi: Racial Peace and Royalty." *Africa Today* 12, no. 6 (1965): 12-15.

_____. "Burundi: Political and Ethnic Powderkeg." *Africa Report* November (1970): 18-20.

_____. "Conflict and Confrontation in Central Africa: The Revolt in Burundi, 1972." *Africa Today* 19, no. 4 (1972): 17-37.

_____. "Rwanda and Burundi: Enemy Brothers Coming Together." *Pan African Journal* 5, no. 1 (1972): 39-44.

_____. "Tensions in Burundi." *Issue* 2, no. 4 (1972): 27-9.

_____. "Ethnicity and Conflict Regulation: The 1972 Burundi Revolt." *Afrika Spectrum* 9, no. 1 (1974): 42-9.

_____. "Rwanda-Burundi: An Aborted Putative Nation." In *Divided Nations in a Divided World*, edited by J. Stoessinger, N. Lebow et al. New York: McKay, 1974.

_____. "Burundi: Alternatives to Violence." *Issue* 5, no. 2 (1975): 17-22.

_____. "Humanitarian Aid and Civil Strife: Politics vs. Relief in Burundi." In *Civil Wars and the Politics of International Relief*, edited by Morris Davis. New York: Praeger, 1975.

_____. "Human Rights in Jeopardy: Burundi and Uganda." *Africa Today* 22, no. 1 (1975): 75-80.

Williams, Roger. "Slaughter in Burundi." *World*, 21 November 1972: 20-24.

Wingert, Norman. *No Place to Stop Killing.* Chicago: Moody Press, 1974.

Wolf, J. "Le Destin Tragique du Roi Ntare V." *Remarques Africaines* 400 (1972): 7-8.

Zarembo, Alan. "Standing on the Brink." *Africa Report*, March/April (1995): 24-29.

Ziégler, Jean. "Un Royaume en Crise: Le Burundi." *Le Monde*, 19 November 1965.

6. Economics and Development

Aerts, L. *L'Évolution Économique du Ruanda-Urundi de 1949 à 1955.* Usumbura: Vice-Gouvernement Général, 1957.

Bell, Philip W., ed. *African Economic Problems: a Collection of Published and Unpublished Works.* Kampala: Makaere University College, 1964.

Blakey, K. A. *Economic Development of Burundi.* Cairo: Institute of National Planning, 1964.

Botte, Roger. "Qui Mangeait Quoi? L'Alimentation au Burundi à la fin du Xixième Siècle." *Cultures et Développement* 15, no. 3 (1983): 455-69.

Chrétien, Jean-Pierre. "La Fermeture du Burundi et du Rwanda aux Commerçants de l'Extérieur (1905-1906)." *Entreprises et Entrepreneurs en Afrique, XIXe-XXe Siècles* 2 (1983): 25-47.

Cierfayt, Albert. *Le Développement Énergetique du Congo Belge et du Ruanda-Urundi*. Brussels: Académie Royale des Sciences d'Outre-Mer, 1960.

Declerk, L. "Note sur le Droit Foncier Coutumier au Burundi." *Revue Juridique du Rwanda et du Burundi* 1 (1965): 38-42.

Durant, A. "Structure Économique du Ruanda-Urundi." *Bulletin de la Chambre de Commerce du Ruanda-Urundi*, 2nd trimestre (1957): 13-18.

Heyse, T. *Bibliographie des Problèmes Fonciers et du Régime des Terres: Afrique, Congo Belge, Ruanda-Urundi*. Brussels: Centre de Documentation Economique et Sociale, 1960.

International Labor Organization. "Rapport au Gouvernement de la Republique du Burundi sur l'Administration du Travail." Geveva: International Labor Organization 1970.

Jaspar, H. "Le Ruanda-Urundi: Pays à Disettes Périodiques." *Congo* 2 (1929): 1-21.

Kayitare, Tharcisse. "Congo-Rwanda-Burundi: Un Nouvel Ensemble Économique en Gestation." *Remarques Africaines* 355 (1970): 151-52.

Lefebvre, Jacques. *Structures Économiques du Congo Belge et du Ruanda-Urundi*. Brussels: Treuvenberg, 1955.

Mottoule, L. "Equilibre de l'Alimentation chez l'Indigène du Congo Belge et du Ruanda-Urundi." *Servir* 1-2 (1945): 25-32, 77-81.

Neesen, V. "Aspects de l'Économie Démographique du Ruanda-Urundi." *Bulletin de l'Institut de Recherches Économiques et Sociales de l'Université de Louvain* 22, no. 5 (1956): 473-504.

Nicayenzi, Zénon. "Le Dévéloppement Économique: Processes Continu ou Discontinu: Le Cas du Burundi." *Synthèses* (Kinshasa) no. 5 (1970): 69-80.

Purnode, J. "L'Intervention des Banques dans le Financement de la Récolte et de la Valorisation du Café au Burundi." *Revue de l'Université Officielle de Bujumbura* 1, no. 2 (1967): 79-84.

"Régime des Investissements au Burundi." *Industries et Travaux d'Outre-Mer* (November 1969): 957-8.

Robatel, J. P. "La Condition Ouvrière à Bujumbura." *Cultures et Dévéloppement* 2, no. 2 (1970): 427-34.

Steward, C. C., and D. Crummey. *Modes of Production in Precolonial Africa.* Beverly Hills: Sage, 1981.

Trouwborst, Albert. "L'Organisation Politique en Tant que Système d'Échange au Burundi." *Anthropologica* 3, no. 1 (1961): 1-17.

_____. "L'Accord de Clientèle et Organisatoin Politique au Burundi." *Anthropologica* 4 (1962): 9-43.

Van Asbroek, J. J. "La Structure Démographique et l'Évolution Économique du Ruanda-Urundi." *Bulletin de la Société Royale Belge de Géographie*, no. 4 (1956): 15-32.

Van de Walle, E. "Chômage dans un de Petite Ville d'Afrique: Usumbura." *Zaire* 14 (1960): 341-59.

_____. "Facteurs et Indices de Stabilisation et d'Urbanisation à Usumbura." *Recherches Economiques de Louvain* 27, no. 2 (1961): 97-121.

Van Tichelen, H.E. "Problèmes du Développement Économique du Ruanda-Urundi." *Zaire* 11 (1957): 451-74.

Wagner, Michele D. "Trade and Commercial Attitudes in Burundi before the Nineteenth Century." *International Journal of African Historical Studies* 26, no. 1 (1993).

7. Linguistics

Albert, Ethel M. "Rhetoric, Logic, and Poetics in Burundi: Cultural Patterning of Speech Behavior." *American Anthropologist* 66, no. 6 (1964).

_____. "Cultural Patterning of Speech Behavior in Burundi." In *Directions in Sociolinguistics*, edited by Gumperz, John and D. Hymes. New York: Holt, Rinehart & Winston, 1972.

Alexandre, P. *Langues et Langage en Afrique Noire.* Paris: Payot, 1970.

Bagein, E. *Petite Grammaire Kirundi.* Bujumbura: Presses Lavigerie, 1951.

Barakana, Gabriel. "L'unification des Langues au Ruanda-Urundi." *Civilisations* 2, no. 1 (1952): 67-78.

Bigangara, Jean-Baptiste. *Elements de Linguistique Burundaise.* Bujumbura: Ministry of Youth, Sports and Culture, 1982.

Bonneau, H. *Dictionnaire Français-Kirundi et Kirundi-Français.* Bujumbura: Presses Lavigeries, 1950.

Bonvini, E., and P. Durant. "L'Enregistrement Sonore dans l'Enquête Linguistique." *Afrique et Langage* 1 (1974): 21-34.

Coupez, André. "Langues Secrètes au Ruanda-Urundi." *Folia Scientifica Africae Centralis* 4, no. 3 (1958): 69.

Coupez, André, and A. E. Meeussen. "Notation Pratique de la Quantité Vocalique et de la Tonalité en Rundi et Rwanda."*Orbis* (Louvain) 10, no. 2 (1962): 428-33.

Eggers, Ellen K. "Temporal Anaphora in Discourse." Ph.D. dissertation, University of Washington, 1990.

Farb, Peter. *Word Play.* New York: Bantam, 1974.

Greenberg, J. H. "Africa as a Linguistic Area." In *Continuity and Change in African Culture,* edited by W. Bascom and M. Herskovits. Chicago: University of Chicago Press, 1959.

_____. "Linguistic Evidence Regarding Bantu." *Journal of African History* 2 (1962): 189-216.

_____. "Linguistics." In *The African World: A Survey of Social Research*, edited by R. A. Lystad. New York: Praeger, 1965.

Gumperz, John, and D. Hymes, eds. *Directions in Sociolinguistics.* New York: Holt, Rinehart & Winston, 1972.

Guthrie, Malcolm. *The Classification of the Bantu Languages.* London: Oxford University Press, 1948.

_____. "Some Developments in the Pre-history of Bantu Languages." *Journal of African History* 2 (1962): 273-82.

Homberger, L. "Les Langues Bantou." In *Les Langues du Monde*, edited by M. Meillet. Paris: Ed. Champion, 1924.

_____. *Les Langues Négro-Africaines et les Peuples qui les Parlent.* Paris: Payot, 1941.

Kimenyi, Alexandre. *Kinyarwanda and Kirundi Names: A Semiolinguistic Analysis of Bantu Onamastics.* Lewiston, N.Y.: E. Mellen Press, 1988.

Kirundi Basic Course. Washington, D. C.: Foreign Service Institute.

Meeussen, A. E. *Notes de Grammaire Rundi.* Tervuren: Musée Royal du Congo Belge, 1952.

_____. *Essai de Grammaire Rundi.* Tervuren: Musée Royal du Congo Belge, 1959.

Menard, F. *Grammaire Kirundi.* Algiers: Maison-Carrée, 1908.

_____. *Dictionnaire Français-Kirundi, Kirundi-Français.* Roulers: De Meester, 1909.

_____. *Guide de Conversation Kirundi.* Algiers: Maison-Carrée, 1910.

Migeod, Frederick W. H. *The Languages of West Africa.* 2 vols. London: Kegan Paul, 1911-1913.

Mioni, A. *Problèmes de Linguistique d'Orthographe et de Coordination Culturelle au Burundi.* Naples: Instituto Universario Orientale, 1970.

Mvuyekure, Augustin. "Ijambo ou le Discours au Burundi." *Que Vous en Semble?* 4, nos. 14-15 (1971): 75-97.

Ntahokaja, J. B. "Le Kirundi: Instrument de Développement Politique, Économique et Culturel." *African Languages* 5, no. 2 (1979): 87-94.

_____. "La Litérature Orale du Burundi." *Etudes Scientifiques* March (1979): 19-28.

Phillipson, D.W. "Archaeology and Bantu Linguistics." *World Archaeology* 8, no. 1 (1976): 65-82.

_____. "The Spread of the Bantu Language." *Scientific American* 256, no. 236 (1977): 106-116.

Rodegem, F. M. *Essai de Dictionnaire Explicatif Rundi.* Bujumbura: Les Presses Lavigerie, 1961.

_____. *Précis de Grammaire Rundi.* Brussels: E. Story-Scientia, 1967.

_____. *Dictionnaire Rundi-Français.* Tervuren: Annales du Musée Royal de l'Afrique Centrale, 1970.

_____. "Le Poker Verbal: Réflexions sur un Colloque." *Cultures et Dévéloppement* 7, no. 2 (1975): 369-97.

Van Bulck, G. *Mission Linguistique, 1949-1951*. Brussels: Institut Royal Colonial Belge, 1954.

8. Literature, Music, and Visual Arts

Belinga, M.S. Eno. *Littérature et Musique Populaires en Afrique Noire*. Paris: Association pour la Coopération Franco-Africaine, 1965.

Boone, Olga. *Les Tambours du Congo Belge et du Ruanda-Urundi*. Tervuren: Musée Royal du Congo Belge, 1951.

Boyayo, A. "Importance de la Poésie Guerrière Rundi dans la Reconstitution de l'Histoire Nationale." *Revue Nationale d'Éducation du Burundi* 3, no. 5 (1966): 4-8.

Bozzini, G. et. al. *Proverbi Rundi*. Milan: Pime, 1980.

Carrington, J. F. *Talking Drums of Africa*. London: Carey Kingsgate Press, 1949.

Chrétien, Jean-Pierre. "Des Légendes Africaines Face à des Mythes Européens." *Cultures et Développement* 3 (1974): 579-87.

Chrysostome, Sœur Jean. "Fabrication de Poterie en Urundi." *Trait d'Union* 21, nos. 3-4 (1953): 15-18.

Collaer, P." Notes sur la Musique d'Afrique Centrale." *Problèmes d'Afrique Centrale*, no. 26 (1964): 267-71.

Curtis-Burlin, N. *Songs and Tales from the Dark Continent*. New York: Schirmer, 1920.

Dechaume, P. "Proverbes de l'Urundi." *Grands Lacs*, no. 78 (1940): 36-7.

Ehret, Christopher. "Cattle-keeping and Milking in Eastern and Southern African History: The Linguistic Evidence." *Journal of African History* 8, no. 1(1967): 1-17.

Finnegan, Ruth. *Oral Literature in Africa*. Oxford: Oxford University Press, 1970.

Gérard, Albert S. *African Language Literatures*. Washington, D.C.: Three Continents Press, 1981.

de Heusch, Luc. *Le Roi Ivre ou l'Origine de l'Etat: Mythes et Rites Bantous*. Paris: Gallimard, 1972.

Jadot, J. M. "Les Arts Populaires au Congo Belge, au Ruanda et dans l'Urundi." *Zaire* 2 (1950): 181-88.

_____. *Les Écrivains Africains du Congo Belge et du Ruanda-Urundi*. Brussels: Académie Royale des Sciences d'Outre-Mer, 1959.

Lord, A.B. *The Singer of Tales*. Cambridge: Harvard University Press, 1964.

Louipas, P. "Tradition et Légende des Batutsi sur la Création du Monde et Leur Établissement au Ruanda." *Anthropos* 3 (1908): 1-13.

MacGaffey, W. "Oral Tradition in Central Africa." *International Journal of African Historical Studies* 7, no. 3 (1975): 417-26.

Makarkiza, André. *La Dialectique des Barundi*. Brussels: Académie Royale des Sciences Coloniales, 1959.

Merriam, Alan P. "Les Styles Vocaux dans la Musique du Ruanda-Urundi." *Jeune Afrique* 7 (1953): 16.

_____. "Music and the Dance." In *The African World: A Survey of Social Research*, edited by R. A. Lystad. New York: Praeger, 1965.

Ndoricimpa, L., and C. Guillet. *L'Arbre-Mémoire: Traditions Orales du Burundi*. Bujumbura: Centre de Civilisation Burundaise, 1984.

Nsuka, Y. M. "Littératures Traditionnelles au Congo-Kinshasa, au Rwanda et au Burundi: Bibliographie Commentée." *Cahiers Congolais* 14, no. 2 (1970): 87-153.

Ntahokaja, J. B. "La Musique des Barundi." *Grand Lacs*, nos. 4-6 (1948-49): 45-9.

_____. "Proverbes et Sentences." *Grand Lacs*, nos. 4-6 (1948-49): 36-8.

Otten, Rik, and Victor Bachy. *Le Cinema dans les Pays des Grands Lacs: Zaire, Rwanda, Burundi*. Paris: L'Harmattan, 1984.

Parrinder, Geoffrey. *African Mythology*. London: Paul Hamlyn, 1967.

Propp, V. "Morphology of the Folktale." *International Journal of American Linguistics: Bulletin*, no. 24 (1958): 4.

Ramirez, Francis, and Christian Rolot. *Histoire du Cinema Colonial au Zaire, au Rwanda et au Burundi.* Tervuren: Musée Royal de l'Afrique Centrale, 1985.

Risselin, J. P. "La Chanson Savante chez les Watousis." *Jeune Afrique* no. 6 (1949): 24-5.

Rodegem, F. M. "Le Style Oral au Burundi: Interview d'un Troubadour aux Sources du Nil." *Congo-Tervuren* 6 (1960): 119-27.

_____. *Sagesse Kirundi.* Tervuren: Musée Royal de l'Afrique Centrale, 1961.

_____. "Syntagmes complétifs Spéciaux en Rundi." *Annales du Musée Royal de l'Afrique Centrale* 68 (1970): 181-207.

_____. *Anthologie Rundi.* Paris: A. Colin, 1973.

_____. "Une Forme d'Humour Contestataire au Burundi: Les Wellérismes." *Cahiers d'Etudes Africaines* 14, no. 3 (1974): 521-42.

_____. *Paroles de Sagesse au Burundi.* Leuven: Peeters, 1983.

Sartiaux, P. "Aspects Traditionnels de la Musique au Ruanda-Urundi." *Jeune Afrique* 21 (1954): 19-26.

Soyinka, W. *Myth, Literature, and the African World.* London: Cambridge University Press, 1976.

Vansina, Jan. *De la Tradition Orale: Essai de Methode Historique.* Tervueren: Musée Royal de l'Afrique Centrale, 1961.

_____, ed. *Les Anciens Royaumes de la Zone Interlacustre Méridionale: Rwanda, Burundi, Buha.* Tervueren: Musée Royal de l'Afrique Centrale, 1962.

_____. *Oral Tradition: A Study in Historical Methodology.* Chicago: Aldine, 1965.

_____. *La Légende du Passé.* Tervuren: Musée Royal de l'Afrique Centrale, 1972.

Werner, Alice. *Myths and Legends of the Bantu.* London: Cass and Company, 1933.

Zuure, Bernard. "Poésies chez les Barundi." *Africa* 5, no. 3 (1932): 344-54.

9. Society

Albert, Ethel M."Socio-Political Organization and Reciptivity to Change: Some Differences between Ruanda and Urundi." *Southwestern Journal of Anthropology* 16 (1960): 46-74.

_____. "A Study of Values in Urundi."*Cahiers d'Etudes Africaines* 2 (1960): 148-60.

_____. "Women of Burundi: a Study of Social Values." In*Women of Tropical Africa*, edited by Denise Paulme. Berkeley: University of California Press, 1960.

Amselle, Jean-Loup, and Elikia M'bokolo, eds. *Au Cœur de l'Ethnie*. Paris: Decouverte, 1985.

Anastase, Frère. "Le Nom et ses Implications dans la Culture Bantoue." *Servir* 22, no. 4 (1961): 129-135.

Arnoux, A. "Quelques Notes sur les Enfants au Ruanda et à l'Urundi." *Anthropos* 26 (1918): 341-51.

Aupens, Bernard. "La Culture Française au Burundi: Analyse Historique et Sociologique." *Culture Française* 2 (1967): 9-18.

Baeck, L. "Quelques Aspects Sociaux de l'Urbanisation au Ruanda-Urundi." *Zaire* 10 (1956): 115-45.

Bahenduzi, Michel. "Les Stéréotypes Idéologiques de la Description de l'Ancien Burundi." *Culture et Société, Revue de Civilisation Burundaise*. Vol. 4. Bujumbura: Ministère de la Jeunesse, des Sports et de la Culture, 1981.

Barth, F. *Ethnic Groups and Boundaries: The Social Organization of Culture Difference*. London: Allen & Unwin, 1969.

Bauman, H., and F. Westermann. *Les Peuples et les Civilisations de l'Afrique: Les Langues et l'Éducation*. Paris: Payot, 1948.

Bay, Edna, and Nancy Hafkin, eds.*Women in Africa: Studies in Social and Economic Change*. Stanford: Stanford University Press, 1976.

Beattie, John. *Other Cultures: Aims, Methods, and Achievements in Social Anthropology*. New York: Free Press of Glencoe, 1964.

Bishop, W.W., and J.D. Clark, eds. *Background to Evolution in Africa*. Chicago: University of Chicago Press, 1967.

Blankoff-Scarr, Goldie, trans. *Ruanda-Urundi: Social Achievements*. Brussels: Belgian Congo and Ruanda-Urundi Information and Public Relations Office, 1960.

Boone, Olga. "Carte Ethnique du Congo Belge et du Ruanda-Urundi." *Zaire* 8 (1954): 451-66.

Bourgeois, R. "Rituel du Marriage coutumier au Ruanda-Urundi." *Bulletin de Juridictions Indigène et du Droit Coutumier Congolais*, no. 6 (1955): 133-46.

_____. *L'Évolution du Contrat de Bail à Cheptel au Ruanda-Urundi*. Brussels: Académie Royale des Sciences d'Outre-Mer, 1958.

Boyayo, A. "La Polygamie en Droit Coutumier Rundi." *Revue Nationale d'Éducation du Burundi* 4, no. 5 (1967): 16-17.

Brain, James L. "The Tutsi and the Ha: A Study in Integration." *Journal of African and Asian Studies* 8, no. 1-2 (1973): 39-49.

Brass, Paul. *Ethnicity and Nationalism: Theory and Comparison*. London: Sage, 1991.

"La Chasse aux Hutu au Burundi." *Revue Française d'Etudes Politiques Africaines* 81 (1972): 103-5.

Chrétien, Jean-Pierre. "La Société du Burundi: Des Mythes aux Réalités." *Revue Françaises d'Études Politiques Africaines*, nos. 163-64 (1979): 94-118.

Chrétien, Jean-Pierre, and Émile Mworoha. "Les Tombeaux des Bami du Burundi: Un Aspect de la Monarchie Sacrée en Afrique Orientale." *Cahiers d'Etudes Africaines* 1 (1970): 40-79.

Chrysostome, Sœur Jean. "L'amour Maternel chez les Barundi." *Trait d'Union* 39, no. 5 (1956): 5-9.

de Cleene, N. *Introduction à l'Ethnographie du Congo belge et du Ruanda-Urundi*. Antwerp: Editions de Sikkel, 1957.

de Clerck, L. *Introduction à l'Étude du Droit Coutumier*. Bujumbura: Université Officielle, 1968.

Coupez, André. "Texte Ruundi: Les Rois du Pays." *Zaire* 11, no. 6 (1957): 623-36.

_____. "Texte Ruundi, 2." *Aequatoria* 21, no. 3 (1958): 81-97.

Delhaise, C. "Chez les Warundi et les Wohorohoro." *Bulletin de la Société Royale Belge de Géographie* (1908): 386-421, 429-50.

Dickerman, Carol. "City Women and the Colonial Regime: Usumbura, 1939-1962." *African Urban Studies* 18 (1984): 33-48.

Dorjahn, V.R. "The Factor of Polygyny in African Demography." In *Continuity and Change in African Cultures*, edited by W. Bascom and M. Herskovits. Chicago: University of Chicago Press, 1959.

Elam, Yitzchak. *The Social and Sexual Roles of Hima Women*. Manchester: Manchester University Press, 1973.

Forde, C. D. *Habitat, Economy and Society*. London: Methuen, 1953.

Gerkens, G. *Les Batutsi et les Bahutu*. Brussels: Institut Royal de Sciences Naturelles Belge, 1949.

Gille, Albert. "Notes sur l'Organisation des Barundi." *Bulletin de Juridictions Indigène et du Droit Coutumier Congolais*, no. 3 (1938): 75-81.

_____. "L'Umuganuro ou Fête du sorgho en Urundi." *Bulletin des Juridictions Indigènes et du Droit Coutumier Congolais* 14, no. 11 (1946): 368-371.

Goffin, J. "Le Rôle Joué par le Gros Bétail en Urundi." *Bulletin des Juridictions Indigènes et du Droit Coutumier Congolais* 19 (1951): 31-53, 61-86, 100-21.

Gourou, Pierre. *La Densité de la Population au Ruanda-Urundi*. Brussels: Institut Royal Colonial Belge, 1953.

Guillaume, H. "Peuplement Indigène, Institutions et Régime des biens au Ruanda-Urundi." *Athenation* (Usumbura), nos. 2-3 (1956): 27-42, 36-53.

Gulliver, P.H. *The Family Herds*. London: Routledge, 1955.

Hiernaux, Jean. *Les Caractères Physiques des Populations du Ruanda et de l'Urundi*. Brussels: Institut Royal Colonial Belge, 1954.

_____. "Racial Properties of the Natives of Ruanda-Urundi." *Anthropos* 50, nos. 4-6 (1955): 967.

_____. *Analyses de la Variation des Caractères Physiques Humains en une Région de l'Afrique Centrale: Ruanda-Urundi et Kivu.* Tervuren: Annales Du Musée Royal du Congo Belge, 1956.

_____. "Note sur une Ancienne Population du Ruanda-Urundi: Les Renge." *Zaire* 10 (1956): 351-60.

_____. "Note sur l'Homme de la Ruzizi." *Zaire* 8 (1957): 845-46.

Jeffreys, M. "The Batwa: Who are They?" *Africa* 1 (1953): 45-54.

Kagame, Alexis. "Les Hamites du Ruanda et du Burundi sont-ils des Hamites." *Bulletin des Séances, Académie Royale des Sciences Coloniales* 2 (1956): 341-63.

Kahombo, Mateene. "Quelques Principes du Choix des Noms Individuels dans Certaines Sociétés Bantu." *Cahiers d'Études Africaines*, no. 50 (1972): 357-61.

Kisyeti, Gérard. "Le Tribalisme au Burundi." *Remarques Africaines* 10, no. 326 (1968): 539-41.

Lemarchand, René. "L'Influence des Systèmes Traditionnels sur L'Évolution Politique du Rwanda et du Burundi." *Revue de l'Institut de Sociologie* 2 (1962): 333-57.

_____. "Status Differences and Ethnic Conflict: Rwanda and Burundi." In *Ethnicity and Nation Building*, edited by W. Bell and W. E. Freeman. Beverly Hills: Sage Publications, 1974.

Leurquin, Philippe. "L'Actif Mobilier des Habitants des Sous-Chefferies Kigoma (Ruanda) et Nyangwa (Urundi)." *Bulletin de l'Institut de Recherches Économiques et Sociales de l'Université de Louvain* 23, no. 2 (1957): 67-94.

_____. *Le Niveau de Vie des Populations Rurales du Ruanda-Urundi.* Louvain: Éditions Nauwelaerts, 1960.

Lowie, R. H. *Social Organization.* London: Routledge, 1950.

Maquet, Emma. *Outils de Forges du Congo, du Rwanda, et du Burundi.* Tervuren: Musée Royal de l'Afrique Centrale, 1965.

Maquet, J. J. "Le Problème de la Domination Tutsi." *Zaire* 6 (1952): 1011-16.

Maus, Albert. "Batutsi et Bahutu au Ruanda-Urundi." *Europe-Afrique* (Bukavu) April (1954): 8-10.

Muhirwa, A. "Une Fille peut-elle Hériter au même Titre que ses Fréres." *Servir* 1 (1946): 41-2.

Murray, H. J. R. "The Game of the Kubuguza among the Abatutsi." *Man* 53 December (1953): 194.

Nkezabera, J. "Le Choix d'un Nom." *Servir* 2 (1953): 49-50.

Nkundikije, André. "Problèmes Ethniques Face à la Revolution Burundaise." *Remarques Africaines* 9, no. 290 (1967): 275-77.

Ntahokaja, J. B. "La Dot au Burundi: L'Institution, ses Avatars, les Tendences Actuelles." *Revue de l'Université Officielle de Bujumbura* 2, no. 7 (1968): 141-49.

Ntahombaye, Philippe. "Le Nom Individuel, Sopport Matériel de Message: Le Cas du Burundi." *Culture et Société*, no. 1 (1978): 12-34.

_____. *Des Noms et Des Hommes: Aspects Psychologiques et Sociologiques du nom au Burundi*. Paris: Éditions Karthala, 1983.

Paulme, Denise, ed. *Women of Tropical Africa*. Berkeley: University of California Press, 1963.

Perraudin, J. "Mort et Furérailles chez les Anciens Barundi." *Missions*, no. 3 (1952): 46-7.

Possoz, E. "Batoa, Batwa, Batswa." *Africa*, no. 3 (1954): 237-59.

Radcliffe-Brown, A.R., and D. Forde, eds, *African Systems of Kinship and Marriage*. London: Oxford University Press, 1950.

Rhodius, George. "The Evolution of the Native Woman in the Belgian Congo and Ruanda-Urundi." *African Woman* 1 (1955): 73-4.

Robertson, C., and I. Berger. *Women and Class in Africa*. New York: Africana, 1986.

Rodegem, F. M. "Nanga Yivuza: Un Secte Synchrétique au Burundi." *Cultures et Dévéloppement* 2, no. 2 (1970): 427-34.

_____. "La Fête des Prémices au Burundi." *Africa Linguistica* 5 (1971): 207-254.

_____. "Sens et Rôle des Noms Propres en Histoire du Burundi." *Etudes d'Histoire Africaine* 7 (1975): 77-87.

Rozier, Raymond. "Structures Sociales et Politiques au Burundi." *Revue Française d'Etudes Politiques Africaines*, no. 91 (1973): 70-8.

Rutynx, J. "Ethique Indigène et Problèmes d'Acculturation en Afrique Centrale Belge." *Revue de l'Institut de Sociologie Solvay*, no. 2 (1958): 309-33.

Ryckmans, Pierre. "L'Organisation Politique et Sociale dans l'Urundi." *Revue Générale Belge* 15 April (1921): 460-84.

Schumacher, P. "Les Batwa." *Congo*, no. 1 (1931): 555-58.

_____. "Les Batwa sont-ils des Pygmées Authentiques." *Aequatoria* 10, no. 4 (1947): 130-33.

Seruvumba, J. N. "A Propos de la Rupture du Mariage." *Bulletin de Juridictions Indigène et du Droit Coutumier Congolais*, no. 12 (1947-1948): 317-74.

_____. "Propriété vente et Bail de Vaches." *Bulletin de Juridictions Indigène et du Droit Coutumier Congolais*, no. 5 (1947-1948): 171-2.

Simons, Eugene. "Note sur les Coutumes Indigènes Relatives aux Dommages-Intérets dans l'Urundi." *Bulletin de Juridictions Indigène et du Droit Coutumier Congolais*, no. 1(1933-1934): 3-5.

_____. "Coutumes et Institutions des Barundi." *Bulletin des Juridictions Indigènes et du Droit Coutumier Congolais*, nos. 7-12 (1943-1944): 137-60, 163-79, 181-222, 237-65, 269-82.

_____. *Coutumes et Institutions des Barundi.* Elisabethville: Revue Juridique du Congo Belge, 1944.

Smets, G. "L'Umuganuro chez les Barundi." *Congrès International Scientifique, Anthropologique, et Ethnologique* . Copenhagen, 1928.

_____. "Quelques Observations sur les Usages Successoraux des Batutsi de l'Urundi." *Bulletin des*

Séances 18 (1937): 729-40.

_____. "Quelques Remarques sur les Techniques des Barundi." *Archeion* 1 (1937): 56-66.

_____. "Le Régime Successoral en Urundi." *Congo* 4 (1937): 453-54, 5 (1938): 297-307.

_____. "Commerce, Marchés et Spéculations chez les Barundi." *Congo* 5. (1938): 568-74.

_____. "Funérailles et Sépultures des Bami et Bagabekazi de l'Urundi." *Bulletin de l'Institut Royal Colonial Belge* 12, no. 2 (1941): 210-34.

_____. "The Structure of the Barundi Community." *Man* 46, no. 6 (1946): 12-16.

_____. "Les Institutions Féodales de l'Urundi." *Revue de l'Université Bruxelles* 1, February-April (1949): 101-12.

_____. "La Eschyle et les Barundi." *Bulletin de l'Académie Royale Belge*, no. 3 (1949): 141-58.

Sohier, A. "La Réforme de la Dot et la Liberté de la Femme Indigène." *Bulletin de Juridictions du Ruanda-Urundi*, no. 9 (1950): 79-87.

_____. "Le Droit de la Vache." *Journal de Tribunes d'Outre-Mer*, no. 9 (1951): 105.

de Sousberghe, L. "Cousin Croisés et Descendants: Les Systèmes du Rwanda et du Burundi Comparés à ceux du Bas-Congo." *Africa* 35 (1965): 396-420.

Townshend, Philip. *Le Jeux de Mankala au Zaire, au Rwanda et au Burundi*. Brussels: Centre d'Etude et de Documentation Africaines, 1977.

Trouwborst, Albert. "La Mobilité de l'Individu en Fonction de l'Organisation Politique des Barundi." *Zaire* 18 (1959): 787-800.

_____. "Kinship and Geographical Mobility in Burundi." *International Journal of Comparative Sociology* 6, no. 1, March (1965): 166-82.

Turner, Victor. *The Drums of Affliction*. Oxford: Clarendon Press, 1968.

Van Bulck, G. "La Promotion de la Femme au Congo Belge et au Ruanda-Urundi." *Zaire* 15 no. 10 (1956): 1068-74.

_____. "Le Troupeau de Vaches est-il un Placement de Capital en Afrique Orientale." *Zaire*.15 no. 5 (1956): 517-23.

Van Mal, G. "Note sur la Coutume Indigène en fait de Dommages Intérets et Droit de Vengeance (Territoire de Ruyigi, Urundi)." *Bulletin de Juridictions Indigène et du Droit Coutumier Congolais*, no. 1 (1935-1936): 13-14.

Verbrugghe, A. "Introduction Historique au Problème de la Nationalité au Burundi." *Revue Juridique et Politique* 25, no. 4 (1971): 435-38.

_____." La Responsabilité Civile des Commettants du Fait de leurs Préposés en Droit Burundais et Belge." *Revue Juridique et Politique* 27, no. 4 (1973): 563-68.

_____. "La Situation de la Feffe Divorcée en Droit Traditionnel Burundais." *Revue Juridique et Politique* 28, no. 4 (1974): 593-99.

Vincent, Marc. *L'Enfant au Ruanda-Urundi*. Brussels: Institut Royal Colonial Belge, 1954.

Waleffe, F. "La Sécurité Sociale au Congo Belge et au Ruanda-Urundi." *Revue Belge de Sécurité Sociale*, nos. 5-6 (1954): 186-220.

Walhin, F. "Note à Propos de la Rupture du Mariage." *Bulletin de Juridictions du Ruanda-Urundi*, no. 5 (1948): 265-66.

_____. "Dommages et Intérêts dus en Vertu des Usages Locaux." *Bulletin de Juridictions du Ruanda-Urundi*, no. 8 (1950): 444-49.

_____. "La Situation des Métis au Ruanda-Urundi en Matière Répressive." *Bulletin de Juridictions du Ruanda-Urundi*, no. 9 (1950): 469-75.

Whiteley, W.H., ed. *Language Use and Social Change*. London: Oxford University Press, 1968.

de Wilde, d'Estmael. *Cours de Juridictions Indigènes du Ruanda-Urundi*. Astrida, Congo: Groupe Scolaire d'Astrida, 1957.

Ziégler, Jean. "L'intégration Sociale et Politique entre Batutsi et Bahutu dans la Région Extra-Coutumière de

Bujumbura." In *Travaux Sociologiques*, edited by P. Atteslander and R. Girod. Vol. 1 Bern, 1966.
_____. "Structures Ethniques et Partis Politiques au Burundi." *Le Mois en Afrique*, no. 18 (1967): 54-68.

10. Religion

Arnoux, R.P. *Les Pères Blancs aux Sources du Nil*. Paris: Édition Saint-Paul, 1948.
Berger, Iris. *Religion and Resistance: East African Kingdoms in the Precolonial Period*. Tervuren: Musée Royal de L'Afrique Centrale, 1981.
Bigangara, Jean-Baptiste. *Le Fondement de L'Imanisme: Religion Traditionnelle au Burundi*. Bujumbura: Ministry of Youth, Sports and Culture, 1984.
Booth, Newell S., ed. *African Religions: A Symposium*. New York: NOK, 1977.
Chrétien, Jean-Pierre. "Pouvoir d'État et Autorité Mystique: L'Infrastructure Religieuse des Monarchies des Grands Lacs." Paris: Société Française d'Histoire d'Outre-Mer, 1981.
_____. "Eglise et État au Burundi: Les Enjeux Politiques." *Afrique Contemporaine* 142, no. 2 (1987): 63-71.
Claver, Rév. Mère. "Traditions des Batusi." *Missions des Pères Blancs d'Afrique* (1907): 177-84.
Dechaume, P. "Imana, le Dieu des Paiens Barundi." *Grands Lacs*, nos. 5-6 (1936): 348-52.
Garnier, C., and J. Fralon. *Le Fétichisme en Afrique Noire*. Paris: Payot, 1951.
Greenland, Jeremy. "The Reform of Education in Burundi: Enlightened Theory Faced with Political Reality." *Comparative Education* 10, no. 1 (1974): 57-63.
Guillebaud, Rosemary. "The Doctrine of God in Ruanda-Urundi." In *African Ideas of God: A Symposium*, edited by Edwin Smith. London: Edinburgh House Press, 1950.

Heyse, T. *Associations Religieuses au Congo Belge et au Ruanda-Urundi.* Brussels: Institut Royal Colonial Belge, 1948.

Janssens, R. "Sur les Coutumes et Croyances de l'Urundi." *Bulletin de Juridictions Indigène et du Broit Coutumier Congolais*, nos. 9-10 (1953-1954): 205-21, 229-40.

Kayoya, M. "Un Problème Très Urgent: L'Orientation de l'Action Catholique au Burundi." *Théologie et Pastoral au Rwanda et au Burundi*, no. 3 (1968): 106-13.

Keuppens, J. "Les Peres Blancs au Ruanda-Urundi." *Bulletin de l'Union Missionaire Clergé*, January (1956): 15-25.

MacGaffey, W. "Comparative Analysis of Central African Religions." *Africa* 17, no. 1 (1972): 21-31.

Mbiti, John. *African Religions and Philosophy.* New York: Praeger, 1969.

P'Bitek, Okot. *African Religions in Western Scholarship.* Nairobi: East African Literature Bureau, 1970.

Péroncel-Hugoz, Jean-Pierre. "Burundi: Le Bras de Fer entre l'Église et l'État." *Le Monde*, 27 August 1987.

Perraudin, J. "Le Culte des Morts Chez les Anciens Barundi." *Missions*, no. 4 (1952): 55-6.

_____. "Imana, Le Dieu des Barundi." *Missions*, no. 1 (1952): 11-12.

_____. *Naissance d'une Église: Histoire du Burundi Chrétien.* Bujumbura: Presses Lavigerie, 1963.

Radner, Ephraim. "Breaking the Power of the Church in Burundi." *Christian Century* 102 (1985): 915-18.

Rodegem, F. M. "La Motivation du Culte Initiatique au Burundi." *Anthropos* 66 (1971): 863-930.

Roy, R. "Notes sur les Banyabungu: Description de l'Initiation au Culte de Ryangombe." *Congo*, no. 2 (1924): 327-47; no. 1 (1925): 83-108.

Smith, Edwin, ed. *African Ideas of God: A Symposium.* London: Edinburgh House Press, 1950.

Tempels, Placide. *Bantu Philosophy.* Paris: Présence Africaine translated from *Banto Filosofie*. 1946. Reprint, Antwerp, 1969.

Zuure, Bernard. "Immâna, le Dieu des Barundi." *Anthropos* 21 (1926): 733-76.

_____. *Croyances et Pratiques Religieuses des Barundi.* Brussels: Bibliotheque Congo, 1929.

_____. *L'Ame du Murundi.* Paris: Beauchesne, 1931.

_____. "Les Croyances de l'Urundi Révélées par les Usages et Pratiques." *Grands Lacs* no. 9 (1948-1949): 66-69.

11. International Relations

Adie, W. A. C. "Chinese Policy Towards Africa." In *The Soviet Bloc, China, and Africa*, edited by S. Hamrell and C. G. Widstrand. Uppsala: The Scandinavian Instituteof African Studies, 1964.

Amate, C. O. C. "The O.A.U. and the Conflicts in Africa." *Africa Quarterly* 33 (1993): 59-75.

Balfour, Patrick. "Tanganyika and Ruanda-Urundi." *The Geographical Magazine* 8 (1938): 42-8.

Bascom, W., and M. Herskovits, eds. *Continuity and Change in African Cultures.* Chicago: University of Chicago Press, 1959.

Bowman, Michael,et al. "No Samaritan: The U. S. and Burundi." *Africa Report*, July/August, 1973.

"Burundi: China's Hand in Spiel." *Internationales Afrika Forum* 3, nos. 9-10 (1967): 439-40.

Ceulemans, Jacques. "Une Campagne Anti-Burundi en Belgique." *Remarques Africaines* 7, no. 234 (1965): 2.

Davister, Pierre. "Le Burundi: Ce Mal Aimê d'une Certaine Belgique." *Spéciale*, 3 October 1973, 30-31.

Duner, Bertil. "The Many-Pronged Spear: External Military Intervention in Civil Wars in the 1970s." *Journal of Peace Research* 20, no. 1 (1983): 59-72.

Larkin, Bruce. *China and Africa 1949-1970.* Berkeley: University of California Press, 1971.

Ogunsanwo, Alaba. *China's Policy in Africa 1958-71.* Cambridge: Cambridge University Press, 1974.

Reuss, Conrad. "La Coopération Internationale au Burundi: 1962-1966." *Revue de l'Université Officielle de Bujumbura* 2, no. 5 (1968): 5-48.

_____. "Réflexions sur l'Aide de la Belgique au Burundi." *Etudes Congolaises* 12, no. 2 (1969): 81-96.

Reynolds, Quentin. "Interview with Tung Chi-ping. *Look*, 1 December 1964, 24.

Sterling, Claire. "Chou En-lai and the Watusi." *The Reporter*, 12 March 1964, 22-23.

Weinstein, Warren. "The Limits of Military Dependency: The Case of Belgian Aid to Burundi, 1961-73." *Journal of African Studies* 2, no. 3 (1975): 419-31.

Weinstein, Warren, ed. *Soviet and Chinese Aid to Africa.* New York: Praeger, 1975.

12. Education

Chrétien, Jean-Pierre. "L'Enseignement au Burundi." *Revue Française d'Etudes Politiques Africaines*, no. 76 (1972): 61-81.

"L'Education des Enfants chez les Baganwa de l'Urundi." *Grands Lacs*, nos. 10-11 (1949): 17-22.

Greenland, Jeremy. *Western Education in Burundi 1916-1973: the Consequences of Instrumentalism.* Brussels: Centre d'Etude et de Documentation Africaines, 1980.

Poelmans, R. "Vers un Enseignement plus Efficient au Ruanda-Urundi." *Actualité Congolaise* (Léopoldville), no. 22 (1952): 4.

Van der Meulen, F. "L'Organisation de l'Enseignement pour Indigènes au Ruanda-Urundi." *Servir*, no. 5 (1953): 171-79.

Vanhove, Julien. "L'Oeuvre d'Éducation au Congo Belge et au Ruanda-Urundi." *L'Encyclopédie Belge* Brussels: 1953.

13. Geography, Geology, and Agriculture

Adamantidis, D. *Monographie Pastorale du Ruanda-Urundi.* Brussels: Ministère des Colonies, 1956.

Aderca, Bernard M. *La Gisement de Terres Rares de la Karonge*. Brussels: Academie Royale des Sciences d'Outre-Mer, 1971.

Adriaens, E., and Lozet, F. "Contribution à l'Étude des Boissons Indigènes du Ruanda-Urundi." *Bulletin Agricole du Congo Belge* 42, no. 4 (1951): 933-50.

Blankoff-Scarr, Goldie, trans. *Ruanda-Urundi: Geography and History*. Brussels: Belgian Congo and Ruanda-Urundi Information and Public Relations Office, 1960.

Chrétien, Jean-Pierre. "Les Années de l'Éleusine, du Sorgho et du Haricot dans l'Ancien Burundi." *African Economic History*. Vol. 7. Madison: University of Wisconsin, 1979.

Deuse, Paul. *Contribution á l'Étude des Tourbières du Ruanda et du Burundi*. Butare: Institut pour la Recherche Scientifique en Afrique Centrale, 1966.

Dubois, L., and Collaert, E. *L'Apiculture au Congo Belge et au Ruanda-Urundi: La Production du Miel et de la Cire*. Brussels: Direction de l'Agriculture et de l'Elevage, 1950.

Everaerts, E. "Monographie Agricole du Ruanda-Urundi." *Bulletin Agricole du Congo Belge* 30, no. 3 (1939): 343-94; no. 4 (1939): 581-615.

Fontaines, Paul. *Les Exploitations Minières de Haute Montagne au Ruanda-Urundi*. Brussels: M. Hayez, 1939.

Frankart, Raymond P. *Aspects de la Pedogenese des Sols Halomorphes de la Basse Rusizi, Burundi*. Tervuren: Musée Royal de l'Afrique Centrale, 1971.

Gevers, Marie. *Des Mille Collines aux Neuf Volcans*. Paris: Stock, Delamain et Boutelleau, 1953.

Guillaume, H. "Monographie de la Plaine de la Ruzizi." *Bulletin des Juridictions Indigènes et du Droit Coutumier Congolais* 18 (1950): 33-66.

Harroy, Jean-Paul. "La Lutte Contre la Dissipation des Ressources Naturelles au Ruanda-Urundi." *Civilisations* 4 (1954): 363-74.

Harroy, J. P., J. Lebrun et al. *Le Ruanda-Urundi: Ses Ressources Naturelles, ses Populations*. Brussels: Les Naturalistes Belges, 1956.

Hiernaux, Jean. "Problèmes d'Anthropologie Physique en Afrique Centrale." *Folio Scientifica Africae Centralis*, Information de l'Institut pour la Recherche Scientifique en Afrique Centrale (IRSAC), no. 4 (1955): 6-8.

Jones, William I. *Farming Systems in Africa: The Great Lakes Highlands of Zaire, Rwanda, and Burundi.* Washington: World Bank, 1984.

Jungers, E. "L'Agriculture Indigène au Ruanda-Urundi." *Société Belge d'Etudes et Expansion*, no. 123 (1946): 323-27.

Kayondi, C. "Murunga: Colline du Burundi." *Les Cahiers d'Outre-Mer* 25, no. 98 (1972): 164-204.

Kisage, H. "Le Deuil Lans la Plaine de Tanganyika, entre Rumonge et Usumbura." *Servir* 6, no. 4 (1945): 199-200.

Lejeune, J. B. "L'Agriculture Indigène au Ruanda-Urundi." *Courrier Agricole d'Afrique* 4, no. 1 (1940): 1-4.

Lismont, J., and S. Gahungu. "La Toponymie au Service de la Géographie et du Kirundi." *Revue Nationale d'Éducation au Burundi*, no. 4 (1971-1972): 12-18.

Maquet, J. J., and Jean Hiernaux. "Les Pasteurs de l'Itombwe." *Science et Nature*, no. 8 (1955): 3-12.

Marchi, F. "L'Élevage du Gros et du Petit Bétail au Ruanda-Urundi." *Bulletin Agricole du Congo Belge* 30, no. 4 (1939): 619-61.

Muhirwa, A. "Opinions d'un Murundi sur les Poisons et l'Anthropologie." *Servir* 8, nos. 4-5 (1947): 198-200, 240-48.

Nicaise, Joseph. "Applied Anthropology in the Congo and Ruanda-Urundi." *Human Organization* 19 (1960): 112-17.

Nicolai, H. "Progrès de la Connaissance Géographique au Zaire, au Rwanda et au Burundi en 1967, 1968 et 1970." *Bulletin de la Société Belge d'Etudes Géographiques*, no. 2 (1971): 263-317.

Peeters, Leo. "Le Rôle du Milieu Géographique dans L'Occupation Humaine du Rwanda-Burundi." *Bulletin de la Société Royale de Géographie d'Anvers* 74 (n. d.): 29-47.

Schantz, Homer L. "Urundi: Territory and People." *Geographical Review* 12 (1922): 329-59.
de Schlippe, P. "Enquête Préliminaire du Système Agricole des Barundi de la Région Bututsi." *Bulletin Agricole du Congo Belge* 48, no. 4 (1957): 827-82.
Schouteden, H. *Faune du Congo Belge et du Ruanda-Urundi*. Tervuren: Musée Royal du Congo Belge, 1948.
Skinner, Snider W. *The Agricultural Economy of the Belgian Congo and Ruanda-Urundi*. Washington, D. C.: Foreign Agricultural Service, U.S. Department of Agriculture, 1960.
Van der Velpen, C. *Géographie du Burundi*. Brussels: de Boeck, 1970.
Vervloet, G. "Aux sources du Nil." *Bulletin de la Société Royale Belge de Géographie*, no. 34 (1910): 108-37.
Waleffe, A. *Etude Géologique du sud-est Burundi: Régions du Mosso et du Nkoma*. Tervuren: Musée Royal de l'Afrique Centrale, 1965.

14. Health and Medicine

Hiernaux, Jean. "La Pression Sanguine des Indigènes du Ruanda-Urundi." *Annales de la Société Belge de la Médecine Tropicale*, no. 4 (1952): 379-88.
de L'Epine, C. "Histoire des Famines et Disettes de l'Urundi." *Bulletin Agricole du Congo Belge* 20, no. 3 (1929): 440-42.
May, Jacques M., M.D. *The Ecology of Malnutrition in Middle Africa*. New York: Hafner, 1965.
Van Dooren, F., and M. Rogowsky. *Etat Cardio-Circulatoire de l'Indigène du Congo Belge et du Ruanda-Urundi*. Brussels: Académie Royale des Sciences Coloniales, 1959.
Vyncke, J. *Psychoses et Névroses en Afrique Centrale*. Brussels: Académie Royale des Sciences Coloniales, 1957.

Waleffe, Fernand, Jr. *La Reparation des Accidents du Travail et des Maladies Professionnelles au Congo Belge et au Ruanda-Urundi.* Brussels: G. van Campenhout, 1948.

Appendix A

Kings (Bami) of Burundi

Dynastic Name	Given Name (if known)	Date of Accession
Ntare I	Rushatsi	1675
Mwezi I		1705
Mutaga I	Seenyamwiiza	1735
Mwambutsa I		1765
Ntare II	Rugaamba	1795
Mwezi II	Gisabo	1852
Mutaga II		1908
Mwambutsa II	Bangiricenge	1916
Ntare IV	Ndizeye	1966

Appendix B

Post-Colonial Heads of State

Dates of office and reason for leaving office:

Louis Rwagasore
(Prime Minister)

September 1961-October
1961
assassinated

André Muhirwa
(Prime Minister)

October 1961-June 1963
resigned

Pierre Ngendandumwe
(Prime Minister)

June 1963-March 1964
resigned

Albin Nyamoya
(Prime Minister)

March 1964-January 1965
resigned

Pierre Ngendandumwe
(Prime Minister)

January 1965-January 1965
assassinated

Joseph Bamina
(Prime Minister)

January 1965-September
1965
executed

Léopold Bihumugani (Biha)
(Prime Minister)

September 1965-July 1966
arrested

Michel Micombero[1] (President)	July 1966-November 1976 overthrown
Jean-Baptiste Bagaza (President)	November 1976-September 1987 overthrown
Pierre Buyoya (President)	September 1987-June 1993 lost democratic election
Melchior Ndadaye (President)	June 1993-October 1993 assassinated
Sylvie Kinigi (Prime Minister)	June 1993-January 1994 not reappointed
Cyprien Ntaryamira (President)	January 1994-April 1994 assassinated
Sylvestre Ntibantunganya (President)	November 1994-October 1996 overthrown
Anatole Kanyenko (Prime Minister)	November 1994-February 1995 forced to resign
Antoine Nduyayo (Prime Minister)	February 1995-present

---

[1]In 1966, Micombero declared a republic; from that time on, the president, rather than the prime minister, became the head of state. The office of prime minister was eliminated completely until the democratic elections of 1993.

About the Author

Ellen K. Eggers is an associate professor of English at the University of Nebraska-Lincoln. She has an M.A. in applied linguistics from Pennsylvania State University and a Ph.D. in linguistics from the University of Washington. She lived in Bujumbura, Burundi, from 1985 to 1986, where she taught English and linguistics at the University of Burundi and collected Kirundi data for an earlier research project on the language's discourse structure.